Patrick Lo
Rebekah Okpoti
Wei-En Hsu
Hermina G.B. Anghelescu
Dickson K.W. Chiu

Inside Hong Kong's Arts & Cultural Scene

Conversations with Hong Kong's Leading Arts & Cultural Administrators, Educators, Producers, and Presenters

nova
science publishers

www.novapublishers.com

Copyright © 2023 by Nova Science Publishers, Inc.

NOTICE TO THE READER

The Publisher has taken reasonable care in the preparation of this book but makes no expressed or implied warranty of any kind and assumes no responsibility for any errors or omissions. No liability is assumed for incidental or consequential damages in connection with or arising out of information contained in this book. The Publisher shall not be liable for any special, consequential, or exemplary damages resulting, in whole or in part, from the readers' use of, or reliance upon, this material. Any parts of this book based on government reports are so indicated and copyright is claimed for those parts to the extent applicable to compilations of such works.

Independent verification should be sought for any data, advice or recommendations contained in this book. In addition, no responsibility is assumed by the Publisher for any injury and/or damage to persons or property arising from any methods, products, instructions, ideas or otherwise contained in this publication.

This publication is designed to provide accurate and authoritative information with regards to the subject matter covered herein. It is sold with the clear understanding that the Publisher is not engaged in rendering legal or any other professional services. If legal or any other expert assistance is required, the services of a competent person should be sought. FROM A DECLARATION OF PARTICIPANTS JOINTLY ADOPTED BY A COMMITTEE OF THE AMERICAN BAR ASSOCIATION AND A COMMITTEE OF PUBLISHERS.

Library of Congress Cataloging-in-Publication Data

Names: Lo, Patrick, author. | Okpoti, Rebekah, author. | Hsu, Wei-En, author. | Anghelescu, Hermina G. B., author. | Chiu, Dickson K. W., 1966- author.
Title: Inside Hong Kong's arts & cultural scene : conversations with Hong Kong's leading arts & cultural administrators, educators, producers, and presenters / Patrick Lo, Rebekah Okpoti, Wei-En Hsu, Hermina G.B. Anghelescu, Dickson K.W. Chiu.
Other titles: Inside Hong Kong's arts and cultural scene
Description: New York : Nova Science Publishers, [2023] | Series: Fine arts, music and literature | Includes bibliographical references and index. |
Identifiers: LCCN 2023041589 (print) | LCCN 2023041590 (ebook) | ISBN 9798891131323 (hardcover) | ISBN 9798891132290 (adobe pdf)
Subjects: LCSH: Arts administrators--China--Hong Kong--Interviews. | Arts and society--China--Hong Kong. | Cultural industries--China--Hong Kong.
Classification: LCC NX770.C62 H66 2023 (print) | LCC NX770.C62 (ebook) | DDC 700.6/05125--dc23/eng/20230929
LC record available at https://lccn.loc.gov/2023041589
LC ebook record available at https://lccn.loc.gov/2023041590

Published by Nova Science Publishers, Inc. † *New York*

Contents

Foreword (1)

It is an honour to have been asked to write a short foreword to *Inside Hong Kong's Arts & Cultural Scene: Conversations with Hong Kong's Leading Arts & Cultural Administrators, Educators, Producers, and Presenters.*

Over the past decade, Hong Kong's arts and cultural scene has reached a new level of maturity. During the nine years I lived and worked in Hong Kong, I witnessed growing confidence across the cultural sector, not just in the unique role the arts could play in enriching and invigorating the city, but also in their ability to speak proudly to the wider world on Hong Kong's behalf. During that time, a whole generation of arts practitioners and administrators reached the highest levels of leadership, building upon a wealth of invaluable experience gained over many years. You will hear from many of them in this book, offering generous insights drawn from rich knowledge, and sharing their always fascinating, and often surprising, career journeys.

The information contained within this volume will provide useful guidance and inspiration for anyone beginning a career in arts and culture, as well as for those thinking of taking the plunge and joining a sector where anything is possible and no two days are ever the same. For readers of a certain age and experience, like myself, this book provides a chance to hear from old friends and respected former colleagues and feel confident that Hong Kong's arts and cultural future is in very safe hands.

Kingsley Jayasekera
Audiences, Branding and Communications Consultant
Edinburgh, 2023

Foreword (2)

Hong Kong's current position as the East meets West capital of the world is truly unique. In recent decades, this "uniqueness" has been quietly embraced by a small but dynamic group of cultural leaders who have been devoted to the task of making their art forms accessible and more relevant to a bilingual society.

Dr. Patrick Lo's "Inside Hong Kong's arts and cultural scene leading arts and cultural administrators, educators, producers and presenters" gives voice to a wide cross-section of arts professionals and educators, who have been raising the level of cultural engagement in an ever-changing Hong Kong society. Some have been making their impact in Hong Kong's more stalwart performing arts companies while others are innovators, driving new and exciting cultural ventures off the ground. Most importantly, Patrick Lo interviews arts professionals who believe in the power of the arts to change lives and promote a more harmonious society. They are passionate and skilled at sustaining creative ventures on a long-term basis with a business minded outlook, a can-do and hard-working ethic, and a heart for the artists they support. Their adaptability and resilience through all the recent local and global changes – the global pandemic and the digital age included – also makes for an inspiring read.

I would like to express my thanks and congratulations to Dr. Patrick Lo for giving Hong Kong's arts professionals and cultural leaders a chance to shine. The valuable insights and experiences shared in this publication will surely enlighten and inspire the next generation of cultural leaders ready to embrace the future!

Leanne Nicholls
Founder, Artistic & Executive Director
City Chamber Orchestra of Hong Kong

Authors' Biographies

Dr. Patrick Lo is the current Director, Liberal & Martial Arts Practice Association. From 2012-18, he served as Associate Professor at the Faculty of Library, Information & Media Science, the University of Tsukuba in Japan. He earned his Doctor of Education from the University of Bristol (U.K.), and has a Master of Arts in Design Management from the Hong Kong Polytechnic University, a Master of Library & Information Science from McGill University (Canada), and a Bachelor of Fine Arts from Mount Allison University (Canada).

His recent publications include the following:

- 以術明道 = *The Artistic and Martial Paths to Dao*. Systech Technology & Publications Ltd. (2023).
- *Stop the War! Performing Artists Across the World Call for Peace in Ukraine*. Cambridge Scholars Publishing. (2023).

- *The Marketing of Academic, National and Public Libraries Worldwide: Marketing, Branding, Community Engagement.* Elsevier. (2023).
- Conversation with Maestro Riccardo Muti (Music Director Chicago Symphony Orchestra). *Music Reference Services Quarterly*, (2022). Vol. 25, No. 4, pp. 132-137. DOI: https://www.tandfonline.com/doi/abs/10.1080/10588167.2022.2085996.
- *Stories and Lessons from the World's Leading Opera, Orchestra Librarians, and Music Archivists. (2-volume set)* Emerald. (2022).
- *Inside the World's Major East Asian Collections in North America.* Emerald. (2022).
- *Literacy and Reading Programmes for Children and Young People: Case Studies from around the Globe.* CRC Press. (2022).
- *Creating a Global Cultural City via Public Participation in the Arts: Conversations with Hong Kong's Leading Arts and Cultural Administrators.* Nova Science Publishers, Inc. (2021).

Dr. Rebekah Okpoti lectures in Musicology at Liverpool Hope University and is Associate Organist at Leeds Cathedral, UK. 2020 saw the international release of the Finding Home Collection released in the UK, USA, China as a Reimagined Last Supper of Miniature 1:12 scale of Sonic Installation Art Pieces. In 2021 SetFootPress released Rebekah's Experimental Organ Music recorded as field recordings during the COVID-19 pandemic. The album Dressing was released as both a limited-run cassette & digital. Rebekah was a Recording and Audio engineer for the Global Sound Movements Uganda Sample Library and was a Score Proof-reader for the Geoffrey Tristram Mass in A flat Published 2022 by Banks of York.

Most recently, Rebekah ran the Arts Council Funded National Lottery Project Organs of Anne Lister Project (BBC's Gentleman Jack) as part of the Anne Lister Birthday Week Festival 2022 where she was commissioned to write a contemporary Organ sonata. Anne Lister's Organ Sonata was premiered at Halifax Minster, England. You can see Rebekah perform in recitals throughout the UK.

As a writer, her scholarly work includes a thesis focused on the Repatriation of Domesticity within Sonic Installation Art and the role of Installed Musical Composition to facilitate engagement with Space, Void, Poise, Sculpture and Composition. Other activities include writing a chapter on Digital Submissions: in Benchmarking Library, Information and Education Services for Elsevier along with writing a series of popular articles about issues associated with being a Female Organist and Engaging new organists as @thegirlyorganist. Anne Lister's Organ Sonata was published in July 2022 by Tim Knight Music Publishers. Rebekah has performed concerts in the UK, Russia, France, Atlanta, and Mozambique.

Wei-En Hsu is Associate Professor at the Hong Kong Academy for Performing Arts and was awarded the Associate of the Royal Academy of Music (ARAM) in 2017. In recent years, Mr. Hsu has established himself as an early music specialist in Baroque opera and the art of recitative for pianists. He is the winner of the 2010 Los Angeles International Liszt Piano Competition, with a Bachelor of Fine Arts from the National University of the Arts, and a Master of Music from The Julliard School and The Royal Academy of Music.

Dr. Hermina G.B. Anghelescu is a Professor in the School of Information Sciences, Wayne State University, Detroit, Michigan. She holds a MLIS and a PhD from the University of Texas at Austin and a degree in foreign languages and literatures from the University of Bucharest. Prior to coming to the United States, Anghelescu worked as a librarian at the National Library of Romania.

Author of numerous articles and co-author of several monographs, Anghelescu is also a member of the editorial board of several scholarly journals, including *Library Trends*, *Libraries: Culture, History, and Society*, *Library & Archival Security*, and *Slavic & East European Information Resources*. Anghelescu has served as an expert and a consultant on Eastern European libraries to various national and international organizations and agencies such as the US Department of State, the Bill and Melinda Gates Foundation (BMGF), and the International and Research & Exchanges Board (IREX). She was involved with the implementation of the Global Libraries project in Romania, a 28.3 million USD project sponsored by the Bill and Melinda Gates Foundation (BMGF). The Presidency of Romania awarded her the Cultural Merit Order for the rank of Knight for her outstanding contributions to the advancement of Romanian civilization, culture, and history abroad. In addition, she was instrumental in securing a 12 million USD grant from BMGF to modernize the public library system in the Republic of Moldova. The Moldovan Government awarded her with one of the highest distinctions in the country.

Dr. Dickson K.W. Chiu received the B.Sc. (Hons.) degree in Computer Studies from the University of Hong Kong in 1987. He received the M.Sc. (1994) and Ph.D. (2000) degrees in Computer Science from the Hong Kong University of Science and Technology (HKUST). He started his own computer consulting company while studying part-time. He has also taught at several universities in Hong Kong. His teaching and research interest is in Library & Information Management, Service Computing, and E-learning with a cross-disciplinary approach involving library and information management, e-learning, e-business, service sciences, and databases. The results have been widely published in over 300 international publications (most of them have been indexed by SCI/-E, SSCI, and EI, such as top journals *MIS Quarterly, Computer & Education, Government Information Quarterly, Decision Support Systems, Information Sciences, Knowledge-Based Systems, Expert Systems with Application, Information Systems Frontiers, IEEE Transactions*, including many taught master and undergraduate project results and around 20 edited books. He received the Best Paper award at the *37th Hawaii International Conference on System Sciences* in 2004. He is the Editor (-in-chief) of *Library Hi Tech*, a prestigious journal indexed by SSCI. He is the Editor-in-chief Emeritus of the *International Journal on Systems and Service-Oriented Engineering (founding)* and the *International Journal of Organizational and Collective Intelligence* and serves on the editorial boards of several international journals. He co-founded several international workshops and co-edited several journal special issues. He also served as a programme committee member for around 300 international conferences and workshops. Dr. Chiu is a *Senior Member* of both the ACM and the IEEE and a *life member* of the Hong Kong Computer Society. According to Google

Scholar, he has over 8,500 citations, h-index=47, i-10 index=180, and ranked worldwide 1st in "LIS," "m-learning," and "e-services." He received nearly 1,000 citations in 2022 and over 2,500 citations in 2023.

Introduction

Hong Kong's cultural scene has a rich and complex history that has been shaped by a variety of factors, including its colonial past, its location as a gateway to China, and its status as a global hub for commerce and culture. Starting as a humble farming village, fishing village, and salt production site, Hong Kong became a British colony in 1841; it has developed into an international financial centre since the 1970s. Hong Kong has always been a transit port for sea vessels and aircraft for China's trade, i.e., serving as a bridge and a channel for connecting the vast mainland and the rest of the world. However, compared to other major international financial hubs, such as New York and London, Hong Kong has often been criticised, over the decades, for the lack of a vibrant arts and culture scene, along with insufficient arts organisations that can help support the long-term development of the local arts and cultural sector (Lo et al., 2021).

During the colonial period, Hong Kong's cultural scene was heavily influenced by British imperialism, with English-language education and cultural institutions playing a dominant role. However, local Cantonese-language newspapers and theatres also thrived, and a unique blend of East and West emerged in Hong Kong's music, film, and art scenes. In the 1970s and '80s, Hong Kong experienced a cultural renaissance known as the Hong Kong New Wave (Gao, 2020). This movement saw the emergence of a new generation of filmmakers, musicians, and artists who embraced local culture and language and challenged traditional artistic forms. The Hong Kong New Wave had a significant impact on the city's cultural scene, helping to establish Hong Kong as a hub for contemporary art (Desser & Fu, 2000).

Over the years, Hong Kong has emerged as one of the art capitals in Asia and also a hub for creative industries driving changes towards a cultural economy. In keeping with its position and reputation as an international financial centre, Hong Kong is actually now recognised as one of the world's biggest trading centres for contemporary art. In the 1990s and 2000s, Hong Kong's cultural scene continued to evolve with the rise of new technologies and the city's increasing integration into global cultural networks. This period saw the emergence of a new generation of artists and musicians who embraced digital media and explored new forms of expression.

The arts and cultural scene in Hong Kong has become increasingly prominent in the City's search for a unique identity since China resumed its sovereignty over the territory in 1997. Ten years after Hong Kong returned to Chinese rule, the local Hong Kong Special Administrative Region (SAR) Government publicly declared its cultural policy, stating its intention to engineer the City towards an international cultural metropolis (Home Affairs Bureau, 2008). Such endeavours carried out by the Hong Kong SAR Government concurred with the notion that for a city to achieve the "world city" status, investment in the cultural and creative industries is necessary (Kong et al., 2006). As noted by Grogan (2022), "Hong Kong's branding campaign as "Asia's World City" sings the praises of its liveability, connectivity, entrepreneurialism and more… Prosperity, security and international influence are all rooted in the powerful trifecta of political values, culture and foreign policy that is soft power, or a country's ability to engage with global audiences. Soft power leaders like the United Kingdom and France know that culture is key to their ability to sway proverbial hearts and minds in their favour."

Hong Kong's Global Art Market and Its Local Art Scene

Hong Kong has a thriving, multifaceted arts scene with a rich history and a diverse population that has influenced its arts and culture. The City has a diverse range of cultural offerings. Some key aspects of the art scene in Hong Kong include contemporary art, with the City playing the role of a hub for contemporary art in Asia, with numerous galleries and museums showcasing local and international artists. Hong Kong is also home to a growing street art scene, with numerous street art murals and installations popping up around the City (Yu, 2022). The annual HKwalls festival showcases local and international street artists (Leung, 2023). Hong Kong has a vibrant performing arts scene, encompassing theatre, dance, and music. The Hong Kong Cultural Centre and the Hong Kong Academy for Performing Arts are two major venues for performing arts in the City. Hong Kong has a long and storied history of cinema, and the Hong Kong International Film Festival is a major event in the industry. In addition, many film festivals take place throughout the year, showcasing local and international films. Hong Kong has a burgeoning literary scene, with numerous bookstores, literary festivals, and writers' groups. The Hong Kong International Literary Festival is a major event in the literary calendar.

Whilst historically, Hong Kong's success has been built largely on finance, transportation, and trade, arts and culture have been overshadowed and overlooked. In the meantime, the Hong Kong (SAR) Government has been embracing a major boost in soft power in recent years, with the aim of raising its status on the global stage (Zhou & Ao, 2022). The successful art market in Hong Kong and its subsequent economic impacts are expected to have an important role to play in building the soft power of this capitalist city. Hong Kong's flourishing art market and cultural environment could be a result of multiple and interconnected socio-economic, socio-cultural, and socio-political factors. It is said that Hong Kong's unique geographical location (proximity to Mainland China), stable multilateral trading system, free-market economy, English-speaking environment, and well-developed institutional and commercial infrastructure have attracted art fairs, galleries, auction houses, and collectors worldwide. According to (E)BrandConnect (n.d.), "The emergence of Hong Kong as one of the world's biggest art trading centres, alongside New York and London, is built on strong cultural and commercial foundations... Now, as Asia and Hong Kong's own art scenes flourish, resourceful financiers and entrepreneurs looking to expand their art collections gather here, alongside artists from East and West, and dealers trading art" (p. 3).

Before the arrival of different international art fairs, auction houses were the major players in Hong Kong's art trade. Furthermore, auction houses, such as Sotheby's and Christie's, historically played an influential role in raising interest in art in the city for over half a century (Poposki & Leung, 2022). The last decade has seen Hong Kong drawing major attention from key international players from different sectors of the visual arts world, including artists, auction houses, curators, buyers, and art enthusiasts. Such international key players also include high-profile art fairs such as Art Basel Hong Kong, the Asia Contemporary Art Show, Art Central and the Affordable Art Fair, etc. In fact, many sources also confirmed that Hong Kong's global art market has in fact overtaken London and is becoming the second-largest contemporary art auction market in the world. Even during the pandemic, Hong Kong saw record-breaking art sales (ArtTactic, 2020; Uttam, 2020; Wang, 2022). According to Wang (2022), "In the first eight months of 2020, Hong Kong's global art market share rose to 26%, from 20% r in the previous year (2019), recording $314.6 million in auction sales, overtaking London's

$303.5 million, in the same period, according to ArtTactic, an art market data analysis company."

However, the Hong Kong art scene extends far beyond these events. In fact, the arrival of international auction houses, art fairs and galleries has not only boosted Hong Kong's global status, but has also significantly impacted the local arts and cultural scene. This thriving art scene not only boasts a wide and exceptional range of art galleries (from classical to contemporary, along with vibrant street) but also exposes both local and foreign audiences to a greater diversity of art, including freelance practitioners, arts educators, arts managers, technical and production crews, etc. In fact, they have now formed the backbone of a strong arts ecosystem, combined with sustained public and private support and partnerships, bringing quality arts experiences to local and international audiences. According to Poposki and Leung (2022), "In Hong Kong's art ecology, the dominance of the top end of the art market has created opportunities as well as problems that have led to a number of challenges in terms of the role of art institutions in Hong Kong... This situation could potentially have a significant impact on the development of art institutions and fine arts practices in Hong Kong, including on the quality of the local art scene in Hong Kong and on supporting and nurturing the development of the arts in Hong Kong." Overall, Hong Kong's arts scene is diverse and constantly evolving, reflecting the City's rich cultural heritage and position as a global hub for the arts.

Hong Kong's Performing Arts Ecology

Hong Kong has a diverse and vibrant music scene with a mix of local and international influences. Some key aspects of the music scene in Hong Kong include:

Cantopop is a genre of music that originated in Hong Kong in the 1970s, blending Cantonese lyrics with Western pop music. Cantopop remains a popular genre in Hong Kong. The City also has a growing indie music scene, with numerous local bands and musicians performing in small venues around town. The annual Clockenflap music festival showcases local and international acts. Hong Kong has a classical music scene, with numerous orchestras, music schools, and venues. The Hong Kong Philharmonic Orchestra is one of the most prominent orchestras in the City. Hong Kong is a popular destination for international music acts, with numerous concerts and festivals throughout the year. The Hong Kong Coliseum is a major venue for concerts in the City. Hong Kong also has a growing electronic music scene, with many clubs and venues hosting electronic music events. The annual Shi Fu Miz festival is a popular event showcasing electronic music acts. Hong Kong's music scene is constantly evolving, reflecting the City's position as a global hub for culture and entertainment.

Benny Lim reported (2017): "In Hong Kong, there are hundreds of professional and amateur non-profit groups, for-profit performing arts companies, drama clubs in schools and universities, and independent theatre makers... Most of the performing arts venues in Hong Kong are run by a government department known as the Leisure and Cultural Services Department (LCSD), which aims to enhance the cultural vibrancy of the city and bring arts to different communities." Perhaps one major project that could potentially reshape the performing arts scene and ecology in Hong Kong is the West Kowloon Cultural District (WKCD). As noted by Poposki and Leung (2022), WKCD is considered one of the world's largest cultural districts and has been in development in Hong Kong since 1998. When completed in 2026, it is set to include 17 venues for music, performing arts, and visual art. The idea of the WKCD was first announced by the Chief Executive of Hong Kong, Chee-hwa Tung, in 1998 in his policy address. According to Tung, the WKCD is expected to serve as a "new state-of-the-art performance venue in Kowloon to boost Hong Kong's status as Asia's entertainment and events capital..." This major undertaking was/is being carried out by the Hong Kong (SAR) Government to "respond to the need to provide more cultural opportunities and exposure for local residents, as well as to put forward a world-class arts and cultural hub for tourists" (Lim, 2017).

Although the WKCD has set out specific aims to provide venues to serve as permanent homes for resident performing arts companies, as well as artists' residencies programmes, many local orchestras (e.g., Hong Kong Philharmonic Orchestra (HK Phil) are still lamenting the lack of world-class venues and are frustrated by the fact that there are still no plans for the promised concert halls at the WKCD). As highlighted by Y. S. Liu, Chairman of the Board of Governors of the Hong Kong Philharmonic Society, "Being a leading orchestra in Asia, it has been a humble wish for the HK Phil to look for a permanent home at a concert hall with world-leading acoustics and purpose build rehearsal spaces built-in. This is important for the future development, maintenance and long-term strategy planning for sustainable growth in its operational, audience and business development as a leading orchestra in the region. We hope we can be a resident orchestra in the WKCD in order to fulfil this lofty ambition..." (Cheng & Fung, 2019).

Aims of the Book

This book comprises a series of insightful interviews with seasoned arts administrators and practitioners in Hong Kong. The interviewees featured in this book include CEOs, chairpersons, founders and chair professors, representing some of the leading cultural and arts education institutions in Hong Kong. These interviews set out to examine the current state, as well as the future development of the ecology of both the art market and performing arts in Hong Kong. In addition to looking into the art and cultural scene in Hong Kong, this book also aims to serve as the most up-to-date platform to understand the current state of the arts and culture industries in Hong Kong. Voices from across a broad spectrum of arts administrators in Hong Kong have been invited to discuss their professional practices, as well as the various risks and challenges they are currently facing. This is significant as the impact is not only on/for the local arts but also for the wider creative industry sector to maintain its edge in the region and as a global player.

This book content is based on a series of face-to-face interviews with leading arts administration professionals practicing in Hong Kong and sets out to achieve the following:

1. Tracing the various social and economic impacts of different local and international music festivals and arts fairs implemented in Hong Kong;
2. Examining if Hong Kong is ideally suited to the centre for arts and culture within Asia and its role within the global arts and cultural world;
3. Determining what directions the arts and cultural industries in Hong Kong are heading.

According to Fok (2018), Art Basel Hong Kong and Art Central have both influenced the production of and trade in contemporary art by emerging artists in Asia. Rather than seeing art fairs just as a space to trade artworks, this book also features several insightful interview chapters that explore the unique characteristics of international art fairs that are particular to Art Basel Hong Kong and Art Central. For example, these interview chapters also investigate other roles these international art fairs have played, their impacts on the local art scene, and their influence on enhancing cultural interaction (e.g., community-wide participation in the arts) and creative industries in Hong Kong.

Arts Management Professional Practices and Developments

Art management, also referred to as art administration, applies business administration techniques and processes to the art world. It entails running the daily business operations of private or public art institutions.

"In the 21st century, it has become common to think of artists and managers as operating in different spheres. Contemporary psychologists have categorised people as "right-brained" or "left-brain," suggesting that artists (the creative ones) would be ever at odds with managers, for whom organisation and accountability are essential tools" (Bindle & DeVereaux, 2011, p. 4).

Arts management as an academic discipline is relatively young. "Only since the late 20th century has the field received the concentrated focus of research and formalised training" (Bindle & DeVereaux, 2011, p. 4). According to Bindle and DeVereaux (2011), "Arts management has been labelled interdisciplinary and multidisciplinary… as such arts management has failed to develop its own set of theories and methods. As a formal field, it is considered to be emerging rather than established" (p. 5). Since arts managers' careers have many variants largely due to organisational size and context, their career paths are known to be convoluted. Arts organisations are distinctive in nature – values, creativity, and imagination – which drives individual passion and motivation to work in the arts or in arts management. Although they are not the ones performing onstage or putting images on canvas, arts managers create performances and exhibitions, organise events that gather people together in circumstances that can be singularly satisfying.

Traditionally, arts management skills are learnt via apprenticeships. Most interviewees featured in this book do not hold formal arts management degrees. They have earned their skills on the job. This book is written on the assumption that arts and management are not opposing concepts, showing the readers how to align resources and oversee and handle the complexities of creating, producing, and presenting arts and culture. In addition to serving as a platform for professional exchange and sharing experiences, this book also aims to identify new and potential areas for networking and collaboration in arts administration. Another objective of this book is to promote best practices in arts administration through strong advocacy, long-term professional development, and fruitful communication, thereby raising the overall standard of arts administration and practices in the region. It is hoped that this publication will bring additional voices and new recognition to the arts administration profession and its previously underrepresented professionals.

This book reflects Hong Kong's cultural scene that continues to thrive, with a diverse range of cultural offerings that reflect the city's unique blend of East and West. From contemporary street art to music, film, and literature, Hong Kong's cultural scene is a testament to the city's rich history and ongoing evolution as a global hub for culture and creativity. The book features many individuals who are deeply involved in diversifying Hong Kong's cultural canvas, thus making it a destination for cultural aficionados.

References

(E)BrandConnect (n.d.). The art of making money: how Hong Kong became a hub for Asia's biggest art deals: An in-depth look at the growth of the Asian market and Hong Kong's role in it. *The Art of Marking Money.* Retrieved from: https://asia hubhk.economist.com/wp-content/uploads/The_art_of_making_money.pdf.

ArtTactic. (2020). The Art Market 2020: A Year in Review. Retrieved from: https://int.nyt.com/data/documenttools/20solowpdf2/5d9d84ff385ca83b/ full.pdf.

Brindle, Meg & DeVereaux, Constance. (2011). *The Arts Management Handbook: New Directions for Students and Practitioners.* London: Routledge.

Cheng, Meggy & Fung, Flora. (2019). Hailed as the 2019 Gramophone Orchestra of the Year, the HK Phil and its Music Director Jaap van Zweden to Tour Japan and Korea in March 2020. *HK Phil Press Releases.* Retrieved from: https://www.hkphil.org/press-release/hailed-as-the-2019-gramophone-orchestra-of-the-year-the-hk-phil-and-its-music-director-jaap-van-zweden-to-tour-japan-and-korea-in-march-2020.

Desser, David & Fu, Poshek (2000). *The Cinema of Hong Kong: history, arts, identity.* New York, NY: Cambridge University Press.

Fok, Silvia. (2018). The roles of international art fairs in Hong Kong in facilitating the production and consumption of contemporary art in Asia. In Lorraine Lim & Hye-Kyung Lee (Eds.). *Routledge Handbook of Cultural and Creative Industries in Asia* (273-82). London: Routledge.

Gao, Sally. (2020). A History of Hong Kong's New Wave Cinema. *Culture Trip.* Retrieved from: https://theculturetrip.com/asia/china/hong-kong/articles/a-history-hong-kongs-new-wave-cinema/.

Grogan, Molly. (2022). The Troubled state of performing arts in Hong Kong. *Zolima Citymag.* Retrieved from: https://zolimacitymag.com/the-troubled-state-of-performing-arts-in-hong-kong-ispa/.

Home Affairs Bureau, The Government of the Hong Kong Special Administrative Region. (2008). *Advisory and Statutory Bodies under the Purview of the Secretary for Home Affairs.* Retrieved from: http://www.hab.gov.hk/en/related_departments_organizations/asb45.htm.

Hong Kong Tourism Board (n.d.). The stories behind Hong Kong's street art. Retrieved from: https://www.discoverhongkong.com/us/explore/arts/the-stories-behind-hong-kongs-street-art.html.

Kong L., Gibson C., Khoo L. M., & Semple A. L. (2006). Knowledges of the creative economy: Towards a relational geography of diffusion and adaptation in Asia. *Asia Pacific Viewpoint*, 47 (2): 173-94.

Leung, Jenny. (2023). Best street art and graffiti in Hong Kong: Discover the most impressive artworks on the city streets. *Time Out*. Retrieved from: https://www.timeout.com/hong-kong/art/best-street-art-and-graffiti-in-hong-kong.

Lim, Benny. (2017). Navigating the Theatre Ecology in Hong Kong: Perspectives of a Singaporean. *Critical Stages/Scènes critiques*. (16). Retrieved from: https://www.critical-stages.org/16/navigating-the-theatre-ecology-in-hong-kong-perspectives-of-a-singaporean/.

Lo, Patrick, Hsu, We-En, Wu, Stephaine, Travis, J. & Chiu, Dickson. (2021). *Creating a Global Cultural City via Public Participation in the Arts: Conversations with Hong Kong's Leading Arts and Cultural Administrators*. New York, N.Y.: Nova Science Publisher.

Poposki, Z., & Leung, I. H. B. (2022). Hong Kong as a global art hub: Art ecology and sustainability of Asia's art market centre. *Arts*, 11(1). Retrieved from https://doi.org/10.3390/arts11010029.

Uttam, Payal. (2020). Hong Kong's Art Market Emerges from a Tumultuous Year with Optimism. *Art Market*. Retrieved from: https://www.artsy.net/article/artsy-editorial-hong-kongs-art-market-emerges-tumultuous-year-optimism.

Wang, Yuke. (2022). Global art sales shift online, NFT prices soar. *China Daily*. Retrieved from: https://www.chinadailyhk.com/article/257798.

Yu, Helen. (2022). Where to find the best street art in Hong Kong. Tatler. Retrieved from: https://www.tatlerasia.com/lifestyle/arts/best-street-art-hong-kong.

Zhou, Mo & Ao, Yulu. (2022). Hong Kong to project soft power. *China Daily*. Retrieved from: https://www.chinadailyhk.com/article/255238.

Chapter 1

Flora Yu, Executive Director, Hong Kong Arts Festival Society Ltd.

Introduction

Launched in 1973, the Hong Kong Arts Festival (HKAF) is a major international arts festival committed to enriching the cultural life of the city by presenting leading local and international artists in all genres of the performing arts as well as a diverse range of "PLUS" and educational events in February and March each year. In addition to partnering with renowned international artists and institutions, the HKAF also collaborates regularly with Hong Kong's own creative talent and showcases emerging local artists. Over the years, HKAF has commissioned and produced over 200 local productions across genres including Cantonese opera, theatre, chamber opera, music and contemporary dance, many with successful subsequent runs in Hong Kong and overseas.

Since November 2022, Flora Yu has been serving as the Executive Director, Hong Kong Arts Festival Society Ltd. In her previous capacity as Development Director of the Hong Kong Arts Festival, Flora formulated fundraising strategies, and led her team in cultivating and nurturing partnerships with corporate and foundation sponsors, donors, as well as other stakeholders and supporters. In the following interview, Flora discusses the brand identity of the HKAF, as well as the challenges faced by a majority of arts and cultural administrators in Hong Kong.

Could we begin this interview by first introducing yourself, for example your professional training and educational background? For example, what did you study at university? Do you come from a family of performing artists, musicians, or creative people?

I come from a family of no artists. I started developing an interest in the arts in my first year in secondary school, when I was asked to learn to play the double bass and join the school orchestra (even though I played very badly!).

My father, a mechanical engineer, and my mother, a homemaker, were kind and understanding and did not stop me from pursuing what I was interested in, i.e., the visual arts, in university. Hence, I have a first degree in Fine Art. I later earned an M.A. in Literary Studies from the University of Hong Kong, and then an M.B.A. from the University of British Columbia in Canada.

I have worked in both the arts field and in the commercial world for many years. I must say that having an academic background in both arts and business disciplines has been extremely helpful throughout my career.

Could you provide a brief introduction to the Hong Kong Arts Festival (HKAF)? What are the missions, visions and philosophy behind the operations and management of the HKAF?

The mission of the Festival is to present an international arts festival of the highest artistic standard that will enrich the cultural life of Hong Kong, act as a catalyst, arouse wider public interest in the arts and encourage cross-cultural artistic exchange.

The Festival always considers the "pursuit of the highest artistic quality" its most important goal. It stages the best artists from around the world from the fields of classical music, jazz, ballet, contemporary dance, theatre, opera, traditional Chinese opera, outdoor events, arts tech programmes, and even popular entertainment. We aim to present a balanced programme each year that will highlight the latest artistic trends and present works not frequently seen in Hong Kong, while also including the more traditional works and art forms. We try our best to ensure there is sufficient variety in our programming each year to meet the needs and interests of different sectors of the Hong Kong community.

The Festival also considers supporting local talent, whether established or emerging, another of its main goals. We have presented more than 250 original local works over the years.

The third most important goal of the Festival is to offer quality arts education programmes to young people in Hong Kong, including primary, secondary and tertiary school students. Our "Young Friends of the Arts Festival" project, which has reached over 800,000 students in the past 30 years, has been making an impact in Hong Kong, especially in building audiences.

Could you describe the brand identity for the HKAF?

Brand identity of HKAF -- A premier arts event in Hong Kong and the region, and an important international arts festival, committed to presenting the highest quality arts programmes and the best artists from around the world and Hong Kong, and committed to arts education aimed at nurturing the next generation of audiences for the city.

Why is brand building so important for any organisations, including arts organisations?

Brand building is extremely important to arts organisations, including the HKAF. A good brand attracts the world's best artists to the Festival stage; a good brand gives confidence to sponsors and donors who are extremely important to sustaining and growing the Festival; a good brand attracts audiences (they trust our programming choices even when they are not yet too familiar with the artists we present); and a good brand attracts good people to join our staff.

Could you describe your career path to becoming the Executive Director of the HKAF?

I once worked for 2 editions of the Hong Kong Arts Festival as an Editor in the earlier stage of my career. Afterwards I joined the Hong Kong Philharmonic where I also worked for two years as Assistant General Manager before going to Canada in 1996 to pursue my MBA degree. At that time, I was not yet determined to stay in the arts field permanently. I was simply too curious about the non-arts world then.

After earning my M.B.A. degree, I returned to Hong Kong and entered the commercial world and held various senior management positions for years, working both in Hong Kong and Mainland China, mainly Shanghai. I learned so much about management and about doing business during those days from my boss, colleagues and business associates! But deep inside, I knew I would be interested in going back to the arts world one day.

That day came in late 2011, when I joined the Hong Kong Arts Festival as its Development Director. It was a challenging but interesting job, so I continued working in that position for 11 years. Then in 2022, Ms Tisa Ho, who has been the Executive Director of the Hong Kong Arts Festival for 16 years, decided to retire. After a series of recruitment exercises and interviews, I was appointed the Executive Director of HKAF effective 14 November 2022.

As the Executive Director of the HKAF, could you describe your main roles and areas of responsibilities?

The Board gives me the responsibility of ensuring that we deliver a quality Hong Kong Arts Festival every year and devise strategies that will lead to further growth of the Festival in a rapidly changing environment. Working closely with the Board and its subcommittees, I am responsible for ensuring there are sufficient financial resources to support the work we now do as well as the bigger projects we would like to pursue in the longer-term future. This means working closely with funders, sponsors and donors, etc. I am also trying to strengthen HKAF's relationships with key players in the arts world and the business community in and outside Hong Kong, to further build the brand of HKAF, and to facilitate colleagues so that they can achieve their own goals at work.

I always ask colleagues about budgets and timelines, but I seldom interfere in the Festival's artistic choices – that part is better left to the experts in the Programme Department and the Programme Committee.

As the Executive Director of the HKAF, could you describe your typical day at work? Is there ever a typical day at work?

I don't think there is a "typical day" at work. There are new challenges every day!

As the Executive Director of the HKAF, could you describe your management and leadership style? Would you describe yourself as a servant leader or a participative leader?

As leaders, we are all expected to communicate our vision, and to set goals and directions for our organisations. But which management style we should adopt really depends on the particular nature of the workforce and the organisation. In the case of HKAF, my "management style" is not so much to "manage," but to "facilitate." This is because almost all HKAF staff are knowledge workers. The more experienced ones are skilled at tackling projects independently, questioning, voicing their views and solving problems with creativity and professional knowledge. The less experienced ones are being trained to acquire these attributes. These types of colleagues cannot stand authoritarian management styles. They expect trust, respect, empowerment, and a reasonable level of autonomy. If we can offer them these, together with suitable structures, processes and the right amount of resources, they will do a great job themselves.

What are the latest trends in marketing and audience outreach/building amongst arts and cultural organisations worldwide? With the convenience brought by Internet connectivity and other mobile technologies, have you witnessed and experienced any major evolutions in terms of marketing/outreach strategies in the context of arts and cultural management?

Just like other arts and cultural organisations worldwide, the HKAF is keen to bring the audience "back to the venues" after years of COVID-19 venue closure.

Loyal audiences are keen to go back to the venues to enjoy live performances, but new audiences, especially younger audiences, have a wide range of activities enticing them every day, and HKAF needs to compete with these to bring them back to the theatres and concert halls.

To young audiences, "digital" is how they live, and it is also how a lot of them consume the arts. Therefore, HKAF has to promote increasingly aggressively in the digital arena, including social media platforms, websites, search engine marketing, eDMs, and even "meta platform" to promote the performing arts.

To compete, arts organisations need to execute both traditional and digital marketing campaigns holistically to develop young audiences while also retaining traditional audiences. Integrated marketing has a different meaning these days.

Arts organisations now spend more resources on content marketing to nurture young and new audiences. This may include short videos, lead-in articles for mobile phone viewers, and interactive games to attract, develop and nurture audiences.

What are the current difficulties and challenges faced by the majority of arts and cultural administrators in Hong Kong?

The biggest challenge is "uncertainty." For HKAF in the past two years, it was hard to predict whether overseas artists could come as quarantine measures were constantly being adjusted to meet changing pandemic situations. Even local programmes were subject to venue closure possibilities. To sell, or not to sell [tickets], that is the question…for almost any arts marketer.

Even when anti-COVID measures have been relaxed gradually, the aftermath of the pandemic still brought great challenges to the 2023 Festival. We believe our audience profiles have changed considerably as many expatriates and professionals have left Hong Kong to avoid COVID-19 measures. We also lost tourist patrons from mainland China and from around the world. We hope they will eventually come back after this year, but we are also putting in greater efforts to acquire new audiences.

The global economic downturn and unpredictable pandemic restrictions also changed ticket purchase patterns completely. Audiences are still interested in going to the shows, but many prefer to buy tickets close to the event date to avoid having to deal with refunds in case of cancellations.

Some young audiences may not choose to go back to the theatre as they have used to "free digital entertainment" during the COVID-19 days. Arts marketers have to really work hard to develop young audiences.

What parts of your job as the Executive Director of the HKAF do you find most rewarding? And which do you find most frustrating?

Most rewarding – seeing the Festival programmes take place before my eyes after everyone in the team has put in so much hard work, and having the assurance that all the money has been raised and all the tickets have been sold!

Most frustrating – I find it a bit hard to answer this question, as I am not the type who easily gets frustrated…

In what ways do you want the HKAF to develop in the next 5 to 10 years?

There are many things we would like to do. But let's just name a few:

We hope the Festival brand will be even better known around the world and also in Mainland China in the next decade; this means devising not merely a clear touring strategy but also further strengthening our international branding and networking efforts.

We hope the Festival will continue to be recognised for the high quality of its artistic offerings as well as its dedication to innovation. We will need to commit more resources to achieve the latter though, and that's not just about commissioning and producing the innovative works; we will have to commit resources and efforts to cultivate the audience for such innovative works.

We also hope to further strengthen our efforts in inclusive arts through the No Limits project, which was launched in 2019 and co-presented by the Festival and The Hong Kong Jockey Club Charities Trust.

The Festival does not have any brick-and-mortar, which makes it difficult for us to do a lot of work such as artist residencies, incubation programmes, or even to find convenient spaces for rehearsals for local productions. So eventually, we hope to raise enough money to have our own Hong Kong Arts Festival Centre. This very long-term goal is also a key goal of the recently set up Hong Kong Arts Festival Foundation.

In what ways do you want the HKAF to contribute to the overall arts and cultural scene of Hong Kong, especially in cultivating the next generation of arts audience in Hong Kong?

For decades, the festival has been investing heavily in arts education and audience development. Our Young Friends of the Arts Festival has reached over 800,000 students in the past 30 years since its inception. We also have many other arts education programmes targeted at primary, secondary and tertiary institute students. I am sure we will continue to enhance our efforts to cultivate the next generation of arts audiences in Hong Kong.

30 years ago versus now – have you witnessed any major evolution in the characteristics of the arts audience in Hong Kong, e.g., their level of appreciation for performing arts?

Thirty years ago, there were fewer arts programme available in Hong Kong. Audiences were eager to grab the chance to watch the outstanding international artists brought in by the Hong Kong Arts Festival. Tickets were sold out quickly, and queues in front of the box office were long. Many people dressed up to go to the performances.

Now, the city offers arts performances and exhibitions almost every day. The pie is bigger in that there are more people interested in going to theatres and concert halls. The atmosphere is more casual (one seldom sees audiences dress up these days). Audiences are still eager for the outstanding international artists featured by the Festival, but there are also audiences who mainly go for local productions. It takes even greater efforts to market the shows because competition is extremely fierce (not just from other arts groups, but also from digital players like Netflix). We have also seen an increase in Mainland audiences in the past decade, and we believe they will come back when the pandemic is over.

I need to emphasise one thing – the loyal audiences of the Festival have always been very sophisticated, whether 30 years ago or now. They have great taste, they understand challenging works, and they show great appreciation for the efforts of the artists and of the Festival.

COVID-19 has turned the world upside down. How has the HKAF been coping with COVID-19?

Because of the first wave of COVID, the 2020 Festival had to be cancelled just a few days before it was due to open in February. We made sure we learned from that experience and everyone in the Festival team became a lot more agile as a result. We learned quickly how to move in-venue shows online, conduct our arts education programmes digitally, and film stage performances for "just-in-case" situations. Those who used to work only at in-venue shows suddenly became film directors; Development staff found themselves creating Festival Openings and Finales online; and we were ready to livestream almost everything when required.

The 2021 and 2022 Festivals were both affected by COVID, but because we had Plan A, Plan B and Plan C in place, we felt quite ready to face any scenarios that came our way. Most programmes became digital offerings in those two years, but we were still able to present some shows in-venue during the second half of 2022 thanks to the tremendous efforts of the entire team.

The Festival is fortunate in that it has had the support of many sponsors and donors still in the past 3 years, despite not being able to present most of the shows in-venue.

In your opinion, what will be the impact of the West Kowloon Cultural District project in Hong Kong, and its potential in creating sustainable arts development in the City?

WKCD plays an important role in Hong Kong's cultural development. The opening of venues such as the M+ Museum and Palace Museum drew international attention and enhanced Hong Kong's branding as a cultural hub. Hong Kong has always suffered from a shortage of suitable performance venues, and we are all eagerly looking forward to the opening of more venues in WKCD.

What would you like to be remembered for when you retire?

Have not thought about retiring yet…

Photo 1. 2016 HKAF local production "Danz Up" [credit: Cheung Wai-lok].

Photo 2. 2018 "Cantonese Opera: Pavilion of a Hundred Flowers" - adapted and directed by Professor Fredric Mao - commissioned and produced by the HKAF [credit: Keith Hiro].

Photo 3. 2019 HKAF Commission and Production – "Always by Your Side," features a talented local cast in a heart-warming original story.

Photo 4. The HKAF organises outreach activities to provide arts education in schools.

Photo 5. "The Plague (English version)." Two versions of "The Plague" – one in English and one in Cantonese - were produced and presented in the same edition of the HKAF during the pandemic in 2021.

Photo 6. "The Plague (Cantonese version)." Two versions of "The Plague" – one in English and one in Cantonese - were produced and presented in the same edition of the HKAF during the pandemic in 2021.

Photo 7. "RUSH" choreographed by Ricky Hu in the Hong Kong Jockey Club Contemporary Dance Series in 2013.

Photo 8. "Morning Glory" choreographed by Ivy Tsui in the Hong Kong Jockey Club Contemporary Dance Series in 2016.

Photo 9. Legendary Cantonese opera artist Yau Sing-po as Artistic Director and main cast in "Cantonese Opera – Li Bai: The Immortal Poet" at the 2016 HKAF [credit: Lawrence Ng @Work House].

Photo 10. "A Floating Family" is a trilogy of plays which portrays a typical Hong Kong family and stars some of the most sought-after names of Hong Kong theatre – an HKAF commission and production at the 2017 HKAF [credit: Lawrence Ng @Work House].

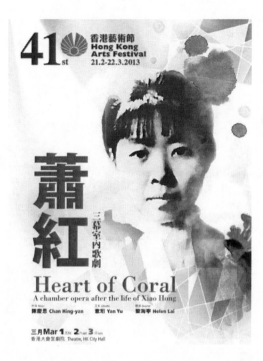

Photo 11. A chamber opera after the life of Xiao Hong, one of the most celebrated Chinese woman writers in the 1930s. The HKAF commission and production features a stellar cast and an outstanding local creative team in poetic verse, staging and original score.

Photo 12. Lecture demonstration by award-winning local dancer and choreographer Alice Ma for student audiences, as part of a Festival outreach programme in 2018.

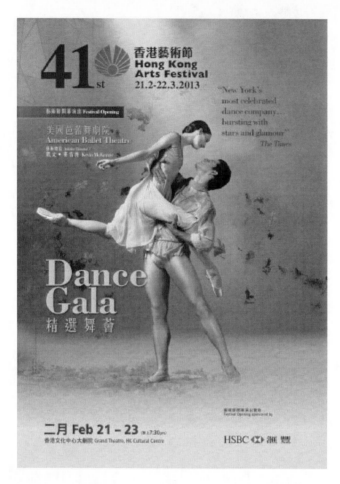

Photo 13. American Ballet Theatre's "Romeo and Juliet" was presented in the "Dance Gala" at the 2013 HKAF.

Photo 14. World-renowned Maestro Gustavo Dudamel performed with the Los Angeles Philharmonic at the 2015 HKAF.

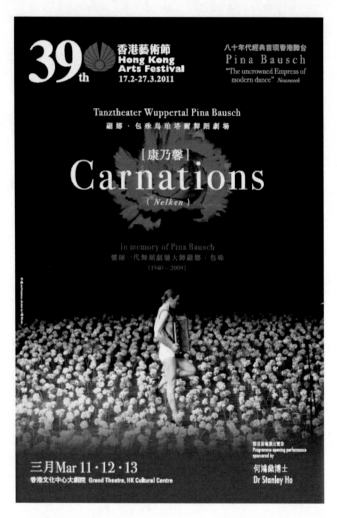

Photo 15. In 2011, legendary Pina Bausch and her Tanztheater Wuppertal's "Carnations" was presented at the HKAF.

Photo 16. The famous opera "Einstein on the Beach" was featured at the 2013 HKAF during its final world tour.

Photo 17. World-renowned conductor Christian Thielemann and Staatskapelle Dresden performed at the 2015 HKAF.

Photo 18. Flora Yu, Executive Director of the Hong Kong Arts Festival.

Chapter 2

Dr. Yu-Chieh Li, MACAH Programme Director, Lingnan University

Introduction

The Master of Arts in Curating and Art History (MACAH) launched at Lingnan University (Hong Kong) is designed for those interested in pursuing an interdisciplinary postgraduate education in art history, and professional careers in museums, curatorial and other art-related industries, etc. Through MACAH, students are given various innovative and creative learning methods to study art theories and collections, curatorial practice, art projects, entrepreneurial initiatives, and professional training -- as MACAH offers students multiple perspectives to explore and engage in the development of art and cultural landscapes in Hong Kong, as well as Asia and beyond.

Since 2021, Dr. Yu-Chieh Li has been serving as the MACAH Programme Director at Lingnan University. Dr. Li holds a Ph.D. in East Asian Art History and an MA in European Art History from Heidelberg University, Germany. Before joining Lingnan University, she was the inaugural Judith Neilson Postdoctoral Fellow in Contemporary Art at UNSW Art and Design, Sydney (2018-2020). She has also held research positions at the Tate Research Centre: Asia, London (2017-2018) and the Museum of Modern Art, New York (2013-2015). Her research engages with aesthetics of performance art in Asia, art historiography emerging from decolonial struggles, and socially engaged practices and curation resisting neoliberal globalisation. In the following interview, Dr. Li discusses the career opportunities for MACAH graduates and the roles that museums play in shaping the future cultural tourism industry in Hong Kong.

Could we begin this interview by first introducing yourself, for example, your professional training and educational background? What did you study at university or film school? Do you come from a family of artists, art educators, art dealers, museum curators, etc.?

I was fortunate to attend art-focused elementary and junior high schools in Taiwan, where I spent my adolescent years dabbling in ceramics, woodblock prints, ink art, watercolour, and drawings. I obtained my BA and MA in art history in Germany, where art history is still divided by regions and mediums.

During this time, I studied classical art historical approaches developed by German, Austrian, and Swiss thinkers, such as iconography, form and style, genre, and techniques, and in addition, Latin and French. The German higher education system differs significantly from that of Hong Kong. The majority of the classes were seminars that focused on critical debates. Thus, I began my first semester at the university with seminars on William Hogarth, Baroque sculptures, and the Bauhaus. I had to study very hard to catch up with class discussions.

During my MA studies, I was exposed to global art discourses at the Heidelberg Centre for Transcultural Studies, which is when I began to consider the role of Asian art in global art historiography. While working on my Ph.D., I was awarded an Andrew W. Mellon C-MAP fellowship at the Museum of Modern Art, a research programme that supported emerging scholars in conducting research that was expected to be related to the interests of the various curatorial departments, including acquisition proposals, publications, and symposia. This was an eye-opening experience as I observed and participated in how the discourses and theories were transformed into exhibitions, conferences, and publications.

What motivated you to pursue a career in academia, specialising in the histories and theories of modern and contemporary art?

When I was working for C-MAP, MoMA, I co-organised conferences and symposia of global contemporary art across regions with scholars specialising in the art of Asia, Central- and Eastern Europe, and the Americas. Through learning from various scholars and curators, I realised that contemporary art theory from a perspective outside of Euroamerica is still an understudied field. Museums depend on scholars trained in art history to expand the Canon. This means more than following institutional critique and New Art History established in the English and German academia; the museum field is looking for solid research on the art of various local contexts.

I am interested in not just how to build bridges among art from various geographies and times but also how the practices excluded from the previous Canon can help us renew the discipline of art history. Becoming an academic and educator is the most practical way to have an impact in the field, as we produce content and educate the next generation of arts leaders.

Could you briefly introduce the Master of Arts in Curating and Art History (MACAH) programme developed by the Department of Visual Studies at Lingnan University (LU)? What are the missions, visions, and philosophies behind MACAH?

The programme is designed to develop emerging arts leaders in the Greater Bay Area and beyond. We offer courses in art history, curating, and museum studies, which combine theory and practice. Students interested in curating, the arts industries, or arts education can apply for an internship and pursue a curatorial project as their graduation project, while those interested in research can write a dissertation.

From the viewpoint of a museum/art gallery curator, are there any core skills that would never become obsolete / outdated for managing art collections, undertaking research, engaging in exhibition projects and spearheading public programmes in museums, galleries and other cultural venues -- regardless of how advanced technology has reached?

Institutional curators are guardians, researchers, and educators of a collection or intangible legacy, and they must first have a strong knowledge of the heritage as well as relevant research skills, which include: critical perspectives of artworks and objects across cultures and time periods, an eye of connoisseur and critic to recognise periodic, regional, and individual styles. A good understanding of work ethics connected to research, exhibition production, and collaboration, is also a key skill/character. In addition, curators' work involves much collaboration and negotiation. They need to be good communicators, listeners, and team leaders.

What are the career paths and career options for a majority of the students who graduated MACAH at LU?

Our alums work as art administrators, arts educators, and other curatorial positions for museums, galleries, auction houses, and art foundations. Some of them also work in the media or finance industries. Many of our current part-time students are already employed by arts organisations and related industries. They enrolled in our MA programme as they feel that continuing education and more professional knowledge of the field are required for them to upgrade to the next stage of their career.

Could you describe your career path to becoming the MACAH Director at LU?

My career has been centred on art historical study. I am the generation of art historians exposed to so-called global art discourse and the emphasis on interdisciplinary research. Aside from the aforementioned art historical training, I was involved in two digital humanities projects in Heidelberg, one on Chinese Buddhist Scriptures led by Professor Lothar Ledderose and the other on Chinese Women's Magazines in the Republican Period led by Prof. Barbara Mittler. These have taught me how to put together a cross-national, collaborative effort in collaborating with engineers to construct a collection database. Data analysis and management skills are significant to museum management and art historian study.

Other prior experience includes research and teaching work (Mellon Fellow in the Department of Media and Performance Art at MoMA, Adjunct Researcher at Tate Research Centre: Asi, Judith Neilson Postdoctoral Fellow in Contemporary Art at the University of New South Wales.) Through these various institutional experiences, I developed my primary research interests in Asian art historiography, intermedia practice, performance art histories, and postcolonial theory.

Aside from these research roles, I was involved in a number of curatorial projects. I co-founded the media art platform SCREEN (2015-), where our curatorial collective has presented performance events and screenings in New York and Berlin. At the Taipei Contemporary Art Centre, I co-curated an exhibition with Shih-yu Hsu and joined their workshop series in Jakarta in partnership with Gudskul (Learning from Peers, 2019). Curating is a collaborative and interventionist approach that allows me to contribute to contemporary art debates. Through these experiences, I discovered a pressing need for academic publications on Asian contemporary art with visions of New Art History.

The paths featured above are rewarding for my current position as Director of Hong Kong's first MA Programme that integrates curation and art history.

Given the recent M+ Museum controversy after introducing Hong Kong's national security law, how do you think this would affect Hong Kong's cultural tourism industry and the City's position as one of the world's top art markets in the long run?

Museums can benefit cultural tourism, however, they also bear the mission of public education. Here I'd like to address the need for community engagement and challenging and fostering the audience regarding the museum scene in Asia. Museums have proliferated in numerous Asian countries during the last decade, from Southeast Asia to Northeast Asia, and each locality faces its own institutional constraints. Cultural workers in many cities are still working hard to nurture an art public. In the long run, what the museum curates and collects must address people and their histories. I believe that additional support should be given to improve Hong Kong citizens' general aesthetic education by expanding history, art, and culture classes in primary and secondary schools. We can maintain and re-interpret intangible legacy through educational efforts and dialogical practices.

We know from the experience of many international and local public museums that it takes decades, if not centuries, of effort by art professionals with public and private support to build a collection that eventually enters and influences art history while also nurturing the aesthetic minds of communities. We're talking about the kind of long-term influence that can't be measured regarding visitor numbers and social media clicks. I believe many new museums in Hong Kong have already established their brands and international profile, and now it is time for them to challenge or expand the public's aesthetic preferences.

Apart from efforts in branding, museums can be more experimental in their programmes, such as revealing lesser-known alternative histories of objects, new perspectives on artefacts and histories, and voices from the frontiers. And this requires freedom for creative practice and critical debates. Otherwise, the audience will only be passive consumers.

In your opinion, who is the greatest and/or most influential art historian of all time?

There are far too many outstanding art historians. I'll just mention two art historians whose works have directly influenced the evolution of my studies on Asian contemporary art.

John Clark, a Professor Emeritus of Art History at Sydney University, greatly impacts the history of Asia's modern and contemporary art. He is a polyglot of Asian languages who has conducted field research in various Asian cities. In his writing, he does not forge essentialist critique or the cliché dichotomy of East and West, nor does he simply borrow one specific discourse, but instead draws from his fieldwork, observation, and comparative study of diverse cultural spaces to analyse Asian modern and contemporary art.

Lothar Ledderose, a Professor Emeritus at Heidelberg University, is a generation of art historians whose work combines archaeology and the German art historical tradition. His research interests are wide-ranging. In rethinking Chinese cultural creation, his concept of a modular structure in *Ten Thousand Things* remains very insightful. What I find most inspiring about his scholarly work is that art history can foster various ways of interpreting heritage (in an interdisciplinary way), rather than just presenting a compilation of data.

These scholars have spent decades developing their research, which is also built on works by their mentors and fellow scholars. I would like to stress that research impact does not happen overnight and cannot always be quantified. I hope all of us, and the leaders in the education and academic systems, bear this in mind: Art history has its role in shaping citizens of civil society. Building art legacies and research traditions takes centuries, but it may only take one night to destroy these efforts.

What are the roles of art historians in society?

There are huge differences among the roles of art and art historians in various societies, so I am afraid my response will appear to be general. In the 20th century, we witnessed multiple waves of institutional critique around the globe developed from "art for art" to the current attempts of the art world trying to justify art's relationships with other disciplines and various communities. Histories suggest art has always played a huge role in various social contexts. Art historians' task is to critically reflect on the results of institutionalisation of art and the impact of art on society (and vice versa), to rewrite or revise previous histories and aesthetic standards, which will transform into textbooks, popular culture, or materials shown in museums. Such knowledge is about who we are and our relationship with the world. Theoretical knowledge, when first produced, will take time until it can directly impact individuals. To conclude, I think the contribution of art historians to society is inseparable from the reception of art.

Photo 1. Dr. Yu-Chieh Li (MACAH Programme Director, Lingnan University).

Chapter 3

Dr. Daisy Yiyou Wang, Deputy Director, Hong Kong Palace Museum

Introduction

Officially opened in July 2022, the Hong Kong Palace Museum (HKPM) is a public museum in the West Kowloon Cultural District, Hong Kong. The HKPM presents over 900 priceless treasures from the National Palace Museum at the Forbidden City in Beijing. The HKPM regularly presents special exhibitions featuring Chinese art and culture, as well as art and treasures from other parts of the world.

Since 2019, Dr. Daisy Yiyou Wang has been serving as the Deputy Director, Curatorial and Programming for the HKPM. Dr Wang is responsible for the HKPM's research, collections, exhibitions, publications, learning and engagement functions supporting the Museum's overarching mission and strategic planning. Before joining the HKPM, Dr. Wang was the Robert N. Shapiro Curator of Chinese and East Asian Art at the Peabody Essex Museum in Salem, Massachusetts, USA. At the Peabody Essex Museum, Dr. Wang oversaw the museum's prestigious Chinese, Japanese and Korean collections and led a dynamic programme of new exhibitions, acquisitions and research projects.

In the following interview, Dr. Wang discusses the missions and operations behind the HKPM, as well as the differences in museum visitors' expectations between the US and Hong Kong.

Could we begin this interview by first introducing yourself, for example, your professional training and educational background? What did you study at the university? Do you come from a family of visual artists, art educators, art historians, scholars, or creative people?

I was born and raised in Mainland China. I earned my Ph.D. in Art History from Ohio University. I specialise in the history of art collecting, Ming lacquer, and Qing imperial portraiture and textile. I have published internationally and received numerous awards, including a Getty Museum Leadership Fellowship, a National Endowment for the Humanities grant, and a Smithsonian Scholarly Studies Award.

Regarding my curatorial experience, I have co-curated the ground-breaking exhibition *Empresses of China's Forbidden City*, which was named the "Most Influential International Exhibition from Chinese Museums" in 2019, and the "Best Thematic/Historical Show" in 2018 by the *Boston Globe*. I co-edited this exhibition's catalogue, which received the Smithsonian Secretary's Research Prize. I am also a leader in international museum professional exchange, and have served as the founding Chair of the American Alliance of Museum's China Programme.

Could you briefly introduce the Hong Kong Palace Museum (HKPM)?

The Hong Kong Palace Museum is of the newest museums in Hong Kong, and it is scheduled to open to the public in early July 2023. We started formally planning in 2017. Part of the planning process included signing an agreement with the West Column Culture District. We broke ground in 2018 and finished the structure of the main building last year. By the end of 2022, we had 22 administrators. This year, we are working on building a team of volunteers. We also recruited approximately 60 staff members; this team is growing well now. One of the immediate goals is to put on some shows. Right now, we are in the process of arranging the insurance as well as the installation of nearly 1,000 treasures from the Forbidden City; the Palace Museum is classified as a world UNESCO heritage site. The Palace Museum is the world's largest ancient palatial wooden structure palatial complex, home to over 1.82 million objects and treasures, and one of the largest and probably the largest depository of most important Chinese art and culture treasures.

So we're fortunate to have such collaborative relationships with the Palace Museum, Beijing. However, we are not a branch of the Beijing Palace Museum; we are one of their key strategic partners. We are also building partnerships with other major cultural institutions worldwide. When this museum opens, visitors will enjoy nine wonderful exhibitions. We have seven exhibitions devoted to the treasures of the Forbidden City and two special exhibitions from the Beijing Palace Museum, which will show, in an unprecedented way, the rarest treasures, including the crowning jewel of the collection. These include 30 ancient Chinese painting clicker pieces that have not travelled often, and have never been shown in Hong Kong; they probably will never again be shown outside of Mainland China. So, we really have this historic moment to celebrate China's culture and art accomplishments. We are also focusing on building other local connections in Hong Kong.

At Hong Kong Palace Museum, it's crucial that this museum is for the people of Hong Kong and to build local connections. With this in mind, we included one exhibition that involves five contemporary mid-career and upcoming Hong Kong artists. These artists are diligently studying the Palace Museum's culture, art, collection, history, and architecture to develop new artistic interpretations, either through digital media or by installing new interpretations of the Forbidden City's culture. This is how we connect the ancient, modern, and Forbidden City to local life in today's culture. We value international collaboration and connection very much; this is an area we are keen to focus on more. Our future work is not just to build connections between Beijing and Hong Kong but also global connections through our museum platform. Hong Kong is unique because of its international global city status for the opening of exhibitions.

We also have a signed agreement with the Louvre Museum. Their director is very supportive, and they have lent us 13 treasures from the Louisville collection under very favourable conditions. We are doing an exhibition called "Art and Cultural Horse." We selected about 100 pieces from the Palace Museum focusing on Chinese horses from the Han dynasty to the 18th century and some Chinese artworks related to horses from the Luffa collection. We're not just about French art but also Islamic and Persian art because horses from other cultures connect Chinese art and culture to the world. The Hong Kong Palace Museum obviously focuses on and is devoted to Chinese art, culture, and history.

HKPM has a contemporary exhibition in the museum, and you select local artists to elaborate on this collaboration. Can you elaborate more on the collaboration and selection criteria?

First, we decide the exhibition's aim and how it will serve the wider museum and sit with the other palace museum collections. We then approached different artists to see who expressed an interest in their works and ideas related to Chinese urban culture, particularly the palace, art, and culture.

We are slightly different from contemporary art museums, although we are doing contemporary art as our starting point is existing art and culture, which is different from contemporary art, which usually starts with artists and concepts, social context, all kinds of things and the contemporary art context you've got a discourse. We are looking at the crossroads and the dialogue part, the intersection of these two fields. That's what we are most interested in, and this sets us apart from the Beijing Palace Museum, which has always focused on traditional art from the past.

Hong Kong has such a dynamic and wonderful contemporary local art scene; we want to make sure we also engage local practitioners as part of the ecosystem. Part of the museum's job is sustaining and supporting art and cultural practitioners. In addition to that, the contemporary and local perspective is not just in one exhibition but in every exhibition. We have also involved Jeffrey Shaw, now a Chair Professor in Creative Media, Art and Technology projects. He works with three other galleries to bring contemporary technology and his perspectives into our traditional art exhibition. We are bringing multimedia, mainly as an engagement tool, to get younger people involved and make people feel like the museum is updated with technology about interpretations.

Gallery 5 is about traditional arts and crafts. We invited Stanley Wong, another big name in Hong Kong, a distinguished designer and artist. He serves as artistic director for G5, mainly with the concept display and graphic design elements. The video tries to show traditional 18th century and even Han Dynasty, such as a 2000-year-old lamp and other objects, from contemporary designers' viewpoint. He also interviews traditional and contemporary artisans, such as carvers of ivory and jade, to bring some contemporary perspective regarding material and techniques to help people understand how 18th-century people dealt with a piece of jade or ivory.

This is another way we invite Hong Kong local artists and creative practitioners to collaborate with us and work on these traditional exhibitions. It also outlines the distinction between the Palace Museums in Taipei and Beijing. We have close professional connections with colleagues, curators, designers, and conservatives. We share the same mission of promoting our collection, Chinese art and culture, and bringing people together to enhance those understandings. These museums have a lot in common.

In what way do you want to educate 200 overarching cultures in Hong Kong, particularly city culture economy and culture tourism?

The museum's founding members and architects have in mind the idea that the museum should contribute in major ways to the Art and Culture of Hong Kong. There is a wonderful existing museum community with two types of museums: government-sponsored and government-affiliated museums under the Hong Kong Leisure and Cultural Services Department (LCSD) and vibrant museums in the private sector, such as the Maritime Museum. The city is excited to have so many museums, making them a global competitor with New York or London. At Hong Kong Palace Museums, we have no real competition with other museums because we are so complimentary and have a clear area of historical outputs.

In what ways do the new art museums or museum curators in Hong Kong collaborate and help each other?

We have a collegiate network among the museum staff. We would like to see a more structured organisation in some ways, for example, regular meetings. Now, we have regular meetings like my museum and LCSD museums because my boss Luis used to oversee all of these museums. He arranged some regular meetings. So, we all understand what's happening here and in other museums. I would like to see more professionalism and some associations and partnerships because it's not just about having the drinks but informal communications.

We would like to see more of your managerial infrastructure in America. I was part of the China programme for American lines of museums. I was there for five years. I was the chairman of the China program, which allowed me to access many policies, professional networks, annual meetings, and forums. Hong Kong should position itself as a regional leader, including greater China. But because there's a lack of museum associations in Asia, Hong Kong needs to claim its leadership in the field and just be bold, as this doesn't take a lot of resources or investment. We can set up professional standards with a group of very committed professionals. We can set up policies and regular meetings among Asian art museum directors and do more to cement our authority on the world stage.

We tend to be homogenous in our organisations, Hong Kong is pretty good in terms of museum visitation, and we can do even better with more museums and cultural facilities. We always complain that we're not doing a good job in Chinese art and culture education. It's a global issue even if you go to China and don't see excellent resources for teachers, and we're doing that not just for the museum's sake but also for Hong Kong and the global community. While we are beefing up local infrastructure and the museum community, the Hong Kong art and culture community needs to be more internationalised, so that it is a unique thing that Hong Kong can contribute.

How would people outside of Hong Kong access your collections? So, does technology serve as a help to you as an enabler to reach this international audience?

I think it's an excellent question, and we're also working on this. So, this will be the general trend, not just in Hong Kong. Mainland China is doing something, but Hong Kong has its unique opportunities and advantages. Hong Kong has this point of opportunity to be a bridge, so we should speak to the international community promoting local and Chinese southern culture and vice versa. When we talk to the international community, we need to promote our own while talking to our local audience, the mainland, Greater China, and even the Asian audience.

What new technologies are being used to serve the HKPM?

Some examples are Robotic cleaners at the museum; Jeffrey Shaw is working on a projection, so that when visitors are detected by motion sensor technology close to a projection, it will trigger some movements of that kind of picture. We are planning to build a gallery with the capability to include virtual reality and augmented reality.

We are also building up our own private and permanent museum, receiving significant donations from generous donors in Hong Kong. So, people really understand our mission and want to support us. It is a good testimony to the local community and collective support. We have had significant artefact donations from international collectors to our new collection.

As a curator and the deputy director of the Palace Museum, is fundraising part of your major responsibility, or do you have a separate staff team like at the Metropolitan Museum of Art? They have a marketing and branding strategy team for fundraising and their businesses.

I came from America, and fundraising was an essential job of mine. I devoted about 50 percent of my time in my previous jobs to fundraising, which is crucial. I do understand the critical importance of fundraising for American museums. When we come to Hong Kong, we do this very differently from traditional museums. This museum needs to look for long-term financial sustainability. Jockey Club provided 3.5 billion Hong Kong dollars mainly for hardware, but we also understand in a cultural business, it's a black hole:

operating costs, people's costs, programme costs, loan fees, shipping, insurance, etc.

Our director and other colleagues are leading the team to have strategies for fundraising and set specific goals. This is very different, exciting, and new brought to the cultural field in Hong Kong. We are pushing curators and other people doing programmes in Concord Park to make the best effort to look for the best exhibition to attract the most people with the biggest impact. However, the visitation number itself doesn't mean impact. There are also many other factors, like the depth of impact and scholarship contribution. So, we have a set of metrics to assess what kind of exhibition we can consider because exhibitions are expensive. One of the criteria is to attract potential donations and funding support. However, that's not the only criterion you have.

How do Hong Kong visitors' expectations compare to the US and other countries? What are the major differences?

There is not much difference because the exhibition is a business of a very narrow field. Museum professionals work on common ground even if you say mainland China, America, or England. The differences are minor. Say you do a diversity report using this or that format; the content is the same. We're so international, our staff is very international, and our project's very international. So, we are very familiar with the practice in mainland China, America, Europe, and locally. Our idea is to bring the best of all worlds together on the platform that is called Hong Kong Palace Museum. Regarding visitor expectations, I would say if this is my experience, I'm glad you asked me because I spent about 20 years in America as a graduate student and a museum professional.

I was actually surprised to find that the Chinese know how to say Qing dynasty, but most American people cannot pronounce it. However, when you go to the next level, you tell me something about teaching history and politics, women's practice, and food binding; then most Chinese don't know. I was surprised when museum visitors came to a very special topic; visitors are not so different. As a curator, it's most important to cover the basic grounds and give people basic and good overviews. In an hour or so, you enlighten them and transform their concept about certain fields. I also learned that I assume you know more about people in Hong Kong. There are many complaints. Hong Kong people know little about Chinese history, and young people need more education.

Hong Kong has a lot of advantages. I also grew up in mainland China. At a fundamental level, on a daily life basis, Hong Kong preserves a lot of traditional cultures, though not palace history. Many things people see daily can be easily connected to palace culture or Chinese traditions, history, culture, or art. People are not aware of that, and they take it for granted. You see them daily because you live in their environment, but Hong Kong preserves much more traditional Chinese culture than mainland China. Hong Kong has great opportunities to enhance local people's understanding.

Can you tell us about your training in the United States? So, would the Hong Kong public be willing to host non-Chinese, non-Asian, and Western art?

There is a thirst now, as both Chinese and non-Chinese are in Hong Kong and the region. I'm talking about Greater China, particularly mainland China even more so, because in major cities with the Shanghai Museum, Palace Museum, and National Museum of China, the majority of 99.9 percent are Chinese art. Even in Hong Kong, we did not have a tradition of collecting non-Chinese art, meaning that you can't use your own collection to tell a story of certain fields of non-Chinese art, culture, and history. So, there is a genuine thirst for non-Chinese culture.

We have lined up a fascinating group of special exhibitions featuring non-Chinese art, some related to Chinese island culture. So again, the dialogue and the connection point are very important to us. For example, we're working with a European princely collection to show some of the best world's best Reubens and van Dyke in Hong Kong later this year. Most museums in this region took package exhibitions in the past, meaning that other museums and curators did the curation. But we want to push a bit at the Hong Kong Palace Museum and be involved with other institutions at the very beginning of the curatorial process. So, our curators become part of the curatorial team even if Reuben's experts do not train them.

But, we want them to learn and collaborate with curators worldwide on equal footing regarding the curatorial concept, exhibition design, and object selection. So we contribute to this princely collection from Europe. We proposed a new curatorial approach to this exhibition, and they are happy.

Is there anything else you would like to share with the readers, like issues we have not touched upon?

I really have a very challenging job, but every day when I hop onto the train, I always feel very safe, even during a pandemic period of Omicron attacks. Second, I feel very lucky to be part of this wonderful transformation of Hong Kong's art and culture scene, and I remind myself of the many tough tasks ahead. However, who has this opportunity to bring in 1000 charges once in history to share with a wonderful community here, and who is paid to do their dream jobs? I came here because I love the Palace Museum, I did my show, and I have worked with my colleagues on the collections for five years daily. When I finished my show, I said, "Oh, would it be wonderful if I could spend the rest of my day like this." I knew it was impossible because I was a curator of Chinese, Japanese, and Korean art.

I also have to do other things and can't just work with the Palace Museum. I feel every day in this job and laugh in my dream about having this opportunity. Can you name your favourite artwork art piece from the Palace Museum in Beijing or Taiwan? There's a focus on palace culture, and I also have a special perspective about ensuring women's contribution inside the Forbidden City is well recognised in all our future projects. So, I try to balance objects used by the emperor and objects used by women inside the forbidden city. In our open exhibition, you'll probably see a good presentation of objects associated with women's history inside the Forbidden City. That's my very small contribution to the open exhibitions from a scholarly point of view.

Photo 1. Dr. Daisy Wang (Deputy Director, Hong Kong Palace Museum).

Photo 2. Hong Kong Palace Museum.

Chapter 4

Professor Laurence James Wood, Associate Head, Department of Cultural & Creative Arts, The Education University of Hong Kong

Introduction

The Department of Cultural and Creative Arts (CCA), Education University of Hong Kong offers a wide range of engaging programmes in Music and Visual Arts that aim to promote and support high standards of professionalism in teaching, learning, research and knowledge transfer, thereby enabling their graduates to take up transformative roles as innovative educators, arts practitioners, and cultural leaders in the region.

Laurence Wood's creative journey started in Leicester in the UK in the early 1980's, as a community mural painter and as a saxophonist with the British 2-tone band The Apollinaires. Since the mid-1980s, his career has embraced painting, publishing, and Higher Education in the Creative Arts. He was a painting finalist in the 8th Artelaguna International Art Prize in Venice, Italy, in 2014, and prior to moving to Hong Kong was a Dean and Head of College at The University for the Creative Arts in the UK. He is currently a Professor in the Department of Cultural and Creative Arts at the Education University of Hong Kong, and a member of the Humanities and Social Sciences Panel at the Hong Kong Research Grants Council. In addition to discussing the career paths and options for CCA graduates, Laurence also talks about how his martial arts training contributes to his art-making in the following interview.

Could we begin this interview by first introducing yourself, for example, your professional training and educational background? For instance, what did you study at the university or art college? Do you come from a family of artists or art educators?

I was born and educated in the UK. From my very academic grammar school in St Helens, Merseyside (where less than 2% of students opted for

"Art" at 'A' level), I went to study for a Foundation Diploma in Art and Design, followed by a degree in Fine Art, Painting, at Leicester Polytechnic (now De Montfort University). Following graduation, I lived and worked in Leicester for three years as a community artist on local government mural painting projects, as a part-time musician, and also setting up an artist's studio facility with a group of fellow graduates.

During that time, my second application for the Master's Degree Programme in Painting at The Royal College of Art, London, was successful, and they kindly agreed to defer my entry due to my commitments with the projects in Leicester. Eventually, I moved to London and took up my place!

The MA (RCA) at that time was a three-year full-time studio programme based in the buildings of the Victoria and Albert Museum in South Kensington. It was an incredible opportunity and a wonderful place to study Painting. Whilst there, I also won a Chase/Taliani scholarship, a three-month artist's residency in Venice, Italy, and a Mercer's Foundation Fellowship, which provided me with a studio space at the RCA for a further year after graduation.

My parents were neither artists nor formal educators. My father was a manager/industrial chemist in a local factory, and my mother worked in the local law courts. I think I was probably 18 years old before I went to an art gallery. An art teacher took three of us from school to visit the John Moore's Painting Prize exhibition in Liverpool in 1976. It was a truly transformative experience for me. I had no idea that contemporary painting could be so exciting. That year, the prize-winning abstract painting by artist John Walker made a huge and deep impression on me. Nearly a decade later, it was a special moment for me when I met him, as he was a visiting tutor at the RCA. I only told him about this experience a few years ago while he showed me new works in New York. He had no idea what an impression his work had made upon a schoolboy from Merseyside!

Although my parents had no particular interest in or knowledge of the world of Visual Arts, they were always very supportive of my chosen direction. I was part of the lucky late 1950's baby boomer generation that was able to go and do things that most of my parents' generation had not been able to do.

There was always music in the house as my father played the piano and my three siblings and I dabbled with various instruments and listened to many pop, rock and classical records. My uncle entertained us with his Flamenco guitar playing too. My mother loved the Rolling Stones and Gerry and the Pacemakers, and we often watched the famous "Top of the Pops" TV music show together as a family. Of course, living in Merseyside in the late 1960's, I also had a Beatles haircut when I was around 11 years old! In that same year as the John Moore's exhibition, I also went to my first live rock concert in Liverpool to watch the UK band 'Dr. Feelgood'. They were very exciting and completely reinforced my determination to follow some kind of creative path, although at the time, I had no idea what that might consist of beyond the first step of attending art school.

Could you briefly introduce the Department of Cultural & Creative Arts at the Education University of Hong Kong (EdUHK)? According to your Department homepage, "The art of teaching is the art of assisting discovery" and "Creativity takes courage" – could you elaborate on these two statements?

The Department has a creative and dynamic learning environment specialising in Music and Visual Arts Education. We seek to nurture skilled, knowledgeable and caring graduates and empower them for future roles such as innovative educators and teachers, enterprising community-based arts practitioners, or for other careers in the cultural and creative industries sectors.

In relation to the two specific statements, my view is that the best thing a teacher can teach you is how to learn by yourself. Receiving instruction and being filled up regularly at the knowledge "gas station" is important, especially in relation to specific skills and processes, but real deep learning is about being inquisitive, open-minded and critically self-reflective. Building confidence and mental and physical stamina are also prerequisites, as taking control of your acquisition of knowledge and expertise, rather than just following instructions, is a difficult challenge. Self-doubt is a very clever and powerful adversary that always stalks us and can really hinder the learning process.

Could you describe your career path to becoming the Associate Head of the Department of Cultural & Creative Arts (DCCA), EdUHK?

I am not a trained art teacher because I don't have a formal teaching qualification, nor am I a trained "academic," in that I don't have a doctoral research qualification. My early academic posts were in specialist art, design and architecture institutions where there was no requirement to be engaged in formal academic research as we know it now. The requirement was to be an active professional in the chosen field; therefore, most staff were part-time.

My career path evolved through a combination of an amalgamation of knowledge and professional expertise from a range of different fields and roles.

Back in the early 1980's, with a few friends and some fellow graduates from the Fine Art department at Leicester, we set up a group studio facility in the city to continue making art, as nothing like that existed there. We all learned a huge amount about the importance of personal and collegiate organisation, and communication and interaction with local government and national funding agencies. Everything was flexible, dynamic, and full of cross-fertilisation, so it worked well. I worked very hard and learned a great deal about some harsh realities of having a professional creative life. After three years, the studio secured some Arts Council funding, which helped create the trajectory for a sustainable facility, which is now more than thirty years old. Playing and recording with "The Apollinaires" was also exciting, but when they decided to disband in 1984, I took up my deferred place at the Royal College in London.

My career in the University sector started with part-time work as a studio technician at the RCA in London shortly after I graduated there along with part-time work as a visiting tutor at a couple of other art schools, mostly teaching studio drawing classes. Simultaneously I was working freelance as an artist, an illustrator and a writer for a few London publishers, and I was also playing some live music gigs and recording sessions with another London-based band, "Champion Doug Veitch" for a short time.

During the late 80's/early 90's I pursued a renewed teenage passion for martial arts alongside my part-time teaching and other freelance work, and I became a professional martial arts coach, an additional element in my broad freelance portfolio. When an opportunity arose for a full-time drawing tutor at one of the colleges where I was a visiting tutor, I applied and got the job. It was really enjoyable and engaging, and just a few years later, I was appointed the Head of Art and Design. The next step was being appointed as the Head of the Canterbury School of Fine Art at the Kent Institute of Art and Design, where I then became the Head of the College (Canterbury) when that Institute merged with another.

This new institution became the second-largest specialist Art and Design University in the UK, and I was appointed as a founding Dean with wide-ranging responsibilities across the new University's five "colleges" covering art, design and architecture. I received a lot of in-service training, especially in the fields of Quality Assurance and Enhancement, Widening Participation, Improving The Student Experience, and International Recruitment. I undertook staff development with senior colleagues in relation to the Leadership, Management and Governance of large complex organisations, Research Supervision, Project Management and Finance for Senior Executives.

The next step would likely have been into the Executive level of University Leadership. I was "knocking on the door" and made the final selection panels for President and Vice-president posts in three institutions in different countries, but I was already aware that this was not really the type of role I wanted. It was becoming increasingly difficult to maintain a fruitful work/life/family balance, especially with a very young daughter. Within my senior role in the UK, there was no allocation of time for professional painting practice or research. The Head of College and Dean roles did not include any formal teaching or academic supervision requirements, so I had minimal contact with students. I decided it was time to step away and return to painting and creative practice. Not long after that decision, an opportunity arose to come to Hong Kong, to EdUHK, as a visiting artist/professor for one year. That was almost a decade ago!

As the Associate Head of the DCCA, EdUHK, could you describe your main roles and areas of responsibility?

I was contracted under a central strategic initiative and based within the CCA department. My role is to support and advise the Head of the Department, especially in relation to Visual Arts, and contribute directly to the teaching and research programmes. I serve on Faculty and University level committees and lead and contribute to specific Departmental, Faculty or University projects as required. Day to day, I am involved in learning and teaching, research, knowledge transfer and community arts projects within a department specialising in Visual Arts and Music. I developed, introduced and taught a new course in community mural arts which annually engages students in experiential learning, creating live large-scale painting projects with partners and communities beyond the University. It is an enjoyable and inspiring role, beautifully aligned with my passions, expertise, and professional experience.

Could you describe the career paths of a majority of the DCCA graduates?

The majority of students undertaking our undergraduate arts education programme graduate as qualified teachers and pursue their careers within the local teaching profession. Graduates from our undergraduate "Creative and Cultural Arts" programme and our music and visual arts-based post-graduate programmes pursue careers and employment within the cultural, community arts and creative industries sectors as freelance creative practitioners, arts administrators, educators, managers and leaders.

According to your online biography, you hold a 5th-degree black belt in Seal Lung Kung Fu, and other hobbies include fishing, shooting, winemaking, and piano playing. How do all these hobbies and personal pursuits (particularly music playing) contribute to your creativity and art making in particular?

As a schoolboy, I found that sport was a great release from the classroom and the academic emphasis at my school, which I found quite boring. I played rugby and cricket and, inspired by early seventies Bruce Lee movies, my friends and I got interested in martial arts and took some classes that were being taught locally. However, once I was at art school, I got so busy with art and music that I more or less stopped doing any serious sport.

Then, after accumulating some seven years of full-time art school, three years of working flat out as an artist/musician, and pushing 30 years of age, I walked past a Kung Fu School in London that had just opened around the corner from where I was living and thought I should take a look inside!

The School's founder and Principal Mr Tony Lloyd was an inspiration and became a great friend. I seriously engaged with it, training for many years, taking all the examinations and eventually coaching courses, and becoming a part-time professional instructor. It was a valuable income source within my freelance portfolio, allowing me to focus on less predictable painting, publishing and writing projects.

It became a very important, fruitful strand in my life. I met my wife in a Kung Fu class, fought and won a Seal Lung London competition, and attended training sessions with world champion Kevin Brewerton in London and with Jonas Nunez's kickboxing team in New York. In 2007, aged 50, I achieved 5th Degree black belt instructor status. Nowadays, hiking and swimming have replaced hard-core martial arts training for me, though I am helping my teenage daughter, who has taken up Hapkido here in Hong Kong.

There are creative elements within martial arts or any sports if you are engaged with them. Creative arts practice relies heavily on critical reflection, and so does making progress in martial arts training. Once you have acquired a reasonable number of physical techniques and developed your body to deliver them, further progress is then reliant on developing the untapped capacities of your mind. This is a fascinating realm to do with the notion of control of your mind, or perhaps the opposite, like a kind of abandonment. Using your mind embraces logic but also intuition. Some martial artists describe it as the "knowing and the unknowing mind." Sometimes when fighting, you try to lose any conscious control of your mind to overcome fear and avoid "freezing" so that one's responses are quicker. Some artists and designers, myself included, go through related distractive preparatory rituals or listen to music to assist in emptying their minds so that ideas can flow more freely.

You also mentioned "Hobbies." Hobbies are even more important! Growing up in the hinterland of industrial Merseyside but luckily close to some remaining pockets of East Lancashire countryside, I always loved to go into the fields and woods to play. My brothers and I became passionate fishermen as teenagers. Much of my early work as a painter was rooted in painting landscape-inspired works, especially the kind of industrial and post-industrial landscapes I grew up with, now sometimes called "edgelands," being a neglected fusion of urban and rural environments. When I moved from London to a rural village in Kent, I arrived in the full-blown countryside, a childhood dream, and became increasingly involved in fishing and shooting. I can't shoot here in Hong Kong, but I like to fish from a kayak. Hobbies are immersive activities that are a fundamental source of well-being for me. In relation to music, I have been an avid consumer since my teens. I dabbled with learning the clarinet and saxophone, the piano, and, at the present moment, the guitar, and my involvement with art school bands in the 80's was exhilarating and very creative. I like to think it could have had a potential longer-term professional trajectory, had I decided to focus on it rather than on painting.

I like to remind students that all creative disciplines require substantial personal discipline, time and commitment. To get really good at something, you really have to give it everything you have, but you also have to take time to reflect upon it, to step back from it to see what you are doing, and to take rest from it to be able to rejuvenate and sustain it. Creative practice has to be fuelled by other things. Bruce Lee coined a marvellous wise rule that we should all take note of; "when you're tired, go and lie down!"

For me, although ironically generally physically active, these other recreational or semi-professional interests are a form of psychological lying down and are refreshing, allowing for reflection and contemplation. They are also FUN which is a much under-used word for many people, and a major part of what we now call "wellbeing." A school teacher once told me, "The things in life that we do, that we don't have to do, are the things that make life worth living."

You have been listed as a notable artist and art educator by Marquis Who's Who – could you describe what this accolade means to you personally and professionally?

I think this dates back to the millennium while I was Head of Fine Art at the Kent Institute of Art and Design in the UK, and the merger we went through created quite a stir. Being asked this question reminds me to update the entry, which is surely out of date! On a personal level, I admit that I am as vain as anyone else when it comes to enjoying any kind of accolade. In my defence, I wish to note that they invited me, and no money changed hands! On a serious point, I don't know that it has had any impact at a professional level. (Oops, now they will probably remove my entry for saying that! It was only a joke!)

Many people still consider Hong Kong a cultural desert. And yet, over the last few years, Hong Kong has joined New York and London as one of the world's top three international art markets, with a diverse range of public art spaces and large-scale art exhibitions springing up across the City – could you describe the contradiction of this very interesting phenomenon? As a practicing artist and art educator from Europe, how would you describe the overall arts and cultural scene in Hong Kong?

I don't agree that Hong Kong is a cultural desert, but I would also argue that an art market alone wouldn't green a cultural desert anyway. For the international art market (trading via large-scale art fairs) to function, you need art, high-quality facilities, potential buyers and free-flowing financial operations. Hong Kong fits the bill for these. I like that Hong Kong is also making great efforts to publicise and widen access to its art fairs. The potential spin-off or trickle-down benefits to other parts of the local cultural landscape are perhaps less evident at present. Certainly, the internationally renowned commercial galleries located here, and the development of the new public museums, galleries and 'art' spaces vastly improve HK's fixed cultural assets and opportunities to engage a wider public, but I think the art and culture scene here is relatively narrow and conservative if compared to London, Berlin, Tokyo or New York, especially once you move out of well-known mainstream assets, or away from the emphasis on local heritage and traditional culture. There seem to be fewer experimental or regenerative sub-cultures here, perhaps.

According to Chow (2022), "Three politically engaged works by Chinese contemporary artists have been removed from an exhibition at Hong Kong's M+ Museum that showcases the collection donated by Swiss mega-collector Uli Sigg…. The three works were Wang Xingwei's New Beijing *(2001), Zhou Tiehai's Press Conference III (1996), and Wang Guangyi's Mao Zedong: Red Grid No. 2 (1989), according to local media service Ming Pao…. [Furthermore], the M+ Museum has been embroiled in a censorship row before, when Ai Weiwei's photography work, Study of Perspective:* Tian'anmen *(1997), drew attack from Beijing loyalists, who accused the work of "spreading hatred against China" under the national security law. The image of the work was removed from the museum's website and it is not featured in the current exhibition."[1] Given the recent M+ Museum controversies after introducing Hong Kong's national security law, how do you think this would affect Hong Kong's cultural tourism industry and the City's position as one of the world's top art markets in the long run?*

The art market is only one part of "cultural tourism" and its primary function is financial, focused on selling art. As long as the goods for sale don't contravene any laws, and Hong Kong remains an easy place for importing and exporting luxury goods, and for processing the finances relative to that, then that element of cultural tourism should remain buoyant. There will likely be cautious pragmatic self-censorship by artists, curators, galleries, and museums so that Hong Kong might be known as a relatively conservative global art hub. Art is often harnessed as a tool of critique of a political, moral or religious status quo, and is used as propaganda by both capitalist democracies and by

---

[1] Chow, Vivienne. (2022). The M+ Museum has removed three political paintings by Chinese artists as Beijing continues its clampdown on Hong Kong. *Artnet News*. Available at: https://news.artnet.com/art-world/political-chinese-paintings-removed-m-plus-hong-kong-2102659.

communist or socialist authoritarian states. Ironically, Hong Kong may well become a hub where artists and their galleries and museum curators will avoid any critique of either the state or big business.

On the plus side, radical, subversive, provocative or politicised art is only one field of art practice. The world is full of an inexhaustive supply of wonderful art dealing with many other aspects of human existence, our environments, our heritage, histories, ideas and shared values.

In relation to the definition of what makes a "top" market, the international art market is a market, and like any market, it will offer for sale what it thinks clients will buy. A gallery or an auction house can present different art and artists depending on the local conditions. It depends on which criteria are applied to determine what qualifies an art market as one of the world's 'top' markets. Such a judgement could be based on financial results, the degree of artistic and political freedom of expression on display, the success in audience building or widening of community participation, or various combinations of all of those.

In relation to Hong Kong's cultural tourism industry, I think many tourists travel around the world to soak up a breadth of cultural heritage within a contemporary notion of "place," that relies on much more than contemporary art market events, and which Hong Kong and the region have in abundance.

As the Associate Head of the DCCA, EdUHK, could you describe your management and leadership style?

In terms of leadership and management in a University, I believe in strategic thinking and placing the quality of the student experience at the centre of that every day. To achieve this, you need devolved management that allows experts in their field to take responsibility and deliver their best directly. One also has to lead by example, and I hope to build trust through fairness and mutual respect, good planning, organisation and communication, and sustained personal engagement with tasks and objectives.

As a visual arts teacher, could you describe your teaching style?

I would say "Active," as I try to share my own passion for life and immersion in creative arts directly with the students and see my role as a catalyst or a facilitator for their own learning process.

Students in Hong Kong versus students in the UK – could you describe the major differences in their self-motivations, learning attitudes, creativity level, and exposure to the arts between these two groups of students?

I don't like to stereotype concerning levels of creativity. Humans are inherently creative. It is our strongest quality and essential to our survival as a species. Many factors beyond a student's physical location determine their level of exposure to the arts, especially now, with our amazing 24/7 online access to the art, design, music, and culture of nearly every remote corner of the world. However, the internationalisation and globalisation that our digital creativity has provided can also be viewed as an opportunity or as a threat by those who control our access to it or who censor particular content, so where you live can clearly have a bearing on your levels of exposure to some art and artists.

The cultures of Visual Arts "Education" are very different between HK and the UK at the University level. The art school tradition in the UK is a tutorial system where the student has a studio space, and tutors go to the students to critique their work. Here in Hong Kong, the emphasis is on students attending regularly scheduled "taught" classes and workshops. Both approaches have pros and cons. I had many students in the UK complaining that we didn't "teach" them enough, and sometimes here I receive requests to teach them less!

You are currently conducting a research project "The Art of Creative Research," with funding from the Faculty of Liberal Arts and Social Sciences at the Education University of Hong Kong, and enabled via a collaboration with The National Institute of Education, Nanyang Technological University Singapore. Could you tell the readers more about this Project?

Yes, the exhibition will be titled "The Art of Creative Research" and feature non-traditional or practice-led research outputs from our VA team here at EdUHK, staff from 3 UK universities, and staff from the National Institute of Education, Singapore, hosting the exhibition in their gallery early in 2023. A dedicated website, a printed catalogue featuring artworks, and participant interviews will be included. The project explores a number of facets of the debate around creative practice as formal research and how staff research or professional practice in the field can enhance the student experience.

In what directions would you like the DCCA at EdUHK to develop in the next three to five years?

Over the past five years, our visibility has increased significantly and we are becoming more recognised for not only preparing students for careers in Art Education but for a broader range of careers in the Creative and Cultural Industries. Our community arts projects and creative collaborations with external partners and institutions, such as the June 2022 'Journey to West Kowloon Community Art Exhibition" project at M+ Pavilion, have presented and illustrated our depth and breadth in the field. In the next three to five years, we will see the increased impact and influence that many of our graduates will be exerting in Hong Kong's CCI's and schools as their careers take shape. Our strategy is to build on this foundation and grow the strength and scale of our connections to HK's CCI's, as this sector will be a primary contributor to Hong Kong's future economic success and its profile as an international "destination" city.

COVID-19 has turned the world upside down. How have DCCA, you and your students been coping with COVID-19?

If we compare our COVID-disrupted lives here in Hong Kong to the lives of many other people around the world under COVID, we have been very fortunate so far. At the University, everybody really pulled together to make the best of the situation as it evolved. The switch to online learning and teaching allowed us to continue to deliver programmes and other activities, and although it created many challenges, especially concerning teaching practical studio-based creative arts and music subjects, we have learned a great deal about the future potential of "hybrid" approaches to learning and teaching, making more use of online and f2f interaction. It was also an opportunity to review course content and try to create new innovative projects that students could undertake outside the formal classroom or studio. This produced some exciting student work.

Why do we turn to art and music in times of crisis?

Many people are more qualified than I to try and answer that question. A "crisis" can be an intensely personal event in one's life, a collective experience such as an epidemic or natural disaster, global warming or a humanitarian catastrophe like war, a combination of all these things and more. Individually, at a personal level, some people may "turn to art and music" because they find something there that helps them reflect upon their situation, and they can engage in a kind of unspoken dialogue or find a distractive background against which they can think more clearly to gain more insight or understanding. The immense power of art, design, architecture and music to inspire or unite people collectively, especially during a war, and whichever side of the battle they are on, is well established. Art, design, architecture and music are also embedded within people's personal histories and significant memories, even if they might not think of themselves as conscious consumers. Artefacts, pictures, films, clothes, favourite rooms, favourite songs are deeply connected to our positive and negative life experiences. Turning towards the positive, familiar and trusted when threatened is instinctive.

What would you like to be remembered for when you retire?

In relation to my academic career, I hope whatever it is that the person remembers me for, it is something that had a positive impact on their working day, creative journey or professional trajectory, and I doubt that I will ever voluntarily retire from professional practice as an artist. There are so many aspects of painting that I want to continue exploring for as long as I can, alongside, of course, fishing, shooting, wine and music making.

The Art of Creative Research

Laurence's 2022/23 research project "The Art of Creative Research" was funded by the Faculty of Liberal Arts and Social Sciences at the Education University of Hong Kong, and enabled via a collaboration with The National Institute of Education, Nanyang Technological University Singapore. It was part of an initiative to share the practice-based research work of creative arts educators with a wider international audience, both within and beyond the realm of academia. With an exciting and important international focus, the exhibition at The Gallery, NIE Singapore (January 2023) showcased a range of works by fifteen staff from the Education University of Hong Kong, The National Institute of Education (NIE) Singapore, The Arts University Bournemouth UK, The Royal College of Art UK, Cambridge University UK, and University College London UK. A dedicated website and printed catalogue supported the physical exhibition, providing an informative collection of video interviews with the exhibitors, and other related project information and links.

https://www.theartofcreativeresearch.com; www.laurencewood.co.uk

Photo 1. Laurence Wood 2020 (Photo by Wong Kai-Yu).

Photo 2. Laurence and family (Christina and Anna) in front of his mural for Shenzhen Design Week, Museum of Contemporary Art, Shenzhen, China, 2018.

Photo 3. Laurence Wood, Mural painting for Yitian Plaza Mall, Shenzhen, China 2020.

Photo 4. (From left to right) Christina, Laurence, Anna with Hapkido Master Ignacio Alba Ruiz, Hong Lok Yuen, 2021.

Photo 5. Laurence Wood.

Photo 6. "Blossom 2022" Laurence Wood 120cm x 120cm (Acrylic on Canvas).

Photo 7. Four of Wood's paintings featured in the exhibition.

Chapter 5

Frank Vigneron, Professor and Chair, Fine Arts Department, the Chinese University of Hong Kong

Introduction

Founded in 1963, the Fine Arts Department at the Chinese University of Hong Kong (CUHK) places dual emphases on studio art and art history. As the first tertiary institute to offer visual arts education in Hong Kong, the Fine Arts Department at the CUHK offers a wide range of courses in Chinese art practices and history alongside Western art history and studio training – with the mission devoted to the exploration of contemporary art while promoting traditional Chinese art and culture.

Prof. Frank Vigneron is the current Chair of the Fine Arts Department at the CUHK. Professor Vigneron received his Ph.D. in Chinese Art History from the Paris VII University, a Ph.D. in Comparative Literature from the Paris IV Sorbonne University, and a Doctorate of Fine Arts from the Royal Melbourne Institute of Technology. In the following interview, Prof. Vigneron highlights the differences between Western and Chinese aesthetics, as well as discusses the future role of the M+ Museum after the introduction of Hong Kong's national security law.

Could we begin this interview by first introducing yourself, for example, your professional training and educational background? For instance, what did you study at the university? Do you come from a family of studio artists, art historians, scholars, or philosophers?

I was born in Hong Kong in 1965. My father was a lawyer working for a shipping company, and my family had lived in London, Madagascar, and Vietnam before coming to Hong Kong. I was about two years old when we left for another posting of my father in Saigon, South Vietnam. That was during the Vietnam War, and some of my earliest memories were of military planes flying over our house or mornings eating breakfast behind sandbags under the stairs. Being so little and living in privileged surroundings, I have personally no bad memories of these times, even though it was tough on my parents. Actually, I also remember my father waking me up in the middle of the night to witness on television the first man on the moon; I was a little over four years old. After that, we returned to Europe, to Antwerp in Belgium, where I received my first schooling. I was eight when we returned to France, first to Lille in the North, before I went to university in Paris in 1982. There I studied Chinese at INALCO (Institut National des Langues et Civilisations Orientales), an institution founded in the early 19th century and equivalent to London's SOAS (School of Oriental and African Studies). It was a choice that had always been obvious to me, although maybe for quite trivial reasons, having grown up in houses full of the Chinese objects and furniture my parents had bought in Hong Kong.

Judging from your last name, I take that you are French. Having grown up in Europe, how did you develop an interest in Chinese Art and eventually decide to pursue a Ph.D. in Chinese Art History at the Paris VII University?

The 1980s were still when Japan was the Asian destination for most students of 'oriental languages,' and few were those studying Chinese then. Although INALCO provided many courses in the Chinese language, it was their civilisation courses that were the most attractive. My family's financial situation was comfortable enough, but it did not allow me to study in either China and Taiwan, and I usually employ that rather weak excuse to explain my lack of communication skills in Chinese. The fact is that I am not a very social person and have always found it difficult to look for opportunities to speak other languages. I also participated in the 1980s by publishing a literary review titled *La Treizième*, edited by the Franco-Brazilian poet Max de Carvalho, whom I had met at INALCO. This naturally led me to love and study literature, which explains my interest in comparative literature. I, therefore, began to audit courses in comparative literature at the Sorbonne and have had no difficulties reading other languages like Spanish, Italian, and Portuguese, while I still can manage – with patience and a dictionary – German and Japanese (as for English, having grown up in fairly international surroundings, I could express myself in this language at a very young age). On the other hand, it was one of the professors of INALCO, François Cheng (程抱一), who introduced me to the wonders of Chinese painting and its theory, a domain that has defined my academic career ever since.

After finishing my MPhil in 1987, under the supervision of François Cheng, I found myself with a degree that was quite useless in France, a country that has chronically experienced very high degrees of unemployment. Having several Brazilian friends thanks to Max de Carvalho, one of them invited me to spend a few months in Rio de Janeiro in 1988 to look for a job teaching French. After spending all my savings uselessly in this beautiful town, which was then experiencing a severe economic crisis, I finally returned to Paris, where I found myself in dire straits. Not wanting to rely on my parents, I barely made ends meet by working for the Wagons-Lits, the company that managed the sleeper cars traveling from France to Italy and back. This was also an interesting experience, as it allowed me to go to Florence, Venice and Rome regularly. Then, in 1989, Tiananmen happened, and many people in Hong Kong were trying to leave for other places, especially Canada. A friend of mine working for Alliance Française in Paris told me that the Hong Kong Alliance Française was hiring many teachers because the Canadian consulate was giving preferential treatment to people who had learnt basic French. It was then 1990, and I decided to return to Hong Kong, where I taught French at Alliance Française for 14 years.

In addition to a Ph.D. in Chinese Art History, you also hold a Ph.D. in Comparative Literature from the Paris IV Sorbonne University, and a Doctorate of Fine Arts from the Royal Melbourne Institute of Technology. How do your research skills and knowledge in Comparative Literature complement what you do in the field of Fine Arts?

Teaching French evenings and weekends, I continued my studies in Hong Kong and obtained my first Ph.D. in Oriental Studies (from Paris VII Denis Diderot University) in 1998. The topic continued what I had started with François Cheng, a study and translation of an extensive treatise on painting written by a late 18th-century Chinese artist. While still teaching French, I began teaching art history at RMIT (the Royal Melbourne Institute of Technology) and the Hong Kong Art School in 2000. Although I started making my drawings in Paris in the 1980s, I only managed to show some of them in Hong Kong for the first time in 1998. Since then, I have had many opportunities to show them locally in China and Europe. The thinking that accompanied my drawing practice had been inspired by my readings on Chinese art theory.

Teaching budding artists for RMIT in Hong Kong, I was encouraged by my Australian colleagues to take the DFA (Doctor of Fine Arts), which I obtained in 2005 with an accompanying thesis that already contained some elements of comparison, thus getting a postgraduate degree as an art practitioner. In the meantime, I was hired by the Department of Fine Arts at CUHK in 2004, an institution where I have worked ever since. Having had the idea of bringing together my interest in both art theory and comparative literature, I also wanted to do a Ph.D. in Comparative Literature on the theme of art theory in China and Europe in the 18th century. I thus began working on a third doctoral degree in 2006 with a supervisor at the Sorbonne (University Paris IV), obtaining it in 2010. Let's face it: no one needs three doctoral degrees. I guess this need came from the fact that I am a profoundly anxious and insecure person who constantly needs to prove himself. However, I think that, in my late 50s, I have finally gotten over it and have stopped pursuing degrees. In addition to my art practice, I am now just publishing academic books and articles, which is not as simple as it sounds since every article and every book needs to be assessed extensively before being accepted for publication, just like a Ph.D. dissertation.

Studying comparative aesthetics resulted from these various encounters and trajectories, even though I am most grateful to François Cheng for being the first to orient me towards an interest in art theory. From the research conducted for the PhD in comparative literature came several books, two in French (*Académiciens et Lettrés. Etude comparative de la théorie picturale en Chine et en Europe au dix-huitième siècle* and *Les traités de pratique picturale en Europe aux 17e et 18e siècles* in 2010) and one in English, titled *China Pluperfect I. Epistemology of past and outside in Chinese art*, which has been published in 2022. A companion volume on contemporary art practices in China and Hong Kong, titled *China Pluperfect II. Practices of past and outside in Chinese art*, has also been published at the same time. Although it was not my initial field, teaching at RMIT and the Hong Kong Art School required me to teach courses in Western Art while taking an interest in the local art world. I also began writing about the local art scene, first in the magazine published by the Alliance Française of Hong Kong and then in other publications such as Art Map. I have never stopped writing about this field ever since, and in addition to additional articles in academic publications, I also published two academic books on local art (*I Like Hong Kong... Art and Deterritorialization* in 2010 and *Hong Kong Soft Power* in 2018).

Western Aesthetics versus Chinese Aesthetics – what are the major differences? Why are pre-modern Chinese paintings and calligraphy so difficult to understand, even for people with trained eyes in art?

This is a very complex issue that should not be generalised. First, using a concept like 'West' is extremely problematic, as was famously pointed out by Edward Said, who traced its origin (and that of its pendant, the 'East') to the ideology developed within European colonialism. For instance, an idea like Hong Kong being the place where 'East meets West' should no longer be accepted in any academic research (this is a point I developed extensively in my two books about Hong Kong art and culture). Moreover, even though it still makes sense to talk about 'Western Europe' and 'China,' it is important to realise that both cultural domains have changed and evolved into widely different forms over the centuries. It is, therefore, impossible to define major differences that would always hold true. In *Académiciens et Lettrés* and *China Pluperfect I. Epistemology of past and outside in Chinese art and China*, for instance, I emphasise and study the fact that knowledge was built alongside very similar lines in the intellectual world of Western Europe and the literati world of China in the late 17th and 18th centuries. This is not the place to elaborate on complex ideas requiring many references and quotes to be understood. However, it can be argued that, even though still different on many points, the way knowledge was pursued in these two worlds presented enough similarities for exchanges to occur during that period. In contrast, cultural exchanges were nearly impossible at other times when these two cultures had nothing, or very little, in common. In the late 17th and 18th centuries, these similarities were not created through exchanges; they just happened at about the same time, but they needed to exist before cultural exchanges could be made. This was precisely the time not only when European painters were active at the court in Beijing, but also when 'Chinoiseries' were prominent in the decorative arts of Europe.

As for the perception of art forms made by people coming from different cultures, it is also something that must be studied with facts; the reception of these artworks is clearly changing over the centuries. Whereas it was impossible for an 18th-century Western European to 'understand' calligraphy, it might not be so impossible today. All the same, it is true that it is extremely difficult to 'understand' calligraphy without some knowledge of the theory and history of that ancient, and yet so contemporary, genre of personal expression. But I believe it is true of any artistic expression. Because of their very visible presence in all forms of contemporary culture (to simplify: from the most 'elite' to the most 'popular,' even though these distinctions are themselves not obvious and generally rely on social structures, as demonstrated by the French sociologist Pierre Bourdieu), non-Chinese tend to believe that it is easier to 'understand' a painting by Monet than calligraphy made, for instance, by the contemporary calligrapher and performance artist Wang Dongling (王冬齡). But believing that we can appreciate a Monet painting 'naturally' is often an illusion born out of habit, as most people actually have no idea of what Monet had in mind, what his theory of art was, when he painted, for instance, the cathedral of Rouen. When non-Chinese people ask me how they can appreciate calligraphy, I often tell them to look at them as if they were abstract paintings while telling them that they are assuredly NOT abstract paintings, the way a French or an American would understand abstraction. Doing so, they obviously have to put aside a great deal of what makes calligraphy so interesting to a Chinese person, but at least they can derive some pleasure from the experience instead of ignoring such works entirely because they know nothing of their history and origins.

Could you briefly introduce the Department of Fine Arts at the Chinese University of Hong Kong (CUHK)? What are the missions, visions and teaching philosophy behind the Department of Fine Arts at CUHK?

Until about ten to fifteen years ago, the Department of Fine Arts at CUHK was the only higher learning institution in Hong Kong where students could receive an education in art. It has a history of over sixty years and was initially created as a unit of New Asia College by the famous scholar Qian Mu (錢穆), who eventually became one of the founders of the Chinese University of Hong Kong in 1963. Its original mission was to study and promote the visual arts of China as part of an effort to preserve Chinese culture, an effort felt necessary when the Communist Party in mainland China was threatening it. It has remained a place for Chinese painting and calligraphy, as well as the teaching of their history for many years; its mission is supported and expanded by the creation of the Art Museum of CUHK in the 1970s. Being in Hong Kong and therefore enjoying unfettered links to the outside, a growing number of its teaching staff began to introduce forms of art that were less directly felt to be part of Chinese culture, often labelling these forms 'Western' with all the issues this may entail. This is how the Department defines its mission on the website: 'Since its inception, the Department has promoted the study of Chinese art and culture. It has also been dedicated to exploring modern and contemporary artistic trends. As the arts have become increasingly internationalised, the Department has revised its curriculum in order to better bridge the connections between contemporary Chinese and Western studios and art history. This all-inclusive approach to Chinese art and culture, traditional, modern, international and contemporary, gives our department its progressive and innovative character.'

In the late 1970s and early 1980s, some of its teaching staff began to introduce much more 'contemporary' forms of art making. By the 1990s, the department was on par with many other similar institutions around the world, even though its emphasis on teaching Chinese painting and calligraphy still managed to put it apart. The other characteristic of the department is that it never stopped teaching the history of Chinese art, while also teaching the history of 'Western' art because of its presence in Hong Kong as part of a curriculum presented as holistic. FAA undergraduate students can choose between three streams of study. The first one has a higher concentration of studio art courses (70% of their credits), and students must complete an art project for graduation. The second one has its concentration in art history courses, and students must complete a graduation thesis under the supervision of an art history teacher to graduate. A third option consists of taking an equal number of credits in art history and studio art and choosing an art history thesis or an art project to graduate. The years 2019 and 2020 were particularly challenging for the FAA because it forced all teachers to revert to online teaching. Although lectures are not particularly difficult to conduct with online teaching, it is nearly impossible to do them properly for classes normally conducted in the studio. The beginning of the pandemic forced the department to attempt studio courses online, which led to such discontent that it became quickly obvious that it could not be continued. With the help of students, and the university's approval, FAA managed to get studio teaching back in the classroom for the 2020-2021 academic year. This feat was made possible by the fact that the FAA is a very small department with a small intake of students, which made social distancing possible in most cases. It was just a matter of opening the same course twice a week for particularly popular classes, so that students could complete their four years of BA studies with sufficient credits for graduation.

The Department of Fine Art consists, in its present incarnation, of eight full-time faculty members, four of them teaching art history and the other four teaching studio arts. Two of these four artist-teachers concentrate on Chinese painting and calligraphy, while the other two teach subjects ranging from drawing and painting to sculpture. To complement that studio art curriculum, the department also employs a small army of part-time teachers who teach courses in various media. If the Department of Fine Arts is probably better known as a studio art institution because of its annual graduation shows (generally in June for undergraduate and MFA students, and in July for its Master of Art in Fine Arts (MAFA) students, a programme that I will present later), it is also an art history department, an identity certainly better projected by its postgraduate programmes. With an intake of between five and ten postgraduate students each year, the Department of Fine Arts has an average of twenty to thirty government-funded research postgraduate students, the majority of whom are engaged in art historical research on subjects ranging from Buddhist art to Taoist art and classical Chinese painting to calligraphy, but also Chinese contemporary art both in mainland China and Hong Kong. Recently, considering that the majority of undergraduate students chose the studio art stream, the department decided to give more opportunities to practicing artists to undertake postgraduate studies. The Master of Fine Arts programme was established in the late 1990s, accepting research-based art practitioners, who usually represented only a small portion of the department's postgraduate population. In the last decade, that population has grown compared to the group dedicated to art history. With practicing artists increasingly comfortable conducting academic research to support their art practice, it became obvious that creating a Ph.D. in art practice was necessary and this option has become available in the 2021-2022 academic year.

As was previously mentioned, and in addition to these government-funded courses, FAA also offers a taught self-financed programme, the MAFA. It is a part-time programme taught on weekdays in the evening and weekends for two years. In 2022, it also offers an additional stream specializing in the practice of contemporary forms of Chinese art such as painting and calligraphy. Unfortunately, the programme cannot offer a space for students to work on their art (whereas the research MA programme allows for space since there are usually less than ten students including year one and year two). This is compensated by the fact that MAFA students are generally more mature students who have to show that they already have an art practice to be admitted, which generally implies that they also have their own space. With their knowledge and experience, the teaching staff supports student peer groups and, through facilitating critical debate and offering practical help and advice, encourages the development of personal projects. The programme is made up of components in art history, cultural theory and group criticism and helps students define or reconfigure their art projects as well as equipping them with the critical tools and practical skills necessary for advanced professional practice. With its intake of about forty students a year, this programme adds about seventy-five to eighty people to the department's student population. This number has doubled in the 2021-2022 academic year due to the recent creation of an additional stream to the MAFA. Even though it already allowed students to dedicate themselves to Chinese media, i.e., Chinese painting and calligraphy, it was decided that creating more specialised courses for these art forms might benefit students and allow them to develop their works in a more specific direction.

In addition to HKBU, the Chinese University of Hong Kong (CUHK), the Education University of Hong Kong (EDUHK), and the Hong Kong Art School (HKAS) also offer degree programmes in Fine Arts, with a strong emphasis on studio art practices. Could you describe the major differences in curricula and staff and student profiles among these four institutions?

Since the University Grant Council (UGC), the funding body of the Hong Kong government, encourages universities to compete for first year-first degree places, the main 'competitor' of the Department of Fine Arts (FAA) has been the Academy of Visual Arts of Baptist University (AVA). The differences between these two institutions are both small and big on different fronts. First, half the faculty of FAA are dedicated art historians, the proportion in AVA being more important in studio art teachers. Half of these studio art teachers are Chinese painters/calligraphers at FAA, while AVA only has one full-time Chinese painter. Therefore, the main difference in the curriculum is a stronger emphasis on Chinese media and Chinese art history at FAA. But this is a very rough comparison that would require a great deal more details to be really significant, and it could be argued that both institutions are trying to strike a balance between art history and studio art, and between Chinese art history and the art history of the rest of the world (this also is an almost shocking generalisation as, in Hong Kong, 'the rest of the world' never includes other continents like Africa or South America).

The main difference is, however, so big that it puts FAA at a clear disadvantage. While FAA's yearly intake of first year-first degree students is around 25, AVAs is closer to 100. Baptist University opened AVA in 2004, first in a beautiful colonial building that gave it a very distinct identity. While it still manages that facility (which is a class 1 heritage building, making it difficult to use for art activities), it is also housed in a building on the main university campus in Kowloon Tong. While CUHK dragged its feet for decades in encouraging art education, Baptist University put enormous financial effort into creating and developing AVA, where facilities are large and extraordinarily well-equipped. It is a fact that the facilities of FAA are inadequate and have been so for a very long time, an issue that FAA department chairs have raised for just as long only to have their recommendations and requests fall on deaf ears. The situation is, thankfully, changing as new personnel at the managerial level of CUHK are finally paying attention. A new dean of the Faculty of Arts, coming from visual culture, is finally supporting FAA in refurbishing its antiquated facilities, while the university itself has applied to UGC for the construction of a new teaching building where FAA will finally be able to offer general education studio courses to all CUHK students. UGC has approved funding for this teaching building in 2022, but its actual completion date is still unknown.

EDUHK has its own Department of Creative and Cultural Arts (CCA), including visual arts and music. Once an institute specialising in educating educators, it now has a more comprehensive set of visual art education courses, offering classes in art making and curatorship at the BA level. They are also better equipped than the FAA and have a highly competent teaching staff, even though it does not seem that many of their students embark in the sort of artistic careers that are more commonly chosen by FAA and AVA graduates.

As for HKAS, I was once very familiar with them as I was the chair of their academic committee for about five years and had even taught for their BA programme offered conjointly with RMIT for several years. Before BU. created AVA, HKAS was once the only option for students wanting to study visual arts in Hong Kong and could not be admitted into the FAA programme. HKAS is not government-funded, and they have had to create self-finance programmes as well as associate themselves with a foreign institution to deliver BA and MFA degrees. They still offer very competitive programmes, even though it is getting far more difficult for them to compete in an environment where UGC has created more art-oriented schools, such as AVA, but also the very large and well-funded School of Creative Media (SCM) at the City University of Hong Kong.

There is no point talking too much about the other non-government-funded school, the American college SCAD (Savannah School of Art and Design), since it ceased operation in Hong Kong in 2019. It offered excellent and extremely expensive art and design courses in its beautiful campus in Sham Shui Po, a campus offered to them by the Hong Kong government who preferred to support a non-local institution rather than a local one like HKAS at the time of its opening in 2009. I can briefly mention the art-related department of the University of Hong Kong to emphasise its specialisation in art history teaching, a fact made clear by its name change in 2020: once also called Fine Arts Department, it is now called the Department of Art History. It would be very complicated in this short interview to talk about the rich interactions taking place between all these institutions in Hong Kong; suffice it to say that this competitive environment is extremely beneficial to local art students, who now have a large array of choices. It is also beneficial to Mainland students, many of them decide to come here to pursue their art studies.

Could you describe your career path to becoming the Chair of the Fine Arts Department at CUHK?

The chair of the Department of Fine Arts, when I joined it in 2004, was a renowned academic of ancient China, Professor Jenny So (蘇芳淑). She had been hired to head the Institute of Chinese Studies, which also contains the Museum of Art of CUHK. It was a time of financial constraints for Hong Kong universities, and CUHK decided to also assign her to the chairmanship of the Department of Fine Arts. As far as I know, she was the only person assigned to that position after being hired from the outside (except an even earlier department chair, Professor Kao Mayching (高美慶), who was also the director of CUHK Art Museum), all other cases were of faculty members of the department who simply became chairs internally (to be precise, notably, the department chair has nothing to do with being chair professor: the chair professor position represents the upper level of the academic hierarchy while department chair merely represents an administrative role given to a faculty member). So, the 'career path' consists merely of having been a faculty member of the Department of Fine Arts long enough and being willing to help. Likely, the next department chair of FAA will also be a member of the present faculty (my own tenure as chair will end in August 2026).

As the Chair of the Fine Arts Department at CUHK, could you describe your main roles and areas of responsibility?

The main responsibility is to act as a conduit between the faculty members of the Department of Fine Arts and the higher echelons of the university through the dean of the Faculty of Arts, of which the department is a unit. Every decision concerning teaching and learning, as well as some aspects of research, is done collegially, and the department chair has no special privileges in that context. However, specific responsibilities are attached to the title of department chair. The first responsibility of the chair is to write a yearly evaluation of the activities of each faculty member (in teaching, research and service) in conjunction with the dean of the Faculty of Arts. Matters of substantiation (which simply means that faculty members no longer have to renew contracts; it is not the equivalent of the American tenure system, since a substantiated faculty member still has to retire at the age of 60 or 65, depending on when they were hired) and advancement are based on these evaluations which need to be made with fairness and accuracy. In addition, many control mechanisms internal to the university are also conducted to ensure the proper functioning of a department and generally demand a certain number of analytical reports to be produced. It is also the responsibility of the chair to write and compile these reports with the help of the department's executive officer.

Moreover, every six years, UGC organises the Research Assessment Exercise, a long process designed to assess, through international panels of hundreds of academics, the quality of research done by all academics in Hong Kong. It is designed to be a competitive process establishing a hierarchy of excellence among the universities of Hong Kong and has consequently financial implications for universities and, ultimately, each unit and department. This process is, therefore extremely important as it has repercussions on each department's budget. Compiling and organising the data to submit for the Research Assessment Exercise is generally the responsibility of the chair. As you can see, there is very little pleasure to get from taking care of these responsibilities, and the department chair is generally simply the one who cannot escape doing them, either because he is the oldest or because he is already a full professor (it basically means that no one in their right mind would want to do it, and the person who takes on that responsibility does it because no one else wants to).

Notably, becoming department chair is not a promotion, even though it can help in obtaining advancement (department chairs are paid a small additional stipend while fulfilling their duties; the stipend disappears when they are on leave while their responsibilities are transferred to the acting head, just another member of the faculty). Department chairs are usually assigned for three years, but since few other faculty members want to take on that role, they often stay for two mandates or more (my predecessor, Professor Harold Mok (莫家良), was kind enough to take on that burden for three mandates, a total of nine years, leaving all of his colleagues the time necessary to teach and conduct research peacefully).

As the Chair of the Fine Arts Department at CUHK, could you describe your management and leadership style?

Everything is done and decided collegially, so I do not believe I have a leadership style or need one. Department chairs are only there to take care of the responsibilities already described. Many of these responsibilities are actually shared with other faculty members. For instance, managing all postgraduate issues is the duty of the Graduate Division Head. Notably, while Ph.D., M.Phil. and MFA (Master of Fine Art) are research-based programmes and are supported by studentships (which allow the departments to employ these postgraduate students as teaching assistants for a few years), MA programmes (Master of Arts) like our MAFA are generally self-financed, meaning that students bear the entire brunt of the tuition fees without financial help from UGC. The MAFA is also managed by another faculty member with the help of the executive officer. So, a large portion of the administrative duties are taken care of by other persons within the department. A very important portion of the administrative duties concerning budget management, student affairs, organising teaching schedules and technical issues (which are an immense responsibility in a department where a large part of the teaching takes place in studios with all sorts of equipment) are dealt with by the department's supporting staff, people without whom nothing would be possible, under the supervision of various faculty members. If there is a management and leadership style to be expected from the department chair, I guess it consists in being friendly with all these wonderful people, making sure that we listen to them and that they listen to each other through regular meetings and good communication (I must say it has been remarkably easy, one of the great advantages of working within a small structure with a fairly small number of people). Similarly, the department chair usually heads meetings organised with students to listen to their requests and expectations, a task that we all take to heart and conduct at regular intervals.

As a teacher of Fine Arts, could you describe your teaching style?

I do not teach studio courses and only give lectures. I'm afraid I am a fairly conventional lecturer and rely on PowerPoint presentations to teach. These PowerPoints are, however, very elaborate, including the entire written content of the lectures and all the images art history courses require. I never read the texts of these PowerPoints aloud in the classroom (which is the best way to put large numbers of people to sleep in a matter of minutes), preferring a more informal way to teach their contents. All the PowerPoints created for my lectures are available for download to all enrolled students, who can keep them for further reading if they are interested. The only slightly original method I put into place is that I let my students choose their own topic for the term paper. In order to make sure they are not either doing something too easy or off-topic (like writing a paper on Renaissance art for a course on Modernism), I discuss with students what they can and should do (by asking them to send me a proposal for their paper one month before the deadline of the completed one, this allows me to give advice and guide their research). Being able to read Chinese, I also allow them to write their papers in their mother tongue. I usually complement the assessment of these lectures by asking students to give a presentation on an article related to the lecture topics, which I provide myself. They are also free to present in either English or Chinese. Throughout the pandemic, as we had to lecture online, I could also see my students take advantage of that situation by recording their own presentations; some even developed these recordings into wonderfully creative short documentaries.

In addition to postgraduate seminars, like the group-taught methodology seminar and one semester of the MFA seminar (based on presentations and discussions), I teach a number of undergraduate courses, like three whole semester courses on 'Western art,' i.e., the arts of Western Europe and North America from the late Gothic period to the present. Considering that it is my own field of research, I also teach courses on art in Hong Kong (from the late 18th century to the present) and a course on 20th-century art in Mainland China. Another of my specialisations is art theory. From time to time, I teach a course on art theory in Western Europe and North America as well as a course on comparative aesthetics based on my previous research in that domain. Recently, trying to open up a certain idea of art making towards more 'popular' applications of our students' talent, I began teaching a course on the history of European and American comics and invited a very popular local comics artist, Stella So (蘇敏怡), to teach a studio course in comics production (these courses have however had to be offered for the first time during the 2019 unrest, and the following year during the COVID-19 pandemic, and have not succeeded in attracting many students, especially fine arts students – there might actually also be a problem of reception of comics in the Department of Fine Arts where teachers and students still consider that form of expression to be unworthy of the attention of 'artists'...).

Three years ago, I also got funding from CUHK to hire a research assistant to start establishing a credit-based internship in socially engaged art, another field in which I have been involved as one of the founders of a local collective called Rooftop Institute, which I will mention again later. Finding local associations and artists willing to take in interns from the Department of Fine Arts is a very demanding job and that same research assistant now manages the programme, Mr. Leung Ho-Yin (梁皓然), one of my former MPhil students, even though I participate in a couple of preparatory workshops with the students who took this credit-based internship as well as evaluate the reports and presentations they wrote as part of their evaluation. A very successful programme, as nearly all the final year students take it each year, it encourages students to dedicate their knowledge of art and art making to the local community, a role that a growing number of visual art graduates are destined to take in the coming years.

Could you describe the career paths of most CUHK fine arts graduates?

I can start by providing simple statistics, as the FAA has been gathering that information for some years. The statistics on the 25 who graduated in 2019 are as follows: Administration/Management 36% (9 students); Art/Design 12% (3 students); Customer Service 8% (2 students); Insurance/Wealth Management 4% (1 student); IT: Multimedia & Digital Entertainment 4% (1 student); Sales/Marketing 8% (2 students); Scientific/Research Work 4% (1 student); Secretary 4% (1 student); Social Work/Community Work 4% (1 student); Teaching: Teaching Assistant 4% (1 student); Teaching: Others 8% (2 students); Others 4% (1 student).

As we can see, most students work in administration/management after graduation, generally working for local galleries or art-related institutions. Other professions are social work and teaching, while very few decide to try a career as professional artists. While quite a large number of the established professional artists of Hong Kong who are in their thirties and forties have graduated from FAA, this is a tendency that is changing as more young professional artists have obtained their degrees from other institutions such as AVA or SCM. Professional, full-time artists such as Chow Chun-Fai (周俊輝), Lam Tung-Pang (林東鵬) or Tozer Pak Sheung-Chuen (白雙全) have graduated from FAA, and even several academics, such as Zheng Bo (鄭波) and Warren Leung Chi-Wo (梁志和) at SCM have obtained a degree from FAA. It is, however, in the domain of socially engaged art, which often is indistinguishable from social work/community work, that is showing a promising new trend. I will describe the professional path in that field of two alumni, the founders of Rooftop Institute, Law Yuk-Mui (羅玉梅) and Yim Sui-Fong (嚴瑞芳).

After graduating from FAA with a BA, they worked for a short while in local galleries before heading to Beijing to expand their experience in the art field. While Yim Sui Fong stayed in Beijing, Law Yuk Mui headed for Tokyo for a long internship at the Mori Museum. After a few years abroad, they decided to return to Hong Kong, where they worked for a while for the collective soundpocket, an institution specialising in sound art established by Yang Yeung (楊陽), who obtained a PhD at CUHK and also teaching in its general education department. While working at soundpocket, they founded Rooftop Institute in 2014, going through the complex process of establishing it as a business, then proving for several years that it was active while not making any money in order to obtain the status of a non-profit organisation. It is now an NGO mostly active in Hong Kong and Asia and keeps creating projects destined to reinforce a sense of community and engage local and international artists in participatory and dialogical art projects. They approached me in 2013 as one of their former teachers at FAA, because it is easier to apply for public funding in Hong Kong while being supported by a well-established academic working in a local institution. I have been active in supporting their efforts in various ways ever since. Applying for funding from institutions such as the Hong Kong SAR government's Home Affairs Bureau, the Hong Kong Art Development Council and other private charities, they have successfully run several programmes involving local and international artists who are working with various communities.

As we often say while being interviewed by these public institutions when applying for funding, we describe the activities of Rooftop Institute as more 'education through art' than 'art education.' Some of these programmes, for instance, brought young students to different destinations in Asia to work and create exhibitions in Hong Kong. Another one brought a local artist, Tang Kwok Hin (鄧國騫), and a Japanese artist, Motoyuki Shitamichi (下道基行), to create a participatory programme with many local participants that was turned into an exhibition at Tai Kwun. But the list of successful Rooftop Institute programmes is now quite long, a feat made even more remarkable by the fact that both its founders and animators, Law Yuk Mui and Yim Sui Fong, are also pursuing very successful personal careers as full-time artists (they have both won the Hong Kong Arts Development Council's Young Artist Awards, Law in 2018 and Yim in 2021).

Although these two artists are quite exceptional in their ambitions and success, it shows that such graduates are very good at using public and private funding to conduct research and creative endeavours. Although it would be exaggerated to say that they 'learnt' that at FAA, it is, however, true that they developed these ideas together while they were students at FAA, and sometimes with the encouragement of their teachers such as Kurt Chan (陳育強) (who reflected on the creation of the identity of 'art facilitator' as part of a proper art education, since not everyone can be a professional artist). It is then probably fair to say that an institution like the FAA provides an environment where it is possible to develop these ambitious plans. With the creation of FAA's internship programmes, and students joining many other socially engaged art associations, developing the capacity to join these programmes and create their own has been developed positively. As a matter of fact, between the extraordinary development of the art ecology of Hong Kong, which made graduates become artists or sent them to work for art galleries and other such institutions, the option of working in the education sector, and the development of possibilities for social engagement, there has been a fairly stable and varied job market for FAA graduates to join. As for the art historians graduating from FAA, they are in their vast majority postgraduate students with an MPhil or, even more frequently, a Ph.D. Most of them continue academic careers in mainland China, since they hail from there in their majority.

Students and the general public in Hong Kong versus their counterparts in France and Australia – what are the major differences in their perceptions and attitudes towards sculpture, installation and experimental film, and multimedia installations in public spaces?

I have never taught (or even really worked at least full time) in France and Australia, having spent most of my adult life in Hong Kong. So, I'm afraid I cannot answer that question.

Many people still consider Hong Kong a cultural desert. And yet, over the last few years, Hong Kong has joined New York and London as one of the world's top three international art markets, with a diverse range of public art spaces and large-scale art exhibitions springing up across the City -- could you describe the contradiction this very interesting phenomenon? As a practicing artist and art educator from Europe, how would you describe the overall arts and cultural scene in Hong Kong?

It is interesting to note that Guangdong province as a whole was considered a cultural backwater in China for a very long time; the Jiangnan area is usually acknowledged as the cradle of literati culture. However, this might have allowed this province to be the most important one when Chinese practitioners could use such methods as oil painting in the late eighteenth century. The very fact that literati culture was not central to the practice of visual art in Guangdong province might have made it easier for artisans in contact with foreign merchants to develop what is now called China Trade painting. But this suggestion would require extensive research to be confirmed or refuted. As for Hong Kong, it was the place many of these studios of professional artisans decided to converge to when it was becoming obvious that photography was just as efficient, if not far better, to make the portraits of these foreign merchants. This statement about China Trade painting and photography, never considered to be on the same level as the 'high art' of literati painting and calligraphy, can partly help us understand where the idea that Hong Kong was 'a cultural desert' comes from: this flawed notion is also based on a very narrow understanding of what art can be. Moreover, even though there were Chinese painters and calligraphers in Hong Kong as early as the fall of the Qing dynasty, they were seldom considered worthy of attention by Chinese art historians who preferred to focus on the artists of the mainland.

All the same, presenting Hong Kong as a 'cultural desert' is clearly an offspring of a colonial spirit, a statement made by mostly non-Chinese people who had no access to the Chinese language and would never be caught dead, for instance, looking at China Trade painting as art. Even during WWII, there were exhibitions of paintings and drawings made by modernist Chinese artists who took refuge in the colony. When we extend the concept of 'art' to Cantonese opera and film, Hong Kong was never a cultural desert. It certainly made sense to an English speaker eager to attend theatre plays and music concerts, but the history of literature, entertainment and also the visual arts in Hong Kong invalidates this notion. In the 1960s, for instance, Hong Kong was central to the renewal of some forms of Chinese painting as many practitioners engaged in what is now called the New Ink Art movement, with artists such as Lui Shou-kwan (呂壽琨), Liu Guosong (劉國松) from Taiwan, Wucius Wong (王無邪) who worked for many years in the US, etc. At the time, mainland China was steeped in chaos, Hong Kong and Taiwan were places where Chinese artists could still practice strategies of renewal and change. Strictly in the domain of visual arts, it might still make sense to talk about Hong Kong from the 1970s to the early 2000s as a cultural desert, but only if we compare it with what is happening now, as many public art galleries and museums are now available to viewers. But even though the 1970s to the 1990s, there were artists engaged in contemporary practices such as installation art and performance (only one example will suffice here: Kwok Mang-Ho (郭孟浩), better known as Frog King, came back from New York in the early 1980s and started doing his own brand of participatory art, even engaging in performances in the mainland on occasions). This very bad and wrong reputation as a cultural desert had genuine consequences concerning the status of artists from Hong Kong.

Until the Umbrella Movement in 2014 and the social unrest of 2019, Hong Kong was often completely ignored by art academics who preferred to dedicate their entire attention to what was happening in mainland China. This was understandable as the PRC's art field was, like its economy, the scene of an extraordinary revival in the years following the announcement of the open-door policy by Deng Xiaoping in 1979. However, it was very unfair to local artists who sometimes even had to resort to moving to Beijing in the early 2000s to be somehow visible to art collectors, who until recently were mostly people living outside China. Even when the local art ecology started to change thanks to the creation of the first large art fairs, most international galleries in the SAR were generally not interested in local artists. It took the dramatic events of 2014 and 2019 to see a new interest in local art practitioners emerge on behalf of the international art market people. How long this will last is as unpredictable as the art market itself. As for academics, they are also starting to take an interest in the local art scene because of the current political situation Hong Kong. To understand the local art ecology, it is essential to analyse the local official art institutions, their connections to the art market as well as how the local educational structure plays into these elements, something I have done in *Hong Kong Soft Power*.

Given the recent M+ Museum controversy art after the introduction of Hong Kong's national security law – how do you think this would affect Hong Kong's cultural tourism industry, as well as the City's position as one of the world's top art markets in the long run?

The M+ controversy was triggered by a pro-Beijing politician at the legislative council who decided that Ai Weiwei's photo of his hand giving the finger to Chairman Mao's portrait on Tiananmen Square insulted China. That politician clearly did not know that Ai Weiwei, in this series of photos titled *Study in Perspective*, was giving the finger to many other symbols of power around the world, like the Washington Monument, but also to less obvious representations of power like a ship of the Viking Lines, a Scandinavian tourism company, etc. I still do not understand that one. In other photos, he even seems to despise symbols of democracy. In what, at least to me, seems like a profoundly questionable attack, he gives the finger to the Reichstag, the German parliament that the Nazis had burned down to become the symbol of German democracy again after the re-establishment of Berlin as the capital of reunited Germany. I can only guess that he did not research that one properly. In any case, the whole series is humorous, sometimes even disorienting, and allows for interesting reflections on the nature of power and its symbols. The clear result of the kind of overreactions we will probably see again and again in the context of national security law in Hong Kong, this attack creates a dangerous precedent and does not bode well for the curatorial independence of that institution, or any other art-related ones in Hong Kong I'm afraid. Beyond that, there is little else we can say.

As for the future of Hong Kong as a centre for the cultural industry and the art market, I don't believe it is being threatened just yet by the politics of the national security law. Once tourism comes back after the pandemic is under control, visitors will hopefully flock to M+ without knowing anything about the Ai Weiwei photo. The only threat to the art market would come from a global economy that would no longer favour the rich, which has not happened during the pandemic. For better or worse (very much for the worse as far as I am concerned), there have never been more super-rich people in the world, and they are still very eager to put their money into the baubles of the art market, even going so far as paying huge sums of money for these new-fangled non-fungible tokens. This trend seems to have largely abated though. All the same, there is already a sense of worry, if not downright fear, in the world of culture in Hong Kong because of these laws, their extreme vagueness making it near impossible to know exactly what is allowed and what is forbidden. Beyond this sense of dread, however, the fact is that straightforward reflections on politics have been a tactic used by a very small minority of Hong Kong artists like Kacey Wong (黃國才), who has chosen to leave Hong Kong and live in Taiwan in 2022. There is little hope that such artists will be able to continue commenting on politics the way they could have been able to until the national security laws kicked in. We can only hope that the attempts at censorship made after the introduction of the national security laws will not have too extensive an impact on the local art scene.

Could the contemporary art scene and art market in China be used as a lens for understanding the changes in the political and social systems in China? If you agree, could you provide examples to illustrate this point?

Like most art historians who came after the 1970s in the Euro-American context, I believe art is very much the product of a social, economic and political environment. So, it is always a lens that can help understand these changes. This is why I analysed the local art ecology in *Hong Kong Soft Power*, making every effort to even situate all the artworks I wrote about on these pages in their context. This is just as true for China as for anywhere else. It is impossible, for instance, to understand the extraordinarily intense production of art that took place in the 1990s in the mainland without understanding how it was in great part conditioned by the emergence of a market economy, something that developed at break-neck speed after Deng Xiaoping's trip to Shenzhen in 1992, where he reiterated China's development in that direction. It would be impossible to even begin to describe in this short answer how this context allowed for what is now widely known as Chinese contemporary art, and since I believe the reader is eager to see this interview come to an end, I will not mention any other example. This question also raises, of course, the issue of agency: are artists capable of creating their art as independent individuals or are they entirely shaped by the environment they live in? Thinking that art-making depends entirely on the social, economic and political environment leaves no room for any kind of freedom, which is quite repugnant to many art practitioners. I'm afraid this is one of the aporias contained in this way of looking at art history, and far better minds than me are still grappling with this problem.

Fine Arts students in Hong Kong versus students in France and Australia – could you describe the major differences in their self-motivations, learning attitudes, creativity level and exposure to the arts between these three groups of students?

Here too, I'm afraid I cannot say anything about students in France and Australia. I can only say that I have never encountered art students who were not motivated and interested in what they were doing. The beginning of the pandemic in 2020 made it quite clear that students were devastated by the impossibility of accessing the campus, which clearly indicates their joy of being here. The Department of Fine Arts decided many years ago that the best learning environment is one that is always accessible. As a result, the FAA studios in the Cheng Ming building are open to students 24/7, an arrangement that has had amazing repercussions on their sense of community. As a rule, FAA students keep extremely close ties even years after graduation, ties that allow them to organise and participate extremely efficiently in the local and international art world. As such, I strongly believe that Hong Kong art students may even have the edge over students from larger countries, where institutions have difficulties creating the conditions for these communities to emerge. I was very surprised, for instance, to learn that the students of the University of the Arts London, on their campus at Chelsea College of Art, all have to leave the facilities before 6 pm (and was even more surprised, horrified actually, to learn that there are no dedicated art history and art theory courses offered there, but that is another story).

Moreover, to tackle this idea of Hong Kong as a ' cultural desert,' it is also important to realise how dynamic the local art field is and how local artists (many of whom graduated from local institutions) have been active in pursuing all sorts of art-related activities, from exhibitions in galleries to socially engaged art in all its forms (including being farmers in the New Territories and growing vegetables and rice in a community setting, like Lo Lai Lai (勞麗麗). It is in great part the community-building possibilities created by institutions such as the Department of Fine Arts, but also the Academy of Visual Arts and other higher learning environments, that has allowed the burgeoning of such a dynamic art ecology. Although it has not been written about enough, the originality and dynamism of the local art field is ample proof that the self-motivation, learning attitudes, level of creativity and level of exposure to the arts of local art students are just as good in Hong Kong as anywhere else we can find higher learning institutions dealing with the arts. Let us hope that it will remain true in the future.

In what directions do you want the Fine Arts Department at CUHK to develop in the next three to five years?

Departments grow in the direction created by the specialisations and interests of their faculty members and history. Its general tendency has been described earlier and will probably not change significantly. In 2019 and 2020, two of its older faculty members reached retirement age, and the department hired two new and quite young scholars to replace them. They both specialise in Chinese painting history and calligraphy and should allow the department to continue producing significant research in the same direction, while providing courses in both history and studio art. Unless the university allows it, which is extremely unlikely, the number of faculty members will remain the same and, therefore, so will its general direction.

The only changes that took place recently and were decidedly new elements in the history of FAA, were the creation of the internship programme in socially engaged art and the addition of courses on comics, which were both initiated by me. There is no guarantee that any of these courses will continue once I retire too, which will hopefully not take place before I reach sixty or sixty-five if the university allows it (professors have to apply for a continuance of their service at sixty years old, and the university only allows them to continue if they can prove they have sufficiently high teaching evaluations and if they have ongoing research projects). Once again, the department chair does not have significant power to make decisions independently.

What would you like to be remembered for when you retire?

Even though I take very seriously all the lectures I teach, all the articles and books I write, and all the drawings I make, I do not take myself that seriously. I do not have any concerns about a possible 'legacy.'

Photo 1. Prof. Frank Vigneron (Chair & Professor, Department of Fine Arts, Chinese University of Hong Kong).

Chapter 6

Dr. Anna Kwong, Programme Director, Centre for the Arts, Hong Kong University of Science and Technology

Introduction

Founded in 1996, the Centre for the Arts (CFA), currently under the Shaw Auditorium Unit, aims to bring art and culture into the Hong Kong University of Science and Technology (HKUST), thereby nurturing students' artistic awareness and appreciation of the arts. To promote arts appreciation and participation amongst the students at HKUST, the CFA organises a wide variety of arts and cultural programmes, including exhibitions, concerts, film shows, seminars, workshops, visits, etc.

Dr. Anna Kwong is currently serving as Programme Director at the CFA, HKUST. She earned both her master's and doctoral degrees in Art History from the University of Innsbruck. In the following interview, Dr. Kwong discusses the important roles that the CFA plays in shaping students' well-rounded education and personal development.

Could we begin this interview by first introducing yourself, for example, your professional training and educational background? For instance, what did you study at the university?

I came across the Italian language when doing my first degree at the University of Hong Kong. After graduation and having worked for a few years, I considered going abroad to pursue further studies; I chose to go to Italy to study a programme named *DAMS – Drama, Art and Music Studies* at the University of Bologna, of which I specialised in Art, i.e., visual arts. The programme aimed to develop an understanding of the three areas of cultural phenomena, theoretical framework, and semiotics. It attracted many international students in the late 1980s and early 1990s due to the famous semiologist Umberto Eco teaching there at that time; I was one of these students.

After a few years in Bologna, I moved to Austria and transferred my studies to the University of Innsbruck, where I completed my master's and Ph.D. degrees in art history.

Umberto Eco (1932 – 2016) was an Italian medievalist, philosopher, semiotician, cultural critic, political and social commentator, and novelist. In English, he is best known for his popular 1980 novel The Name of the Rose. Why do you think his literary works are so influential worldwide? What was the most valuable lesson that you have learnt from Umberto Eco?

It has been over four decades since *The Name of the Rose* was first published, and many studies have been done on the novel. It has sparked a new current of historical fiction (think of Ken Follett's *Pillars of the Earth* (1989), Dan Brown's Angels and Demons (2000) and The Da Vinci Code (2003), among others), in which academic historical facts are blended into an imaginative fictional plot through a detective popular culture story, this satisfies the interests of readers of many levels.

The novel was based on Eco's years of research into the Middle Ages, a period of time when religion and superstitious beliefs dominated everyday life. To solve murder mysteries, the main character (Brother William) uses knowledge and rational thinking to find the right way out of the labyrinth (a recurrent motif of medieval culture). The novel has been read as a postmodern novel, where text can be interpreted on multiple levels, and context is constantly constructed to unfold the story.

The most valuable lesson Umberto Eco taught me is that a good scholar has to read and think incessantly.

Mastering the theoretical framework of the semiotics – what part does it play in general research and scholarly studies of visual arts and art history?

Semiotics has brought the polysemy of meaning into art history. It opens up multiple levels of interpretation of art as signs that can be understood within a context. This is in fact not new in art history; think of Jacob Burckhardt's *The Civilisation of the Renaissance in Italy* of 1860, in which the whole "culture/civilisation" of the Renaissance was presented as the contextual background for the rise of Renaissance art.

After the spread of semiotics, art historians became conscious of two parallel and complementary approaches to interpreting art: formal analysis and contextual analysis. The former uses the language of art to describe the visual/formal elements; the latter requires building a context to understand the purposes and meanings of the visual/formal elements. The success of decoding art depends on the context, and the scope of this is subject to the knowledge and intellectual capacities of art historians.

Umberto Eco demonstrated that an enormous knowledge base was essential for capturing the depth and complexity of how visual culture was constructed across time and space. In *History of Beauty* (Rizzoli, 2004), he examined the idea of beauty in Western culture through visual arts with parallel quotations from writers and philosophers of all eras, drawing into the discussion concepts that shaped the cultural milieu and spirit of different times.

Could you briefly introduce the Centre for the Arts, The Hong Kong University of Science and Technology (HKUST)?

The HKUST Centre for the Arts (CFA) was founded in 1996 with Danny Yung as its first programme director. Over the years, CFA has played an important role in enriching the cultural life of the HKUST community.

What are the missions, visions and philosophy behind the Centre for the Arts, HKUST?

Our mission is to bring art and culture into this business and science-oriented university, thus nurturing students' artistic awareness and appreciation of the arts.

To what extent have the programmes of the Centre for the Arts integrated into HKUST's total curricula?

The University acknowledges one of its responsibilities is to provide a well-rounded education that enhances the development of creativity, critical thinking, global outlook, and cultural awareness for the students. The wide range of programmes CFA runs greatly and benefits the University in this respect.

For example, we held around 50 events annually to serve audiences of 4,000 to 5,000. The most significant event is the annual HKUST Arts Festival which takes place from mid-March to April with a cluster of programmes and activities organised under a theme. The theme of Arts Festival 2021 was *Art,*

Despite the Pandemic, with which we wanted to remind people of the beauty of art and music despite the challenges posed by COVID-19.

The exhibition *"Between Europe and Asia: Traditional Music and Costumes from Central Asia, Caucasus and the Middle East"* was a major event of AF2021. It brought our audience to the three lesser-known regions between the big continents and allowed them to read about cultures of Turko-Persian tradition and see rich artefacts from these cultures. In preparation for the exhibition, CFA reached out to the consulate generals of Iran, Turkey and Kazakhstan in Hong Kong. This helped the University to establish a tight working relationship with these countries and assist in consolidating academic and research exchange between our University and tertiary education institutes in these countries and regions.

The exhibition was accompanied by a series of performances and workshops featuring music and dance from these regions, e.g., *My Dear with Passionate Eyes: an Afternoon of Central Asian Dance by Pasha Umer and Eugene Leung* and *Lovers' Complaint: a Musical Tour Through Central Asia, Caucasus and the Middle East by Nur Collective*. Through these events and activities, our audience will feel the respect for diversity and world cultures of our University, and students will learn to share these values.

According to the Centre's homepage, "We hold exhibitions, concerts, film shows, seminars, workshops, and arrange visits and many more to serve the art-loving HKUST community... Our mission is to bring art and culture into this business and science-oriented university, thus nurturing students' artistic awareness and appreciation of the arts." How would this benefit HKUST as an educational institution, when the whole University is geared towards Science and Technology? What benefits would your Centre bring to the students' personal, academic, and social development in the long run?

Intellectual qualities like creativity, critical thinking, global outlook, and cultural awareness are necessary across disciplines, so even a university geared towards science and technology, like HKUST, views training students to acquire such qualities as essential. Our programme can fulfil this aim and purpose.

Nurturing students' artistic awareness and appreciation of the arts. -- How can science, technology and business students benefit from their increased participation and appreciation of the arts in the long run – in the context of their social, academic and personal lives?

Socially, students participate in many arts and cultural events and make friends with fellow participants. Academically, they can broaden their interests and consider new areas of study after coming into touch with arts subjects. Personally, the arts enable them to experience beauty, express their thoughts and give them consolation.

Could you describe your career path to becoming the Programme Director at the Centre of the Arts at HKUST?

In my second year of study at the University of Hong Kong, I became a volunteer helper at Hong Kong Arts Centre, assisting in translating programme notes, editing work and providing library services. Upon graduation, I joined the publicity department for six months. This job allowed me to attend arts and cultural events and earn valuable work experience through promotion and marketing.

In 2011, I worked as a part-time instructor at the School of Humanities and Social Science (SHSS) at HKUST, the then Director of Student Affairs intended to expand on arts and creativity education. I was subsequently hired to become Senior Lecturer (SHSS) and Programme Director of the Centre for the Artsunder the Student Affairs Office then.

You also serve as a Senior Lecturer at the Division of Humanities, HKUST. Senior Lecturer at the Division of Humanities and Programme Director at the Centre of the Arts – how do these two roles complement each other?

I introduced many outside classroom activities into my courses and recommended my students join CFA activities to broaden their horizons in/through the arts. For example, in the first few years of my work at CFA, I received complimentary tickets for Hong Kong Art Fair and later Art Basel Hong Kong shows and distributed them to students and the HKUST community. With the official status of the programme director of CFA, it is easier to organise and promote such activities to students.

As the Programme Director at the Centre of the Arts at HKUST, could you describe your main roles and areas of responsibility?

I am responsible for the overall planning of the CFA programme, discussing event proposals and details with artists and potential co-organisers of events, approving programme contents and controlling budgets. I also write up the content for the publicity materials and supervise the Centre's daily operation and running of CFA events.

Many people still consider Hong Kong a cultural desert. And yet, over the last few years, Hong Kong has joined New York and London as one of the world's top three international art markets, with a diverse range of public art spaces and large-scale art exhibitions springing up across the City -- could you describe the contradiction this very interesting phenomenon? As a practising artist and art educator from Europe, how would you describe the overall arts and cultural scene in Hong Kong?

I do not believe that Hong Kong is a cultural desert. If you look at LCSD venues and other performance/exhibition venues, there are events going on every day. Many are government-funded, additionally, non-profit and private organisations are organising arts and cultural events throughout the year, along with many people attending the cinema regularly every year. Therefore, from the perspectives of the number and days of cultural events being organised and the audience sizes engaging with the events, it would point to Hong Kong as a place with a vigorous cultural life.

I feel that the art market itself is not an indicator of whether a place is a cultural desert. The art market is not where art happens but only where art is treated as a commodity, and I doubt how much the essence of art and its true value are being discussed and advanced there. As for its coverage, the art business in general, especially art auctioning, focuses on artworks of high market value and has, therefore, a high profit margin. Bologna, for example, has been holding an annual art fair, the Arte Fiera, since the 1970s. When I was studying DAMS, local people were not interested in the fair even though admission was free. I once asked my fellow Italian classmates if they wanted to attend with me, and they commented that it was like a furniture showroom and was meaningless. In Hong Kong, art fairs are only held for a couple of days a year. The majority of the attendees are foreigners, and only a small group of local people participate. As mentioned in the previous paragraph, these people may or may not overlap with the event organisers and audience.

Nevertheless, the growth of the Hong Kong art market in recent years has aroused people's attention to the arts in a more generalised sense, and it is inspiring more people to work in the arts and culture field. With large-scale investment into arts and cultural facilities and collaborative projects with overseas institutions, initiated by the government and private organisations, the area is expanding rapidly, and I am very optimistic about its development.

As the Programme Director at the Centre for the Arts, could you describe your management and leadership style?

I would say I am quite democratic with my staff. I encourage them to give advice and fine-tune the work processes to achieve optimal results.

As an art history teacher, could you describe your teaching style?

My teaching is lecture-based, and I try to prompt students to speak up in class and to think critically by asking questions frequently.

Students in Hong Kong versus students in Italy and Austria – could you describe the major differences in their self-motivations, learning attitudes, creativity level and exposure to the arts between these three groups of students?

This would not be a fair question to pass comment on as I have not taught students majoring in art history or visual arts in Hong Kong. It would be an unfair comparison between HKUST students and students in Italy and Austria.

In what directions do you want the Centre for the Arts, HKUST to develop in the next three to five years?

HKUST is opening the 800+-seated Shaw Auditorium in November 2022, and CFA will be part of the future management team. In the next three to five years, I foresee a huge expansion of our programme. Internationally renowned artists will be invited to frequently perform or exhibit their works at our new venue. We also aim to become a cultural hub in the district, serving audiences from Sai Kung and the whole community of Hong Kong.

COVID-19 has turned the world upside down. How have the Centre for the Arts, HKUST, you (as the Programme Director), and your students been coping with COVID-19?

During the past year, CFA developed a series of online workshops and concerts to raise morale. We substituted the more frequent face-to-face events with large-scale projects and were able to provide events.

The aforementioned *"Between Europe and Asia: Traditional Music and Costumes from Central Asia, Caucasus and the Middle East"* exhibition was a major event of HKUST Arts Festival 2021. Much of the planning work was completed via Zoom early before we had face-to-face meetings or paid visits to the consulate generals for their loan of display items. With the reduced number of programmes, we could deploy resources to explore the less well-known cultures of eight countries from the three regions. We also developed applications of digital technologies for creating interactive experiences in the exhibition.

Students in my courses were not so fortunate, as I could sense that their learning motivation dropped over the three terms, understandably due to Zoom fatigue. I have modified my courses and adopted alternative assessments, e.g., instead of traditional exams, they were asked to do group presentations, write up project reports, join consultation meetings, write comments on peer presentations, write essays on certain concepts, etc. The assignments were scheduled over the term so that their learning interest and engagement remained high until they could return to individual face-to-face meetings.

Why do we turn to art and music in times of crisis?

Because art and music appeal to our senses and remind us of the beauty of life.

Photo 1. Dr. Anna Kwong at the opening ceremony of one of the exhibitions co-organised by HKUST Center for the Arts and the Library.

Chapter 7

Professor Louis Nixon, Former Director, Academy of Visual Arts, Hong Kong Baptist University

Introduction

The Academy of Visual Arts (AVA), Hong Kong Baptist University, provides professional visual arts undergraduate, postgraduate and research degree programmes linked to international exchange and the fast-growing creative industries. AVA is the first academy of its kind in Hong Kong, as its programmes seek to break down the boundaries of concepts, beliefs, traditions, perceptions and hypotheses through art. AVA students gain the confidence to perceive, appreciate and articulate – thereby widening students' perspectives and creating awareness and respect – allowing them to work with the contemporary issues of society – be they local, regional or global.

Prof. Louis Nixon served as the Director of AVA from 2018 to 2022. Prior to AVA, he was the Associate Dean of Research at the Kingston School of Art, Kingston University. In the following interview, Louis Nixon discusses the visual arts programmes offered by the local higher education institutions in Hong Kong, as well as differences in local students' perspectives and attitudes towards the arts compared to their British counterparts.

Could we begin this interview by first introducing yourself, for example, your professional training and educational background? For instance, what did you study at the university or art college? Do you come from a family of artists or art educators?

I am currently Professor and Director of the Academy of Visual Arts at Hong Kong Baptist University. I studied undergraduate painting at the Chelsea School of Art and then a Postgraduate degree in Sculpture at The Slade School of Art in London during the mid-late 1980's. Having studied across different media, my practice encompasses painting, sculpture, installation, and experimental film, often presented as multimedia installations in galleries and public spaces. After graduating, I founded the artists' collective Space Explorations and participated in large-scale interventions as an artist and curator in response to specific sites across London. Since 2001, I have worked independently and exhibited widely in the UK, Europe, Australia, Chile and China. I came from a family of artists and educators; my parents are both artists and are still practicing and exhibiting their work now. They both worked in the Arts education sector from the 1970's until the 1990's.

Could you briefly introduce the Academy of Visual Arts (AVA) at the Hong Kong Baptist University (HKBU)?

The Academy of Visual Arts (AVA) is the first university academy of its kind in Hong Kong to provide professional visual arts undergraduate, postgraduate, and research degree programmes. The Academy is closely linked to the international and local creative industries, and we offer a broad range of practical and studio-based courses and programmes combined with Critical and Historical Studies. AVA was founded in 2005 and is still a very young Arts School. At AVA, we take an open-minded, inclusive and holistic approach to visual arts education, combining studio-based research, critical and historical studies and sustainable service for the cultural and creative sectors as well as for the community at large. At AVA, we encourage our students to experiment and work across disciplines, and we try to break down the boundaries between disciplines and approaches to widen perspectives and create awareness and respect, encouraging students to work with the contemporary issues of society – be they local, regional or global.

Could you describe your career path to becoming the Director of AVA at HKBU?

Before joining HKBU, I was the Associate Dean for Research at Kingston School of Art, and before that, I was the Head of the School of Fine Art from 2007-14. Before that, I had worked in Higher Education in teaching and research positions at numerous UK Art Schools. I visited Hong Kong for the first time in May 2018 and was then approached to apply for the role of AVA Director. After visiting the Academy and meeting staff and students, I was very impressed with the energy and vibrancy of the Arts School and saw great potential for the Academy, particularly in building the research community and developing the curricula and resources to embrace new technologies and building and furthering our international links. HK seemed such an exciting context for an Arts School, particularly with the broader investment in the Art and Culture sector in Hong Kong (M+, Tai Kwun, etc.) At that time (2018) there was also a lot of interest from international Art Schools and Artists working and collaborating with HK, so it was an exciting place to live and work.

As the Director of AVA at HKBU, could you describe your main roles and areas of responsibility?

As Director, I have overall responsibility for the Academy; a similar title would be Dean of a Faculty. I set strategic priorities in teaching, research, facilities development, recruitment, and internationalisation. In addition to the academy's leadership, I enjoy working with the students in a teaching capacity at all levels of BA, MA and PhD, and feel it is important to understand the academy through the student's eyes and experience. I also enjoy working with younger artists, watching them develop, and seeing what makes them tick. In my 35 years working in art education, I have stayed in touch with many of my former students, and I find it very interesting to follow their careers and watch them develop over time.

According to your online biography, your art practice encompasses painting, sculpture, installation, and experimental film, often presented as multimedia installations in galleries and public spaces. What is the definition of experimental films in the age of YouTube, Tok-tok, particularly in an era dominated by digital technology in the form of mobile devices?

My films are experimental in how they are made and exhibited. I film a lot using combinations of fixed cameras on cars or vehicles that simultaneously capture different viewpoints and directions. The films are often durational and shot over days on long journeys on roads or motorways circumnavigating countries or landmarks. I edit them systematically and exhibit them using different display technologies such as projectors/CCTV monitors/ or LED Screens. I also work a lot with sound, often creating or combining sounds with films to make immersive experiences for the viewer.

I am increasingly working with found footage, and in the age of YouTube or TikTok, the availability of and access to found footage opens up many possibilities. Generally, the proliferation of films across media is a good thing. Access to moving image material and easily available and user-friendly editing software is exciting, as anyone can shoot, edit, and publish film material, opening up many creative possibilities. I am also interested in the proliferation of instructional videos on YouTube, which I turn to when I want to find out how to do a specific thing or how something works. These are invaluable resources. On the negative side, we increasingly live in the spaces of our screens, and interaction with the physical world seems to decline as a consequence. The immediacy and reach of making and publishing moving images can lead to mediocrity, clickbait disinformation, and increasing issues with screen addiction and privacy.

Students and the general public in Hong Kong versus their counterparts in the UK – what are the major differences in their perceptions and attitudes towards sculpture, installation and experimental film, and multimedia installations in public spaces?

There are a lot of similarities, and I think the similarities outweigh the differences. But I have noticed that the HK students seem more methodical in their working out and less risk-taking. They use art more to tell personal stories, and there is a general need for things to have specific reasons behind them, rather than just doing something to see how it looks and then responding to it. In the UK, the students I taught were more diverse and came from different backgrounds and experiences.

For art audiences in the UK, I think they have generally been more exposed to work in museums and galleries, so they are possibly more discerning and perhaps more critically engaged than in HK. I think in both the UK and HK. The public is appreciative that there are museums and galleries to visit, and as we have seen from the success of spaces like Tate Modern and Tai Kwun, these spaces become important places not just to see great art but to congregate, socialise, entertain, and enjoy and all great cities need these kinds of public spaces.

Could you describe the career paths of a majority of the AVA, HKBU graduates?

As AVA is a young institution, our early Alumni are now reaching the midpoints of their lives and their career paths are very varied. Our graduates tend to work in a number of fields, and it often takes a few years for graduates to establish and settle on a career path. Mainly they work in Arts, Crafts and Design related jobs independently or in teams, some go into teaching, further study or the Museum and gallery sector, and of course some of our graduates are finding great success as practicing artists and galleries and collectors supporting their practice.

In addition to HKBU, the Chinese University of Hong Kong (CUHK), the Education University of Hong Kong (EDUHK), and the Hong Kong Art School (HKAS) also offer degree programmes in Fine Arts, with a strong emphasis on studio art practices. Could you describe the major differences in curricula and staff and student profiles between these four institutions?

There are many differences between these programmes brought about by institutional contexts, historical developments, student and staff profiles, curricula, resources such as space facilities and funding, etc. I don't know all the details of these factors at the other institutions because I get most of my impression from the outside, looking in through the lens of the student's work. At AVA, we try to provide and promote skills and competencies in materials and processes, self-initiated studio practice, rigorous research, knowledge of critical and historical studies and experimental and collaborative work. We put a lot of emphasis on peer learning and try to get our students to take the sort of risks with their work and ideas that can be more difficult to undertake in life outside the Art School. From my previous experience working in London, where there are 16 Art Schools, HKAS and AVA have the most in common with those.

Many people still consider Hong Kong a cultural desert. And yet, over the last few years, Hong Kong has joined New York and London as one of the world's top three international art markets, with a diverse range of public art spaces and large-scale art exhibitions springing up across the City. Could you describe the contradiction of this very interesting phenomenon? As a practicing artist and art educator from Europe, how would you describe the overall arts and cultural scene in Hong Kong?

One of the reasons I came to work in Hong Kong in 2018 was because of the rapidly developing arts and cultural scene; it reminded me of London in the 1990's when artists, galleries, art schools, curators, collectors and museums were all pushing in the same direction, and there was a lot of focus and opportunity across the sector. HK certainly isn't a cultural desert, but the art market remains strong with International Art Fairs and Auction houses. The galleries and museums sector has been revitalised and added too significantly. There is a lot of international focus and attention through Tai

Kwun, M+, and the numerous public art projects that have taken place here. There is a much broader and deeper infrastructure, and I've seen it progress in the past four years. I think many experienced and energetic people are working in HK to make it a global focus for Art and Culture, and the scale of investment and development is significant and impressive. It's also a supportive and close community where we each work to benefit the other as part of a creative ecology. Developing and engaging new audiences and ensuring that there are wider benefits to society as well as the economy is perhaps more of a challenge long term.

Given the recent M+ Museum controversy after introducing Hong Kong's national security law, how do you think this would affect Hong Kong's cultural tourism industry and the City's position as one of the world's top art markets in the long run?

This is very hard to predict. Many museums across the globe have controversy in what they display or don't display, and operate within specific frameworks, so I don't think this is a unique problem to Hong Kong. However, the NSL is a new consideration for everyone coming to terms with and working out. During this time, there is a degree of uncertainty, and I worry more about artists and institutions and the amount of HK artists wanting to leave HK as an immediate reaction to the NSL.

On the other hand, I speak to many artists who are very committed to staying and helping to build and contribute to the developments here, and they are excited to be working in HK as a vital part of this ambitious project. Time will tell how the NSL will affect the cultural tourism industry and the city's position. I think it's too early to predict whether international audiences will stop visiting. Much will depend on the kind of projects and artists shown, what is communicated through the museums and the press, and how the government responds.

As the Director of AVA, HKBU, could you describe your management and leadership style?

I have tried to be flexible and adapt quickly to the unprecedented changes and challenges in HK and Internationally over the past 18 months. Having worked in the Education sector for 35 years, I have tried to bring my experiences to the benefit of the Academy and build a confident and diverse team. I try to listen and learn and be consensual, but also, I have to make decisions based on my understanding and experience. Running an International Arts School and being an outsider means I rely a lot on the very experienced and professional staff from HK. We face many challenges ahead, but I believe through working together and in constant dialogue with our internal and external stakeholders, we can navigate a successful path ahead for AVA.

As a visual arts teacher, could you describe your teaching style?

I try to be supportive and not too critical of students because learning to be an artist is very hard. I try to build self-awareness and confidence, encourage experimentation and enjoyment, and get the students to learn from and work with each other. I think it's important for students to know that in creative education, you are always learning and the same problems they are facing – what idea do I want to work on? What form will it take? Is what I made what I want to see? Is it any good? How do I survive financially? All these questions recur throughout one's life as an artist, so I try to teach them how to prepare for their life ahead.

Students in Hong Kong versus students in the UK – could you describe the major differences in their self-motivation, learning attitudes, level of creativity and exposure to the arts between these two groups of students?

Hong Kong students seem less confident working independently at first and are more cautious; they are less questioning of their teachers and the world around them and more inward-looking and self-reflective. In London (and other big UK cities with Arts Schools), the students are more diverse as it's a much more diverse education system and population. Hong Kong students impress me greatly with their commitment, resolve, and ability to talk and communicate their ideas. I think they are similar regarding exposure as it is so easy now to access and research most things remotely. We have some students who leave to study postgraduate courses abroad and return. These students are really interesting as they have worked and benefited from both contexts.

In what directions do you want the AVA and HKBU to develop in the next 3 to 5 years?

The role of technology and the growth of 'Art Tech,' and how this impacts curricula and practice is exciting for us. As a 'traditional' Art School with all the established technologies (glass, ceramics, print, photography, etc.), how these merge and combine with AI, VR, AR and Robotics, this combination of old and new technologies is very interesting for us. We are investing heavily in creative robotics, physical computing, AI, and creativity, but we have kept hold of all our traditional technologies and still value the potter's wheel and the bronze foundry. I think this combination will enable us to do exciting things in Art Design and Craft Education and research in the future.

COVID-19 has turned the world upside down. How have AVA, you and your students been coping with COVID-19?

We moved everything online for months at a time, using a range of digital tools and resources. We also sent the equipment back to students' homes so they could continue to physically make things, we held a lot of international virtual events and projects, and the students (and the staff) introduced a lot of new elements to the curriculum, many of which we will continue in post-pandemic. The students and staff found it hard to adapt at first, but creative people are good at adapting, and we have developed many positive outcomes. Students didn't receive a normal arts school education. Although it wasn't ideal, a lot of student work seemed more focused and developed, perhaps because the students had less to distract them. We are all looking forward to returning to the tried and tested ways, but many of the new digital tools and resources and virtual projects we have introduced will stay, and we have advanced rapidly in many ways as a result of COVID. The biggest issue we face now is travel and being able to send our students out of Hong Kong and receive International Artists. At AVA, we have a very good exchange programme and visiting scholars' scheme, which has been on hold for nearly two years.

Why do we turn to art and music in times of crisis?

This is a very good question. When the pandemic hit, I started to learn the guitar as well as carry on my artistic practice. I know a lot of people who took up new creative hobbies, I think because we simply had more time at home, and it's also a way of making sense of the difficulties of the situation, doing something constructive to occupy time, developing new skills, find enjoyment in the chaos of it all.

What would you like to be remembered for when you retire?

I would like to be remembered as making a positive contribution to the lives of all the students I worked with. I always remember my teachers at Art School, and I am still in touch with many of them; they helped me a lot as an artist and a human being. At AVA and other Art Schools I have led, I have always tried to make the best environment for the students with the resources I have. I have also built two distinctive Ph.D. programmes (at Kingston School of Art and AVA), and I hope that I have positively contributed to improving the quality and acceptance of artistic research within academia and advancing the field itself.

Photo 1. Louis Nixon in his studio at The Academy of Visual Arts. (2021).

Photo 2. Louis Nixon at The Academy of Visual Arts. (2019).

Photos 3 & 7. The Academy of Visual Arts Kai Tak Campus. (2020).

Photo 4. Students and staff at the entrance to the Academy of Visual Arts (Kai Tak Campus). (2020).

Photo 5. Academy of Visual Arts, Kai Tak Gallery. Exhibition 'New Art Now.' (2020).

Photo 6. Academy of Visual Arts, Kai Tak Gallery. Exhibition Opening of 'New Art Now.' (2020).

Chapter 8

Elaine Yeung, Former Deputy Director, Leisure & Cultural Services Department (Culture), Government of Hong Kong

Introduction

The Leisure & Cultural Service Department (LCSD) is responsible for formulating the overall policy and strategic proposals for funding and developing all leisure- and culture-related facilities and projects in Hong Kong.

The Cultural Services Branch under the LCSD conducts a wide variety of services, including planning and managing cultural projects throughout Hong Kong, research related to cultural resources, and funding and managing international festivals. It also oversees the Performing Arts Division, the Heritage and Museums Division, responsible for managing film archives and museums, and the Libraries and Development Division, responsible for planning and managing public libraries. The Cultural Services Branch currently manages a total number of 16 major performing venues for cultural and art performances, 17 museums, and 82 public libraries.

Elaine Yeung is the current Deputy Director of the LCSD in charge of the Cultural Services Branch. In the following interview, Elaine Yeung discusses her exceptionally long career in managing the city's performing arts, as well as her devotion to educating the next generation of arts consumers in Hong Kong, thereby raising the overall standards for arts appreciation for this international city that was once a tiny fishing village.

Could we begin this interview by first introducing yourself, for example, your professional training and educational background? What did you study at the university? Do you come from a family of musicians or performing artists? Are you also a trained musician yourself?

I am currently serving as the Department's Deputy Director in charge of the Cultural Services Branch of the Leisure and Cultural Services Department (LCSD) in Hong Kong, which has a unique connection to culture and the arts. At the University of Hong Kong (HKU), I studied English Literature, but my career aspirations moved me away from what I studied at university. In 1983, I applied for a civil service post with the Hong Kong Government, starting as an arts festival assistant, and a year later, I joined the then Urban Services Department as a civil servant.

When I was young, my mother encouraged me to develop an interest in music, as she was a lover of vocal music and a member of the HK Oratorio Society. My schoolteachers also encouraged me to develop an interest in the performing arts world by attending live performances.

Before the establishment of the Hong Kong Cultural Centre in 1989, there were two extremes in the local arts and cultural scene in Hong Kong during the 1980s. It appeared that Western classical music (e.g., piano recitals, orchestra concerts, operas, etc.) was mainly catered to the white elites (i.e., well-*educated, middle-class expatriates living in Hong Kong). On the other hand,* Cantonese Opera and other forms of traditional Chinese performing arts (including music) were found to be more popular among the laymen and local Chinese people of working-class background in Hong Kong. This gave us the impression that the *better-educated and more sophisticated audience* tends to be more receptive to Western classical music.

I joined the Urban Services Department (USD) in 1984; my first post was serving as the Assistant Manager at the Tsuen Wan Town Hall. Tsuen Wan was an area of Hong Kong that I was very unfamiliar with. *Tsuen Wan was a* typical old district surrounded by industrial areas. During my initial years working at the Tsuen Wan Town Hall, I found this district to be old, very rundown, and almost no culture could be found there. I initially found the Tsuen Wan Town Hall and the surrounding areas untidy. During the 1980s, Tsuen Wan Town Hall did not function like a cultural centre. It was more like a public building where people could just come in to socialise without real aims or purposes. Most of the time, they would come in and sit near the entrance -- just to enjoy the free air-conditioning, and not for our arts and cultural activities.

However, from a different perspective, the people from the local area made my job more interesting. During the 1980s, when concerts were being held at the Tsuen Wan Town Hall, we had to prepare locally manufactured white sneakers for the audience, in case some of them would show up at a performance wearing slippers (flip-flops), because the local Chinese audience was not aware of the proper etiquette for attending formal concerts at that time. My ultimate goal was to help educate them, as well as to raise the overall standards of appreciation for the arts amongst the local general public in Hong Kong, via different pre- and post-performance workshops and educational programmes.

Could you describe your career path to becoming the Deputy Director, Leisure & Cultural Services Department (LCSD), HKSARG?

A combination of both vision and opportunity, coupled with a little luck, has made me the Deputy Director of the LCSD. My career has included the grand opening of the Sha Tin Town Hall (1987) and the Hong Kong Cultural Centre (1989), as well as working for the Shanghai Expo 2010. Shanghai Expo 2010 was the first major cultural exchange project between Hong Kong and Mainland China, where Hong Kong sent different performing arts groups to perform for the Expo for six months (i.e., three different programmes a month, in tandem with various exhibitions).

For the Shanghai Expo in 2010, we knew nothing about how things could/should be done in Mainland China, so we had to start everything from scratch. At the Shanghai Expo, we managed to create a very successful Hong Kong Week via our unique performing arts performances and made an excellent impression on the audience in Mainland China. Then, we were invited to launch our performance (featuring artists from Hong Kong) in other major cities throughout Mainland China, including the Greater Bay Area.

Looking back at my career, the most challenging task I ever undertook was looking after the Hong Kong Chinese Orchestra (before it was corporatised) when I was still serving as a junior manager. The artistic director and conductor curated the Hong Kong Chinese Orchestra (HKCO) programmes, and I (as a junior manager) had to help manage the HKCO musicians.

At that time, HKCO musicians mostly came from Mainland China (whereas now, many are graduates of the Hong Kong Academy for Performing Arts). Because of that, the working morale and discipline could be low. All sorts of unpleasant accidents could happen, e.g., HKCO members not showing up on time for rehearsals (being stuck in traffic, sick, or absent for any reason). As you can imagine, if just one major player was absent, the artistic standard of the whole performance would be seriously affected!

Could you describe the mission and vision of the LCSD (Culture)?

The Cultural Services Branch comprises three divisions which are responsible for the planning and management of museums, performance venues, public libraries and indoor stadia; promotion and presentation of museum exhibitions, arts festivals, film, literary and performing arts programmes and intangible cultural heritage activities; conservation of cultural heritage; management of the Music Office and operation of the URBTIX ticketing system.

Our vision is to provide quality leisure and cultural services commensurate with Hong Kong's development as a world-class city and events capital. In other words, apart from providing good quality services in arts and culture, we also aim to provide wonderful experiences to enrich the life of the general public in Hong Kong. Through our museums, libraries, and concert halls, we aim to bring them meaningful educational experiences via art and culture. The high standards of professionalism amongst our LCSD staff are evident in each exhibition and performance we provide to the general public.

Our mission is to:

- Enrich life by providing quality leisure and cultural services for all;
- Promote professionalism and excellence in leisure pursuits and cultural services;
- Promote synergy with sports, cultural and community organisations in enhancing the development of the arts and sports in the territory;
- Preserve the cultural heritage;
- Beautify the environment through tree planting;
- Achieve a high level of customer satisfaction;
- Build a highly motivated, committed and satisfying workforce.

We achieve our mission by embracing these core values:

- Customer focus
- Quality

- Creativity
- Professionalism
- Result oriented
- Cost-effectiveness
- Continuous improvement

As of 2022, I oversee 17 museums, including the visual art centre, with an art promotion office. There are also three small museums, including the Law Uk Folk Museum (former Hakka village house in Chai Wan, Hong Kong). In addition, there are 14 performing arts venues, including the Hong Kong City Hall and two stadia (Hong Kong Coliseum and Queen Elizabeth Stadium). My work also encapsulates 82 public libraries (including the Hong Kong Central Library, district libraries, mobile libraries, plus remote ones located on the surrounding islands like Cheung Chau). There are five other music centres (dedicated to music education) and the Hong Kong Film Archive.

*Could you describe the total staff population of the **LCSD** (Culture)?*

I oversee the cultural services with approximately 3,000 permanent staff and about 500 contract staff, i.e., under 4,000. Performing arts are managed by some 340 cultural services managers. There are almost 240 curators for visual arts and heritage, and another 380 librarians.

As the Deputy Director of LCSD, could you describe your main roles and areas of responsibility?

My roles and areas of responsibility sound enormous, but the Government trusts my propensity for the appointment. I am responsible for overseeing the delivery of cultural services as well as the management of venues, including the Hong Kong Film Archive, performance venues, public libraries and the Music Office; promotion and presentation of cultural programmes and intangible cultural heritage; and planning of new cultural facilities. It is a tough job, and there have been many difficult times. But I love my work, because I know that I am making valuable contributions to our city's culture and future. Through the years working as an arts administrator at the LCSD, I am so lucky to have become friends with many internationally renowned artists, musicians, film/theatre producers, etc. Many expressed their interest in returning to Hong Kong to work with me and the LCSD again.

In 1997, Tan Dun was invited to conduct the Concert, celebrating the handover of Hong Kong. I met him in 1995, two years prior, as he was working as a guest conductor with the Hong Kong Chinese Orchestra. Tan Dun and I have known each other for almost 30 years. Throughout the years, we have continued working together on very different projects, particularly at the New Vision Arts Festival. We are going to launch a big event featuring Tan Dun's earlier work, Buddha Passion, at Chi Lin Nunnery, hoping to bless the people of Hong Kong after going through such trying times caused by COVID-19.

Over the years, the general public in Hong Kong has voiced their opinions over the work carried out by the LCSD. During the early 1980s, we, as civil servants, appeared to be invincible! No one would criticise our work. Today, the situation is totally different. The *"complain culture" has grown to* become too common, and people are encouraged to voice feelings even at a young age. It is common to receive comments from people via different channels (email, Instagram, Facebook, etc.), telling us, "Oh, I like your programme, or I don't like it." We listen, observe, and find ways to improve as much as possible because many ideas and comments given by our audience are valid and worth noting.

For example, recently, someone raised the issue of why LCSD does not allow people to take photographs at concerts. We reviewed the practice immediately. We do not let people take pictures during a show to avoid disrupting the performance, but the audience can do it at the curtain call now. Previously, no mobile phone signals could come into a concert hall, but now we have to let the signals in because we are doing a lot of live streaming of our performances.

What are the core professional knowledge, skills, and personality traits necessary to become the Deputy Director, LCSD?

As a devoted arts administrator, every day, you learn something new. And you try to learn as much as possible; you are like a sponge in every situation. As a senior arts administrator, there is no textbook or curriculum package to tell you what you should do on your job daily. Of course, the LCSD provides general holistic training sessions for newcomers, but it depends very much on one's personal aptitude, as well as how much time one wants to invest in improving one's skills and professional knowledge and connections, etc. It all boils down to how much devotion and passion one has for the arts, and you believe a career could be built upon that. Or you are just doing it as a job for a living. To do this job well, one must have an appreciation and a strong appetite for the arts.

I think the key to the success of LCSD has been my dedication and professionalism. In order to have a high level of professionalism, one must have the professional knowledge, curiosity, and language to master the art form, as well as to liaise with the artists/creators. Possessing a great sense of appreciation and respect towards the art form and the artist is equally important. Furthermore, following the latest trends and artistic endeavours is important to understanding the story behind specific art forms. If you don't know how to appreciate what you are presenting (regardless of whether it is a dance, drama or opera), how are you going to promote or publicise it from different perspectives and make it appealing to different audience groups? Hence, it is quite demanding when some newcomers have not yet understood how to do it.

Are there any other interesting and inspiring stories regarding LCSD (Culture) that you wish to share with the readers?

The LCSD has been very proactive with cultural exchange for over ten years by organising a major event called *Hong Kong Week* in different cities almost every year since the Shanghai Expo 2010. We sent local artists from Hong Kong to foreign cities to facilitate artistic exchanges and collaborations. We also maintain our presence in the international arts arena, intending to reinforce Hong Kong's position as a facilitator in the global networking of arts institutions and practitioners in the region and beyond. We are going to host the mid-year congress of the International Society for the Performing Arts in mid-2022 (the first time it was in 2006). All the members taking part in this International Society for the Performing Arts Congress are arts practitioners and performing artists from different parts of the world. This International Congress provides a great opportunity to showcase our local artists and programmes from Hong Kong. Despite the COVID-19 crisis, we still created an opportunity to work closely with the Manchester International Festival to create an online production in 2021. The first online collaboration between Manchester International Festival and the LCSD has fully demonstrated our professionalism. This online project has not only led to closer friendship between the two parties, but also created more opportunities for future collaboration.

Looking back on my career history as a seasoned arts administrator, I remember one moment in particular: my working experience with Yukio

Ninagawa (蜷川 幸雄, 1935-2016), a great Japanese theatre director, actor, and film director. We planned to invite Ninagawa and his world-renowned theatre company to perform in Hong Kong for almost ten years. Unfortunately, he kept saying that he did not have the time, and he kept on postponing due to his busy schedule. Then, around 2008, an opportunity came up, and we managed to invite his second-tier theatre (the first-tier comprises mature actors; the second- and third-tiers comprise young and senior actors, respectively). We managed to invite both junior and senior actors to come and perform in the show called *Ravens. We Shall Load Bullets* in 2014, and it was a very great show. The actors were probably aged from 57 to 80. Ninagawa was particularly known for his Japanese language productions of *Shakespeare's* plays. (The Hong Kong Academy of Performing Arts (HKAPA) staged his version of *Medea* in the 1990s).

Finally, he agreed with the senior actors and the theatre company to come to Hong Kong to perform. Unexpectedly, he got very sick when he was in Hong Kong and had to be admitted to a hospital. The Japanese Government eventually arranged a special chartered flight and a crew to escort him back to Japan. When this incident happened, we all got very worried. However, when he returned to Japan, he said, "No matter what, my *Macbeth* has to be performed in Hong Kong! The company has to come here!" Sadly, Ninagawa passed away shortly after, and these were among his last words. An artist of his calibre celebrated our city with dedication and integrity. I take some pride in that. Finally, we presented Ninagawa's *Macbeth* in 2017, after his death.

What would you like to be remembered for when you retire?

If a legacy is to be recounted, I would like to be remembered as a fun person with an amiable attitude that could get things done. I chose this as my lifetime career and have turned it into one of meaning.

Photo 1. Elaine C.L. Yeung (Former Deputy Director, Leisure & Culture Services (Culture), Government of the Hong Kong).

Photo 2. Elaine C.L. Yeung (Former Deputy Director, Leisure & Cultural Services (Culture), Government of Hong Kong).

Chapter 9

Sandy Angus, Chairman, Angus Montgomery Arts

Introduction

Sandy Angus is Chairman of Angus Montgomery, a privately owned 124-year-old family business, active in running trade and consumer events on five continents and its arts division, Angus Montgomery Arts, which specialises in events in the contemporary art market and is committed to delivering high quality, regional art fairs that serve the needs of collectors and galleries. With more than 50 years of experience in the event and exhibition industry, Sandy Angus has worked extensively in the contemporary arts sector since the 1980s.

Continuing to seek out new art markets, Angus co-founded Art Hong Kong in 2007, which was later taken over by Art Basel. He has co-founded and invested in a wide range of regional art fairs, and more recently, focusing on the Asia-Pacific region. Angus Montgomery Arts' current portfolio includes Art SG, Tokyo Gendai, Taipei Dangdai, India Art Fair, Sydney Contemporary, Aotearora At Fair, PHOTOFAIRS New York, PHOTOFAIRS Shanghai, Photo London, Art Central Hong Kong and Art Düsseldorf, making Angus Montgomery Arts the largest art fair organiser in Asia.

Sandy Angus has served as the President of the Union of International Fairs (UFI), Chairman of the UK Association of Exhibition Organisers and is a recent Chairman of the National Association of Exhibition Management of the USA. Angus has been recognised with a Lifetime Achievement Award from the AEO, the Pinnacle Award from IAEE, the Medal d'Or from UFI and the Hall of Leaders from the Convention Industry Council. In the following interview, Agnus discusses how the fall of the USSR and the opening of communist China changed the overall event and exhibition industry around the world.

Could we begin this interview by first introducing yourself, for example, your professional training, educational background, and what you studied at the university? Do you come from a family of artists, art historians, museum curators, or art dealers?

I was born in India, so part of my education was done there. I then returned to the UK and went into the family business, which ran exhibitions. My family was very into the arts, especially contemporary art. I didn't go to university, but during my university-type days, I was surrounded by art, learnt what contemporary art meant, and had the enjoyment of meeting artists and going to galleries and so on. That was my youth in the sense that I went straight into a family business that ran exhibitions. In those days, they were largely industrial exhibitions, but in the 80s, we took it into art fairs in London and Los Angeles. During that period, we got to know a lot of galleries, artists and collectors, mainly in Europe and the US.

Could you tell me more about the 'family business'?

The family has been running fairs since 1895, and it has a long tradition of running exhibitions, but we did not initially get into the arts. The head of the family was very interested in contemporary arts during the 1960s and 70s and encouraged everybody to become fascinated. Our offices were always covered in contemporary art and had lots of activity.

According to your online biography, you have more than 50 years of experience in the event and exhibition industry and have worked extensively in contemporary art centres since the 1980s. How has the industry evolved in the last 50 years, particularly in light of globalisation and the emergence of digital media?

Social media has come into prominence within our industry, but really only in the last five to ten years. Over that time, the changes in the industries were relatively small. But digitalisation has greatly affected the industry, and COVID-19 has sped that process up dramatically. Online platforms have become a very standard way of looking at art, and I think there's no doubt that as they improve, they will continue to play a crucial part in the process of looking at, buying, and collecting art. If you look at Sotheby's statistics, online activity in their auctions has dramatically increased.

During the eighties and nineties, there was a major movement in video art and installations. Are they still a trend?

Video art has never taken the prominence that I thought it would. Obviously film has, but other forms of video art have certainly become collectable. They're less popular than more traditional forms of art, but I think photography has also grown dramatically over the last 20 years as a collectable entity.

Can contemporary art in art fairs — for example, Art Central Hong Kong or Art Basel — be used as a lens for understanding the political economies of a geographical region?

Yes. Artists have a way of looking at things, which is much clearer in many ways than the rest of us. They study to see how different situations impact their lives and try to record them. They can be used as a lens to understand what's going on, and we see that in particular areas where strife and upheaval occur.

Could you provide a brief introduction to Angus Montgomery Arts and the mission and philosophy of the operation?

Angus Montgomery Arts was conceived when we started in Hong Kong in 2008, but before that, Montgomery had created an art fair in London in the 1980s and one in Los Angeles. The one in Los Angeles became highly reputable and attracted a lot of famous American collectors, and Eli Broad was certainly a moving force in making it a success. But both those fairs got really knocked on the head by the economic downturn of the nineties. It wasn't until 2007 that we decided we would try to run an art fair in Hong Kong, ideally as a regional hub in Asia, to create something that would serve the broader Asian art market at the highest level.

Could you describe your career path in becoming the chairman of AMA?

The Montgomery group is a very diverse group that works across many industries in different countries. We're geographically spread broadly from Africa throughout Asia and headquartered in Europe. I've been running the business since 1995, when I took over as Chairman. I have been instrumental in a lot of the expansion of the business and particularly into the art world, where we have a diverse portfolio, largely in Asia Pacific from Sydney all the way to Delhi.

Could you describe your primary roles and areas of responsibilities as the Chairman of AMA?

I oversee the growth and regionalisation of the art portfolio. I am responsible for the strategic look of what we're doing regarding networking; I identify and use my contacts. I acquired a wide network of contacts as President of the Union des Foires based in Paris in 2000. This was at the same time China was developing its exhibitions industry. I used my role as President to help Chinese cities appreciate the benefits that exhibitions and events can bring to their city. Over the years, there was a massive expansion of the industry which is now the largest in the world. I knew Hong Kong very well because we ran many exhibitions there, and it is being able to build on those experiences and recognise where art markets can be centred.

Could you describe your management and leadership style?

I try to lead by example, and I wouldn't ask anybody to do anything I wouldn't do myself. I'm hugely optimistic and hope to translate that to the people I work with. Essentially, I hope I give people the confidence to deliver on what we are promising and do it as a team. We should work together, be flexible, and be determined to see things through, as you don't always succeed. It's essential to learn from your mistakes and keep going when others feel they've had enough.

What was the motivation behind AMA to found Art Hong Kong? Were there any challenges?

The biggest challenge was finding a venue because Art Basel was constantly approaching the Hong Kong Convention and Exhibition Centre.

Many people still consider Hong Kong a cultural desert. Over the last few years, Hong Kong has joined New York and London as the top three international art markets worldwide, with a diverse range of public art places and large-scale exhibitions. Could you describe the contradiction between this phenomenon?

I don't think I've ever heard Hong Kong described as a 'cultural desert'. When we first arrived in 2007, people were quite sceptical, but there were so many benefits to opening a gallery in Hong Kong to serve the broader Asian market and Mainland China. There were benefits from a taxation point of view for dealers and no complex bureaucracy or censorship to transporting art in and out of the country.

At that time, the West Kowloon project was emerging as an ambition for the city, which gave people real confidence that many cultural things would evolve here. The Art HK exhibition opened many people's eyes to the potential of Hong Kong, and many major galleries opened up. I think Hong Kong is now very much the cultural centre of Asia and has the headquarters for all the major auctions and galleries. It's a fact that when the annual Art Basel and Art Central run each year, the hotels, restaurants and general economy are massively culminated by the number of people who come in for those events.

Given the recent M+ Museum controversy, how do you think introducing the National Security Law will affect the Hong Kong cultural tourism industry and the city's position as one of the top markets in the long run?

People are looking to see the impact, but I believe Hong Kong will settle back into the role it has played all along. All the advantages that Hong Kong offers to the art world are still there. You could argue that there will now be a degree of censorship, but I think having worked in Shanghai as well as Hong Kong, you learn to work with legislation and exist within the constraints of whatever will evolve.

Could you briefly introduce Art Central Hong Kong initiated by AMA?

There's no doubt that Art Central is a satellite fair to Art Basel. When we initially agreed to sell Art HK to Basel, one of the agreements was that they would allow us to run a satellite fair simultaneously. I think satellite fairs broaden the appeal to buyers and collectors because not everybody can afford to spend fifty thousand or a million dollars for a painting or sculpture. You have to have different levels of art represented. That's really what Art Central has done.

I like to think that we provide a different vibe to Art Basel. It's got a much more 'village-y' feel than the more corporate feel at Basel. We still attract very high-quality galleries because they want to see the major collectors come in and be part of something different but still attractive and entertaining. Art Central has its own crucial place in the art world.

Would you say the audience or clientele of Art Central and Art Basel are different?

Many of the major collectors who see Art Basel come to Art Central. They enjoy it as it has a very different vibe. We get a lot of young collectors as well as younger, edgier artists.

We concentrate very much on collectors, but the interesting element about Art Central is that there are people who are simply buyers. Collectors have a grand plan and work very closely with particular dealers — that's a particular ambition. If you're just a buyer of things you like and enjoy, then you're just a buyer of art without preconceptions of trying to be grand. Art Central provides that. We look for people who want to buy art on an occasional basis rather than a regular basis. They're inevitably a little younger with less money, but they're intrigued, and it's the early stages of turning people into collectors. That's a significant part of what Art Central provides.

COVID-19 has turned the world upside down. How have AMA and Art Central Hong Kong been coping? Has COVID-19 impacted the art market?

We have just run Art Central, the first event we ran in fourteen months. All our activities worldwide have ground to a halt, and we haven't been able to run any of our launches. Singapore had to be put off (Art SG has since launched successfully in January 2023), and we were also planning to launch in Seoul. COVID-19 has impacted the art markets. It's been far less impactful than people might've thought because of the digitisation and digital platforms that have been created. But I think this has broadened the appeal of the art fairs. If they can have a digital existence, they can increase the number of days in a year that people can access art, and it also helps promote the fairs. Apart from the very social activities during the fair, I think it has ultimately broadened the number of people who will be a part of the art fairs in the future without necessarily visiting them.

Do you think there's a tendency for people to turn to art in times of crisis, such as COVID-19?

Artists produce some of their best works in times of crisis. Artists reflect the time they're living through and record them in diverse ways. For lockdown here in the UK, various artists have run programmes on television to encourage people to use art to help come to terms with their living restrictions.

You have received many lifetime achievement awards and accolades. What do they mean to you on a personal and professional level?

It's always very nice to be recognised. I always feel many people do a lot of things that don't get recognised, so there are controversies with that. They mean a lot to me, and it's nice when your peers recognise the work you do, but I don't think the reason one does these things is for the awards. It's because one believes in them.

Which part of your job as the Chairman of AMA do you find most rewarding or frustrating?

Most rewarding is, without question creating new fairs in new markets. There's nothing more exciting than creating something and seeing it succeed. We're providing a stimulus that makes a quantum difference to the importance of Hong Kong as an art hub in Asia. We've jointly worked to create fairs in Singapore, Sydney, Delhi, and Shanghai as a team. We've probably got the most interesting data on collectors and galleries in Asia. We have the most diverse operations across Asia.

What criteria do you use to measure whether a fair is successful?

I'm afraid to say that fairs are judged entirely by the amount of art sold. Some art fairs show wonderful art and are stimulating to see and create critical acclaim, but otherwise, the longevity of art fairs is judged by their commerciality. If galleries don't sell, people won't support the fair in the future. They're not doing it for altruistic reasons.

What would you like to be remembered for when you retire?

I would love to be remembered for expanding people's knowledge and appreciation of contemporary art in broader ways and across as many continents as possible. I've still got ambitions to do things in other parts of the world, but in Asia, I think we've been particularly successful because of the timing of our endeavours. It's a time when money has allowed a lot of young artists to thrive. If we've done anything to increase people's appreciation of the arts and the joys of contemporary art, then it was a worthwhile objective.

What are the major differences between going to a museum and going to an art fair?

You get more feedback from the artists from an exhibition. You'll get information at a museum, but it won't be as thorough — at an art fair, you often get to speak to the artist, or the gallery will have very intimate details about them and their background. Art fairs are one of the major ways to educate people and bring them as close as possible to the artists.

Are there any interesting stories regarding Art Central or Art Basel you would like to share with the readers?

I think Art Basel has created the ability for people to work together in the arts, and that was proven when we ran Art Central, Art Basel, and Christie's at the HKCEC. I think Hong Kong appreciated we had all gone out on a limb as it wasn't a commercial exercise but one to keep the community alive. It showed alternatives to a normal art fair to which people had become accustomed. During these times, the galleries that had the faith to come did very well, and we all felt very satisfied that we'd made the effort we had made under quite difficult circumstances. We all persevered, so it was very gratifying to see them succeed. I think that was a great lesson for people to work together and complement one another. My hope for the future is that fairs will return to a level before COVID-19. I think the excitement that Asia offers is unique. When I look at all the different markets in Asia, they're in many ways very aspirational and enthusiastic. I hope more artists can emerge from Asia, as I believe they'll have a very dominant effect on the world.

Photo 1. Sandy Angus (Chairman, Angus Montgomery Arts) – Art Central Hong Kong.

Chapter 10

Thomas Warren, Regional Head of Archives, the Hongkong and Shanghai Banking Corporation Limited (HSBC)

Co-authored with:
Zhang Xueqian (Shirley)
Kung Po Fung (BoBo)
Li Kwun Hung (Joe)
Cheng Wong Ping (Kate)
Tang Mimi (Sherry)
Leung Wai Kwong (Tom)

Introduction

The Hongkong and Shanghai Bank was established in British Hong Kong in 1865 and was incorporated as The Hongkong and Shanghai Banking Corporation in 1866; and has been based in Hong Kong ever since. HSBC is now the largest bank incorporated in Hong Kong and one of Hong Kong's three note-issuing banks. The HSBC Group archive is one of the largest and most important business collections of corporate archives, witness to the history of HSBC's identity and preserving the legacy of its predecessors. The HSBC Archives are overseen and managed by four teams located in London, Paris, New York, and Hong Kong, and are open to researchers by appointment. The Archives Gallery in Hong Kong offers a visitor engagement programme within the bank as well as externally for clients, stakeholders, regulators, and certain public groups.

The HSBC Archives collection in Hong Kong focuses on the historical records of The Hongkong and Shanghai Banking Corporation Limited and the modern records of HSBC in the Asia Pacific region. Its collections include historical documents and photographs of Hong Kong since 1865 and contemporary archival records related to the Asia-Pacific region since the 1970s. Special collections include complete sets of banknotes issued by HSBC and drawings, watercolours, and paintings by Chinese and European artists, such as the 19th-century painter George Chinnery (1774–1852), as well as a small contemporary art collection. Collection highlights include the minutes of the bank's board of directors and the first customer ledger from 1865. In this interview, Thomas Warren (Regional Head of Archives ASP HSBC) explains the collections' cultural and historical importance, as well as its unique features.

Could we begin this interview by introducing yourself, your professional training, and your educational background?

My name is Thomas Warren. I am the current Regional Head of Archives, Asia Pacific, for HSBC. My background is in History. I earned a BA in history with a European language from the University College of London. I spent a year in Germany because German is the language I selected for my BA. I followed up with a Master's at the London School of Economics, where I specialised in History and International Relations. I have no formal archives education. My education is all history-based. With this knowledge, I came into this role.

The HSBC ASP Archives was looking for a temporary researcher in 2009. So, my whole HSBC career has been right here with this team. I joined in 2009, and it was supposed to last only six months. Then my contract was extended twice. Afterwards, it became a permanent role and they changed the position title to History Manager and, finally History and Art Manager. The position was revised over the years, and the nature of the responsibilities and scope also changed, then I assumed the Regional Head role in early May (2021) this year. I did have some experience (via maternity cover) in this role before accepting the full-time job.

I was born in Sweden, and grew up in Malaysia, Brunei, Sweden, and Hong Kong. In terms of my family background, there is no archivist in my family; no historian either. My father was a professor of English Linguistics at the Polytechnic University of Hong Kong. He is now retired. He was very keen on History and Politics, which may have rubbed off on me. History was always my favourite subject in school. I grew up in Hong Kong, so we moved here when I was about 12, and I went to high school here, so I have quite a connection to the place. When I moved back here in 2009, it seemed like a good opportunity.

How does your childhood experience in Hong Kong contribute to your current work as the Regional Head of Archives, HSBC?

I think I became interested in telling HSBC's story because it's so closely linked with the story of Hong Kong's development, which was part of my childhood. HSBC was always a familiar place to me. I think I had one of the old passbooks at home, which helped nourish my interest in this position. Getting the opportunity to look into the history of Hong Kong was definitely appealing when I joined.

Can you provide a brief introduction to the HSBC Archives?

In Hong Kong, the core collections are basically paper documents showing how our client base was created, how our operations ran and were structured, what decisions were made and why, and how our staff worked and lived. The key source for this would be our collection of board minutes, which go all the way back to the founding of the back and up to almost the present (the Corporate Secretary keeps the latest minutes for an agreed period before they come to us). We have some original minutes on display in the HSBC Gallery. Other paper records in the collection encompass journal reports, architectural drawings, plans, maps, marketing materials, chairman's papers, key strategy documents, etc.

The very first board meeting minutes would date back to August 1864 (the peak of the Victorian era). That is when the original committee first met before the bank officially opened. That was definitely a very interesting time in Hong Kong. I believe in 1866 (a year after the bank opened), there was a global financial crisis, and six of the 11 foreign banks in Hong Kong collapsed. HiBC survived that and then grew beyond that. This evolved into a fascinating period regarding financing, trade, and the first foreign bank to be headquartered in Hong Kong, which was significant for this part of the world.

How many different archives does HSBC have worldwide?

There are totally four teams in the HSBC global archives. Here in Hong Kong, we have a total number of five team members. The HSBC Archives in London has the biggest team and biggest repository. This is because they look after archives from banks that HSBC acquired in the past. Midland Bank collection is a major component of the London collections. It was acquired by HSBC in 1992, founded in Birmingham, and is, in fact, older than HSBC. In that sense, if you look at our collections in London, they contain banking records that go back further than similar records in Hong Kong. One colleague in Paris manages the CCF archives, Crédit Commercial de France, which we acquired in 2000. We have a team of two in New York. They manage the US collections, which include the archives of Marine Midland Bank, a New York state bank acquired by HSBC in 1980. Here in Hong Kong, we manage the historical records of The Hongkong and Shanghai Banking Corporation Limited, which is the mother company of the group, as well as the modern records of the bank in Asia.

Was HSBC the very first international bank established in Hong Kong?

HSBC was the first international bank headquartered in Hong Kong. Before HSBC, other foreign banks were already operating in Hong Kong, but they were just regional branches, not headquarters. Their headquarters were typically based in either India or Britain. HSBC was established by Sir Thomas Sutherland (1834–1922), a young Scotsman working for a large shipping firm in Hong Kong. He had never held a bank account himself, but while sailing along the South China coast in 1864, he read an article on Scottish banking that inspired him. Local and foreign trade in Hong Kong and at ports in China and Japan had increased rapidly in the preceding few years, and Sutherland recognised that businesses needed better local banking facilities.

However, a year after we opened in Hong Kong, in 1866, there was a global financial. There were 11 or 12 foreign banks operating in Hong Kong at that time (all, except for HSBC, headquartered overseas), and over half of them collapsed during this crisis. Being headquartered in Hong Kong and quickly opening in Shanghai meant we were embedded in the region and could communicate much more quickly with customers. We expanded our network rapidly. Within the first decade, we had branches in multiple countries, including Japan, India, China, the USA, and Europe, so we established a global network very early.

In what ways do the archives collections contribute to the services and operations of HSBC on a daily basis?

Well, in quite a few different ways, many of them intangible. For example, our visitor programme effectively drives engagement for our staff, particularly newcomers, who perhaps know HSBC as just an acronym and don't necessarily understand the institution's long history, heritage, and culture. In that sense, it really helps new joiners to come through here and get a sense of connection to the company.

We also work quite widely (i.e., we have many projects in different countries where the bank operates because the bank has a long history in many countries). So, we do many things, like celebrating anniversaries in countries through exhibitions and publications, etc. And we also have a heritage display, a standardised exhibition that we place at head office premises in different countries. This continues to be a major project for us.

This year, we are launching four such displays in Malaysia, Korea, Shanghai, and Egypt. These are standardised exhibitions that tell HSBC's story focusing on the particular location in which they are deployed. The curatorial aspect of these exhibitions is quite significant, and also involves communication work, including marketing campaigns or staff communication, internal communication, and social media. HSBC actively promotes its heritage because it helps you differentiate yourself from competitors and add value. We deal with a lot of enquiries from different departments. Departments will come to us with questions about what we have, how we used to do X, Y, Z in the past, etc. So, bringing up past evidence of HSBC's decision-making is very useful for the departments that come to us with enquiries. We also work quite closely with the legal team on things like proving bank copyright, or bank ownership of certain financial concepts.

Have you digitised your archives holdings?

We have a digital archives team based in London and a digital repository. In fact, tomorrow is the official public launch of the HSBC history website. So, this website has been a huge 2-year project, finally coming to fruition. It involved the whole global archive team. We are putting a lot of our collections online, including online exhibitions and virtual tours of this gallery, so there will be a lot of content out there. As a result, users can search the collections by keying in queries. It will hopefully be a big success that we are very proud of, and it will all be within HSBC.com.

When HSBC was first established in Hong Kong during the mid-19th century, who were its first clientele?

We have the bank's very first customer ledger here. It is quite a unique piece in the collection: the first list of our main clients from 1865. During the first year when HSBC was established, many of our first clientele were Parsees, Indians, Americans, British, German, and other Europeans and also Jewish merchants from a variety of regions, but no Chinese are listed. The ledger features the early days of the banking phenomenon now synonymous with Hong Kong.

Are the local Chinese who eventually became HSBC customers already involved in international trade or just doing other local businesses?

That's a good question. I haven't seen any evidence of Chinese merchants dealing with HSBC at that level in the earliest years of our operations in Hong Kong. I know in Canton, China, there were some extremely wealthy merchants involved in international business in the pre-HSBC era. But in Hong Kong, we don't have any evidence, records, or listings of them as being linked to HSBC. Our first customer ledger is a unique artefact—definitely one of the highlights of our collections in Hong Kong. It reads as a 'who's who' of large businesses in Hong Kong in 1865 and 1866; for example, one early customer was the Hong Kong Shanghai Hotel Company that established the Peninsula Hotel.

Is there any reason why one could find a large collection of valuable artworks in the HSBC Archives collection?

The genesis of our art collection at the Hong Kong location is actually our Chief Manager in the 1920s, who was an art lover himself. He started purchasing art pieces for his own residence in Hong Kong, and he was a particular fan of George Chinnery (an English painter who spent most of his life in Asia painting in the China-Trade style, especially in India and southern China). As a result, we ended up having one of the world's largest Chinnery collections, which is awesome. And then, over the following decades, HSBC followed a considered strategic pattern of acquiring art in the China-Trade genre. So, it happened more organically than suddenly. It was planned. We also have a small contemporary art collection, mostly displayed inside offices.

Obviously, budget is a limiting factor, and the contemporary art market is very expensive, particularly in China.

Does HSBC purchase art for investment or for decorating the offices?

It's a combination of the two, but driven by the requirements of our premises, the décor, and the available project budget. We look at the lasting qualities of artwork—and the approach must align with our collecting policy. We also occasionally need to account for the personal tastes and opinions of senior management and make recommendations accordingly.

We still have value for our work, particularly in Hong Kong, when we displayed the China trade collection with the head office and senior officers. We learned from museums and cultural institutions, occasionally, mostly from the Hong Kong Maritime Museum. They had an exhibition on the silver trade. We launched Smart Works to that. We try to lend art where appropriate because many of these geometric paintings are old, and some are fragile. But my position is history and art manager. Those roles exist; we are recruiting for them now. That has been renamed again, so it's now for the heritage manager, because we have had to basically reduce the art component, overall, just because of the lack of resources to allocate to it. In short, it (art) is always challenging because it is a subjective view, but what was archived was more objective.

As the Regional Head of Archives, could you describe your roles and responsibilities?

There are four key areas:

1. Ensuring the Archives team all work to align with our strategy; complying with international archive and collection standards; delivering engaging projects to support HSBC's strategy, brand, and culture; and developing the collections);
2. Designing uniform collection policies aligned with Asia's different countries and departments (that is a huge task and challenge);
3. Managing our strategic collection development, including selecting and transferring records from key departments (another major process for us); and
4. Setting and monitoring global policies and procedures that we implement. This covers a wide range of governance, including

environmental copyright, environmental conditions, and responsibility for deploying those policies.

Overseeing the visitor engagement programme led by our Heritage Manager is also important. We also constantly receive a stream of enquiries, both informed within the bank and externally from academics, scholars, educators, and researchers, to use the Archives collection for research and scholarly purposes.

As the Regional Head of Archives, could you describe your management and leadership style?

I have been managing people for three years now. I would say flexibility is a key part of my management style, because we have many things going on simultaneously at HSBC. Hence, we have to be flexible to adapt to circumstances and planning according to different priorities and countries. I would say I provided calm, steady leadership, which was particularly relevant during the COVID-19 crisis—it was a very difficult time for everyone to navigate. My flexible leadership style was appreciated when I was trying to lead the team through these difficult times. I also try to foster a supportive environment where the team members feel free to speak their minds to be open about challenges.

There can be challenges at work, but team members also face emotions in their personal lives, especially last year, when everyone was struggling with the impacts of the COVID-19 crisis. I think my background does help me see things through the lens of another culture, because I have the experience of growing up in Asian cultures, which helps me see other people's perspectives and try to show both empathy and understanding. Finally, I think I am quite good at trusting the expertise of my team. I hired them for certain skills and trusted their judgement based on informed decisions. I think that is particularly important because I don't have formal archives training. I learned a lot on the job, but I feel confident I now have good professional advice from the team to execute my role effectively. I think those are the main characteristics of my management and leadership style.

Could you describe the highlights of the HSBC Archives collection?

I think a particular highlight is the money collection. People are very excited about it whenever they come; it goes back to the 1860s, and even further back when you look at the coins and bullion. It covers Hong Kong and other countries in which we issued currency. It is undoubtedly a fascinating topic for people to see. The first customer ledger (as mentioned earlier), as well as certain components of the art collection, are definitely other highlights. Our board minutes from the 19th century are also significant (particularly for our staff), and we use them a lot for our own research work. In fact, we have all the board minutes indexed, and they are very valuable indeed, especially the early minutes, which contain very granular details of all of the decisions made by the bank in those early days.

As the Regional Head of Archives, Asia Pacific, what part of your job do you find most rewarding, and which do you find most frustrating?

The rewarding part is being able to work with a diverse range of people within the bank. I work with many different teams across HSBC. I would also say being able to see our HSBC Archives collection increasingly come to life online is very rewarding.

In terms of frustrations in this role, I would say the pandemic (COVID-19) was a significant one. This is particularly due to its impact on the visitor programme, which had to be on hold for many months. In my current role, I am further away from the reason I joined the team in the first place, which was research and curation. Sometimes, I miss that side of the research work, which I just don't have the time to do and must delegate. That is something I miss, but on the whole, I would say I still find it enjoyable. I have a good team that is also quite young. So, I'm optimistic for the future.

I understand HSBC Archives also provides visitor and educational programmes to the local school. What would you expect the local school students to learn from the HSBC Archives collection?

Just seeing and experiencing primary resources is pretty interesting for them. I think that is an enormous appeal because we take them into the repository and show the original materials, explaining why primary resource research is important. I think that's a real learning experience for them. Also, we cover topics that they might not cover so closely in school or their regular textbooks. We look at historical photographs and the development of currency over time. This is particularly interesting for teenagers who have spent their whole financial lives just doing online banking, using apps, etc. Looking at pieces of silver, a solid currency, is quite fascinating for them. We also highlight some early history of Hong Kong and Hong Kong's occupation, which is partially covered in schools, but we go into some interesting detail.

HSBC was founded in Hong Kong in the mid-Victorian era (1850–1870) during Britain's "Golden Years," and China was in the Qing dynasty period. Could you describe the major differences in the banking system being operated by HSBC compared to the traditional banking system in Mainland China during the late Qing dynasty?

I think one reason HSBC did well in China in the early years was that we provided more sophisticated options for traders in terms of doing international business, more reliable and structured for sure. HSBC operated with a professional approach to banking, as well as being more systematic. Even in its early days, HSBC already had a reputation for being global but also reliable. I think the banking industry in China then didn't have the depth of skill and sophistication to meet the evolving demands of doing international business, particularly for the clients HSBC was serving. Large international firms and merchants were looking for a bank to make them money and support their businesses, and HSBC ticked these boxes, particularly for trade finance.

We didn't venture into retail banking until after World War II. We didn't have any branches in Hong Kong until we opened in Mong Kok (as the first branch in 1948). That was the first full branch. We had one sub-branch before that inside the Peninsula Hotel, which opened in 1929. The rapid branch expansion period after opening in Mongkok certainly strengthened the bank's reputation among Hong Kong's citizens, as did our response to the duress notes issue. And particularly after the war, there were still notes issued illegally by the Japanese in circulation (we have some on display in our HSBC Archives Gallery), which we decided to honour in cooperation with the government.

At that time, HSBC put up 16 million Hong Kong dollars, which rescued a lot of people's savings and helped prop up Hong Kong's post-war economy. Our bronze lions are a famous symbol of HSBC in Hong Kong. When they were returned to Hong Kong at the end of WWII after being removed from Japan for scrap metal by the Japanese military, it was on front-page news, and we have that page on display. HSBC has also become symbolic of Hong Kong itself. In fact, our 1935 HSBC building was featured on postage stamps and postcards, and as such a symbolic premise, it was selected as the Japanese military headquarters during Hong Kong's occupation. This intertwining of Hong Kong and the bank is a powerful thing, and quite a unique thing in global history. I can't think of anywhere else in the world where a bank has been so tied into the social fabric of a place.

Photo 1. Thomas Warren.

Photo 2. HSBC Asia Pacific Archives Repository.

Photo 3. HSBC Hong Kong Archives Gallery Centre.

Photo 4. HSBC Hong Kong Archives Gallery Centre.

Chapter 11

Benedikt Fohr, Chief Executive, Hong Kong Philharmonic Orchestra

Introduction

The Hong Kong Philharmonic Orchestra (HK Phil) is the largest professional symphony orchestra in Hong Kong. Established in 1947 as an amateur orchestra under the name Sino-British Orchestra, it was renamed the Hong Kong Philharmonic Orchestra in 1957 and became a professional orchestra in 1974 with government funding.

Benedikt Fohr has been serving as the Chief Executive of the Hong Kong Philharmonic Orchestra (HK Phil) since April 2019. Before joining the HK Phil, Benedikt was the Orchestra Manager (CEO) of Deutsche Radio Philharmonie Saarbrücken Kaiserslautern for 12 years. Previously, he was the General Director of the Luxembourg Philharmonic Orchestra, Secretary General of the Camerata Salzburg and Managing Director of the Ensemble Research Freiburg. Benedikt was educated in Germany and holds an MBA from the University of Mannheim. He studied the violin and viola until the age of 18. He now enjoys performing with amateur orchestras and playing chamber music. In 2021, he joined the SAR Philharmonic Orchestra. In addition to discussing his working relationship with the Music Director of the HK Phil, in the following interview, Benedikt also compares the current difficulties and challenges faced by most arts and cultural administrators in Hong Kong and Germany.

Could you first introduce yourself, for example, your professional training and educational background? For instance, what did you study at the university? Do you come from a family of musicians or performing artists? Are you also a trained musician yourself?

I studied Business Administration at the University of Mannheim, Germany, and at that time, the idea of managing an orchestra was not on my radar. At the time, pursuing a career in a bank or an international company was the obvious choice. My parents didn't play any instruments, but they regularly went to concerts and wanted all four of us siblings to play an instrument. I learned the violin and viola until 18, then continued playing in amateur orchestras and chamber ensembles. Our parents showed us the beauty of culture, music, arts and archaeology. Of the four siblings, we all studied law or business; three of us work in music specifically, and my younger sibling is a media artist.

Could you describe your career path to becoming the Chief Executive at the Hong Kong Philharmonic Orchestra (HK Phil)?

Looking back, it seems to be quite a natural and consistent development. It is difficult to plan and predict a career in the arts, as it depends on many factors, personal situation and motivation, connections and also luck. It started when I was approached during my studies by a friend of a musician who wanted to form a new contemporary music ensemble. He was looking for someone who could manage the administration, contracts, finances, etc. I had no idea about contemporary music; I couldn't name a single living composer, but it was a great experience. I managed the ensemble Recherche; they are still among the best groups. Over the five years I was involved, we toured all important European festivals. I then moved to Salzburg and took over the management of the Salzburg Camerata, a chamber orchestra mainly performing classical repertoire. It received almost no subsidies, meaning all income needed to be earned through engagements or box office. This is only possible if the group always performs at the highest artistic level combined with the best-known international conductors and soloists. A challenging but also rewarding time! After another five years, in 2001, I started working with the Luxembourg Philharmonic Orchestra. This was my first experience with a government-funded symphony orchestra. On top of that, in 2005, we were given the chance to move into the newly built Philharmonie Luxembourg, a wonderful concert hall. n 2006, I was asked to merge with a radio orchestra in Germany, so we moved back to Germany and lived for 12 years in Saarbrücken before moving to Hong Kong in March 2019.

Before joining the HK Phil, you served as the Orchestra Manager (CEO) of Deutsche Radio Philharmonie Saarbrücken Kaiserslautern (DRP) for 12 years (2006-2019), and the General Director of the Luxembourg Philharmonic Orchestra (2001-2015), and also as the Secretary General of the Camerata Salzburg (1996-2001). How do all these professional experiences contribute to your current work as the Chief Executive of the HK Phil?

It is the experience gained over the years in the industry; much of my learning has been through learning by doing with each of these ensembles and orchestras. If you run a superb professional orchestra like HK Phil, it is good to know how artistic planning, orchestra operation, financial budgeting, contracts, fundraising and marketing work and how they are connected. I have overseen the production of more than 70 CDs and streamed multiple concerts. Knowing how all the cogs connect is especially important; looking to the future where the online presence of ensembles/orchestras is ever more important. The situation in every country and every team is different, but having a deep understanding of the different tasks in orchestra management helps one to do the job and gain the respect of the musicians, staff, the executive board, and other stakeholders.

Last but not least, and maybe most important, is the network you have built over the years. This is so valuable to you as a manager; building an international network of artists, agents and presenters is indispensable if you want to further improve the international profile of an orchestra.

Orchestral players in Germany enjoy a civil-servant-like status. Is it also the same case for the Luxembourg Philharmonic Orchestra and HK Phil? DRP versus HK Phil – how does the employment status (civil-servant-like status) affect the turnover rates, working attitudes, job satisfaction and job security amongst the players between these two orchestras?

In Germany, Luxembourg and most European countries, the musicians of the orchestras are run by the commune, the department, the government or radio stations, and enjoy a civil-servant-like status. This means under normal circumstances, they cannot be terminated after passing the probation and the contract finishes with the musicians' retirement in Germany; currently, this is at 67. With the HK Phil, it is slightly different; our musicians have 5-year contracts. And there is no official retirement age at the HK Phil.

My experience is that the working attitude and job satisfaction are very similar among all orchestras; it also depends a lot on the individuals, the team spirit within the orchestra, the artistic leadership and the vision. A supportive and understanding administration as well as a respected contact between management and musicians, is essential for a healthy atmosphere. Like the turnover rate, globally, musicians try to step up to the next artistic (and financial) level until age 35. Then the move often becomes more of a challenge, as they start having families and the competition in auditions with the younger applicants is getting harder.

DRP versus HK Phil – what are the major differences in the operations behind the artistic planning and administration between these two orchestras? What are the signature repertoires of these two orchestras?

The DRP is a radio orchestra financed by public radio stations, unlike most other European orchestras that the community or government funds. As such, all concerts are recorded for the radio archive, and others are live broadcasted. One of the main reasons for the existence of radio orchestras is the repertoire, which typically has a more diverse range of music across genres.

Previously radio orchestras played and recorded a lot of contemporary composers and compositions in addition to the mainstream, what we would call 'musical discoveries.' Often radio orchestras have their own studios, which may only fit 400 – 600 audience members, equipped with excellent recording facilities and purpose-built acoustics. These "studio concerts" are not meant to attract thousands in the audience; the main purpose is to record this repertoire. Nowadays, radio orchestras are in stiff competition with the philharmonic orchestras in terms of audience and recognition; they also want to attract big-name conductors and soloists - many of whom are not able or willing to invest their time in learning new works just for one performance – so increasingly soloists and conductors are focusing on the usual core repertoire. The DRP has a long history with the contemporary repertoire.

Hans Zender, one of the most recognised German composers, has been the music director for 16 years. The DRP still performs in its "Studio Konzerte" quite some full programmes with a lesser-known repertoire in both classical and contemporary genres. This approach is something that we cannot often "risk" with HK Phil, as we have to attract an audience of 4,000 each weekend. With the HK Phil, we tend to perform more core classical repertoire with international soloists and conductors or other attractive projects with movies or special guest artists. Of course, we include well-known conductors and soloists from Hong Kong and Mainland China in our series. And we increasingly commission local composers, which we then integrate into our subscription concerts. This keeps the audience curious without deterring them.

Besides the repertoire, there is a difference in the financial structure. Professional orchestras in Europe are usually subsidised by 80% or more by the Community, the Government or one of the public radio stations. This figure is much lower in Hong Kong (around 55%), so we have to put a lot of effort into marketing and development (sponsorship). Therefore, more people are working in the office, especially in these two departments. I don't see much difference between the two orchestras in terms of repertoire and financial structure.

Every single orchestra has its own distinctive, unique sound. Could you describe the overall sound quality of the DRP and the HK Phil?

I agree many orchestras have a specific sound, and it mostly depends on an acoustically excellent home, a venue where the orchestra and the musical director can develop its sound regularly in rehearsals and concerts, which is very important for a first-class orchestra. When I first heard HK Phil, I was astonished that the wind/brass and string sections are equally excellent and homogenous. This is unusual in my experience and has resulted in the unique, full sound we hear when the full orchestra is on stage.

As the Chief Executive of the HK Phil, could you describe your main roles and areas of responsibility? Could you describe your typical day at work? Is there ever a typical day at work?

In the last two years, "typical days" have been uncommon due to COVID-19. However, almost every day comes with new challenges and questions. My main task as CE is to oversee all the orchestra's operations, secure financial reliability, set up strategies for future planning and development, and keep the information moving around the departments, including support staff, musicians, the board and stakeholders. A typical day would start with answering my emails, then weekly meetings with the senior management, discussions with conductors at the beginning of the rehearsal, office work in the afternoon, and more (Zoom) meetings with staff and international partners (agency, presenters), in the evenings I might attend either the HK Phil concerts or another performance in Hong Kong. My job normally would also include travelling to potential presenters, artists or agents.

As the Chief Executive of the HK Phil, could you describe your working relationships with the Music Director of the HK Phil?

The Music Director is responsible for the artistic profile and artistic development of the orchestra. This requires close communication between the Music Director, the CE and the Director of Artistic Planning. Many factors, such as budget, availability of the venues, availability of guest conductors and soloists, tour projects, programmes, etc., must be discussed and considered in the regular contact – and it usually takes place several times a week. When the Music Director is in Hong Kong, we have many face-to-face meetings.

How does the change in senior management (e.g., Chief Executive & Music Director) affect the operations and organisational culture of a performing arts institution like the HK Phil?

The change of Music Director affects an orchestra more than the change of the CE. Each Music Director has their own style of artistic leadership, and they will choose a different repertoire, appear with new soloists, and communicate with the audience differently. External stakeholders will see and hear the change immediately. All marketing efforts concentrate on the orchestra and its new Music Director. But if the CE joins a stable and well-established organisation with long-term staff and an experienced board, the CE will be well-advised to continue to lead the ship in the 'same' direction. You do not start the job by questioning or changing everything, so the influence of the CE is not that obvious at the start. Ultimately, it is not about the CE, and it is about the orchestra. As time goes by, the CE can set new priorities in terms of audience development, fundraising or international touring for instance, which will hopefully positively impact the HK Phil's status and development.

Could you describe your management and leadership style? Would you describe yourself as a servant leader or a participative leader? What is the ideal leadership style best suited for a non-profit performing arts organisation like HK Phil?

I am certainly more of a participative leader. Before I make a decision, I like to hear the opinion of the staff concerned. Obviously, most of the decisions are in agreement with colleagues. It is important to acknowledge their professional expertise – and in my case, my colleagues have a deeper understanding of the local conditions. They also need to understand that I am in the job because I have a certain international view and experience, and therefore might decide to go in a different direction. "Servant leader" sounds very devoted, but there is something true about it. We in the administration must understand and accept that it is all about the orchestra. Nobody is interested in an administration without the orchestra. But it is good for audiences to remember that when the orchestra operates smoothly, plays a great concert, and we see an exciting full house, it is down to the work of a much larger team, not just the players on stage; there is a hardworking, professional administration team behind the scenes. The musicians are smart; they appreciate what they have in the back office and treat the team staff equally and respectfully.

Since HK Phil is a non-profit performing arts institution, what external and/or internal factors do you use for measuring the successes and achievements of HK Phil?

Good question: what is successful artistic planning? Is it to plan what you, as Music Director, CE or Artistic Planning Director, would like to perform and hear? Is it what most of the audience would like to hear? Is it what other orchestras in the city don't play or should it be the same as all the other orchestras?

As a public-funded symphony orchestra, we are obligated to perform for all of Hong Kong. We should reach out to all generations and present a seasoned programme that speaks to many different audiences regarding interest, experience and ethnic background. The core repertoire will always be the symphonic repertoire; the continuous time on these works guarantees the orchestra's quality. Besides this, we have to offer many other programmes, ranging from film music to contemporary music, to remain relevant and reach wider audiences. Regarding soloists and guest conductors, we have to provide a good balance between artists from Hong Kong, mainland China, and international guest artists, from young talents to big names. If we present to the public a well-balanced programme for the season, the HK Phil will be considered an important and indispensable player in Hong Kong's cultural life and live music scene. If Hong Kong is proud of its orchestra and international reputation, these would be external factors for a successful programme strategy.

Internal factors would be the attractiveness of the orchestra for guest conductors and major soloists. Other factors are the working atmosphere within orchestra and office, as well as the turnover in the orchestra and management, which is certainly a benchmark for job satisfaction.

Germany versus Hong Kong, could you describe the overall arts and cultural scenes between these two places – in particular, the concertgoers and operagoers in Hong Kong and Germany – what are the major differences in terms of their levels of appreciation and appetite for Western classical music?

In Germany, we have around 150 professional symphony orchestras, and almost every city with more than 100.000 inhabitants has its own orchestra. Most of them are integrated into an opera house that presents opera, ballet and theatre. And, of course, symphonic concerts. Many of them have existed for 100 years or more. Western music has a long tradition and plays – still – a very important role in the communities. I say still, as the audience in Germany and Europe gets older, the fear is that it will lose its importance for the younger generation. It is an ongoing discussion. Many say that it was always the older generation of 50 years old or more, who finally had the money, less stress in the job, no more kids at home, and therefore have the time to enjoy concerts. But meanwhile, the average concertgoer is 60 to 65, and we feel that the generation of the 45 – 60 is missing. And if the older generation doesn't transmit their love for music to the younger generation, they will have no reason to be interested in classical music when they get older, so we will lose the audience – and then there is a break which is probably irreversible.

In Hong Kong and the Mainland, the tradition of classical music is much younger. Most orchestras are 50 years or younger, so we are asked to do a lot of outreach and educational work to let people know about the classical repertoire and the enjoyment they can appreciate with concerts. And it is very encouraging that in Hong Kong, many young people learn instruments, many more than in Europe these days. So, if we can invite these young people to concerts and they can experience the joy of making music in youth orchestras, we can look very positive in the future. Right now, the appetite for classical music might still be higher in Europe, but we see signs that this might change soon.

Germany versus Hong Kong – what are the major differences in current difficulties and challenges that a majority of arts and cultural administrators in Hong Kong and Germany have been facing?

The current challenges because of the pandemic are different; honestly, I am not sure which is the better place for making music. There is almost no quarantine in Europe, and travel for artists between most countries, even between Europe and the US, is possible. Currently, indoor audiences are very restricted due to the relatively high infection rate. Still, as most orchestras have their own rehearsal and concert venues, they can at least do recordings and offer online concerts.

In Hong Kong, our infection rate is almost at "0." Since March, we can have live concerts with a 75% audience, so around 1,200 people are in the hall, which is the good part. The difficulty is the quarantine, which keeps almost every international artist away from Hong Kong. It is the same in the Mainland, but as the Mainland is huge, with many first-class soloists, conductors, and many orchestras and concert halls, it can keep its concert activities on an average level, even without involving artists from other countries.

"HKAPA x HK Phil Nurturing Orchestral Talent" – could you share with the readers about the missions, visions and philosophy behind this programme? What are the funding sources? Did HKAPA initiate this programme? How would you like the HKAPA to benefit from this programme? Why is it important to the nature of local music talents?

The Orchestra Academy (TOA) is initiated and co-directed by the Hong Kong Philharmonic Orchestra (HK Phil) and The Hong Kong Academy for Performing Arts (HKAPA) to provide professional training for distinguished HKAPA Music graduates and facilitate their career development in the orchestral field.

TOA is funded by "TrustTomorrow" of The Swire Group Charitable Trust (Swire Trust) over a 3-year period.

The Orchestra Academy consists of two programmes: under the Fellowship Programme; candidates have to undergo a competitive selection process, which features two rounds of auditions. The six selected Fellows will receive intensive orchestral training with the HK Phil in its 2021/22 season, learning about the expectations and protocols of a professional orchestra, while performing a wide range of symphonic repertoire. In the mentorship scheme, each Fellow will pair up with an assigned HK Phil musician to gain insights into the professional lives of orchestra players.

The other programme, The Young Pro Platform (YPP), offers the selected 15 to 25 musicians per season a versatile season-long of full ensemble concerts with Philharmonia APA (PAPA) and a series of chamber concerts. The Platform encourages players to commit to high-calibre performances and to take an active role in curating specially designed concert programmes.

The additional practical training in master classes and lectures will help the young musicians of both programmes understand more about the professional life of an (orchestra) musician and apply more successfully for jobs with top professional orchestras worldwide.

What parts of your job as the Chief Executive of the HK Phil do you find most rewarding? And which do you find most frustrating?

Successful concerts and tours, with artistically satisfied artists, motivated staff and an enthusiastic audience, are rewarding moments in our professional lives. Presenting a well-balanced season with major star artists, exciting rising talents, known repertoire and new discoveries is rewarding. In the last two years, we had many frustrating moments, where carefully and long-term planned projects disappeared within hours. But even in normal times, you face less attractive work or tasks, like in any other job. Salary negotiations, disciplinary discussions, budget applications and audits, just to name a few. These are also part of the job and the responsibility.

Why do we turn to music in times of crisis?

Because it is a language everyone understands, it unites people of different backgrounds, education and political convictions and brings harmony, emotion and peace to our lives. Culture – music, fine arts, literature, architecture – is society's backbone. If we care about the arts and convey this to the next generation, we keep communication and understanding for each other going.

Are any other interesting and inspiring stories regarding DRP and the HK Phil that you wish to share with the readers?

After working with orchestras in 4 different countries, you realise that the way the orchestras think, behave and work are pretty much the same. This might be because the musicians travel a lot and study in different country's orchestras, so an orchestra usually has many nationalities. You find the same kind of personalities in every orchestra. The core repertoire of the orchestras is very much the same; of course, the conductors jump from orchestra to orchestra and spread their influence. Conversely, the local realities influence the administration, how it is funded, its structure, venues, ticketing system, marketing channels, etc. And, of course, the audience is very different from place to place. So, while it seems easier to adapt from one orchestra to another, it takes a lot more time to understand how the administration and the teamwork.

What would you like to be remembered for when you retire?

No one will care when I retire. But when I leave an organisation, I wish most colleagues would appreciate what we have achieved during my term.

Photo 1. HK Phil Chief Executive Benedikt Fohr.
Photo credit: Cheung Wai-lok/HK Phil.

Photo 2. HK Phil Music Director Jaap van Zweden conducts Mahler's First Symphony at "Swire Maestro Series: Jaap | Mahler 1" (18 & 19 Nov 2022). Photo credit: Keith Hiro/HK Phil.

Photo 3. HK Phil Music Director Jaap van Zweden conducts Beethoven's Symphony no. 9 at the 2022/23 Season Opening concert (9 & 10 Sep 2022). Photo credit: Ka Lam/HK Phil.

Photo 4. HK Phil Music Director Jaap van Zweden conducts Beethoven's Symphony no. 9 at the 2022/23 Season Opening concert (9 & 10 Sep 2022).
Photo credit: Ka Lam/HK Phil.

Photo 5. HK Phil's mega outdoor concert *Swire Symphony under the Stars* 2022, conducted by HK Phil Principal Guest Conductor Yu Long. (12 Nov 2022).
Photo credit: Andy Lam/ HK Phil.

Photo 6. HK Phil and Hong Kong Ballet co-present Carmina Burana. Under the baton of HK Phil Resident Conductor Lio Kuokman, acclaimed soloists, dancers, two choruses and the HK Phil present the world premiere of *The Last Song* by HKB's Choreographer-in-Residence Ricky Hu Songwei and Artistic Director Septime Webre's dance masterpiece *Carmina Burana*. (14-16 Oct 2022). Photo credit: Keith Hiro/ HK Phil.

Photo 7. HK Phil Resident Conductor Lio Koukman conducts Richard Strauss' *An Alpine Symphony*, along with stunning images of the Alps by photographer Tobias Melle. (21 & 22 Oct 2022).
Photo credit: Keith Hiro/ HK Phil.

Photo 8. HK Phil and Utopia Cantonese Opera Workshop join forces to present the inter-disciplinary production: Raining Petals – An Orchestral Re-Imagining. (23 & 24 Dec 2022).
Photo credit: Ka Lam/ HK Phil.

Photo 9. HK Phil Music Director Jaap van Zweden conducts Bach's *St Matthew Passion.* The concert assembles world-class soloists, together with State Choir Latvija, The Hong Kong Children's Choir and HK Phil Chorus to perform this masterpiece. (3 & 4 Feb 2023).
Photo credit: Ka Lam/ HK Phil.

Photo 10. HK Phil Music Director Jaap van Zweden leads HK Phil's first performances of Messiaen's *Turangalîla-Symphonie*, along with pianist Jean-Yves Thibaudet, and Cynthia Millar on the ondes Martenot. (10 & 11 Feb 2023). Photo credit: Ka Lam/ HK Phil.

Chapter 12

Vennie Ho, Executive Director, Hong Kong Philharmonic

Introduction

Vennie Ho is currently serving as the Executive Director of the Hong Kong Philharmonic Orchestra (HK Phil) and Chairman of the Hong Kong Arts Administrators Association (HKAAA). Vennie Ho joined the HK Phil in 1975 when the Orchestra had just turned professional. In her early years with HK Phil, Vennie was among the small group of administrative staff spearheading the many important initiatives of the Orchestra. With her professional qualification in Accountancy, she takes charge of not only the Society's finance but also the overall administration. In the following interview, Vennie told us about her working relationship with the past and current Music Directors of the HK Phil, as well as her passion and vision for the Orchestra.

Could we begin this interview by first introducing yourself, for example, your professional training and educational background? Do you come from a family of professional musicians or accountants?

I was born into a humble family, with my father running a small printing business. All family members would offer whatever they could to help run the business to lower costs. Being the eldest child and having a keen interest in numbers, I helped my father in bookkeeping, laying the groundwork for my later studies and career in accounting.

In my childhood days, there were no "monster parents" as such, but I was given the opportunity to have painting and singing classes in a neighbourhood community centre after school. Later, at secondary school, I joined the school choir and guitar and dance clubs. I was a soprano singer in the school choir and was actively involved in competitions, performances and musicals. I was particularly thrilled to be singing solo by the side of the school grand piano. After school, I managed to find some time to give private tuition to small kids to make money to pay for my piano lessons. Since we did not have a piano at home, my music teacher was so nice to let me practise in the music room during the lunch hour. After completing my secondary school education, I joined the Accounting Department of a big conglomerate company. However, I later found the job to be extremely boring and monotonous.

In 1975, I joined the Hong Kong Philharmonic (HK Phil) when the Orchestra had just turned professional. At that time, HK Phil did not have its own management office, and I was among the first few staff members being recruited. As far as I can remember, the recruitment process, which Dr. Darwin Chen supervised, included a written test done in a room on the high block of the City Hall, followed by two rounds of interviews. German Conductor Hans-Gunther Mommer was one of the interview panellists. I was so fortunate to be part of the small management team and was responsible for setting up the first set of books of accounts for HK Phil. Looking back, I feel I was fortunate and honoured to be the first accountant to work for the HK Phil Management.

Can you describe your career path in becoming the Executive Director at the HK Phil?

When HK Phil turned professional in the 70s, the then City Hall Office presented and promoted orchestra performances. HK Phil's Management Office started with only five staff members, including myself, General Manager, Executive Secretary, Librarian, and Administrative Assistant. Although my main role was Accounting, I also performed a list of other duties. The size of the Management Office was extremely small, occupying just one of the dressing rooms inside the Hong Kong City Hall Concert Hall.

While working full-time for the HK Phil during the day, I took evening classes to further my studies in Accounting and Personnel Management (Human Resources Management as it is known today). As the HK Phil continued to grow and develop, I also began to take up more responsibilities with multiple managerial roles. I not only take charge of HK Phil's finances, but also the Orchestra's overall administration as a whole, e.g., managing the operations of the Orchestra, organising concerts, and overseas tours, as well as overseeing marketing campaigns and ticket sales operations. The Eighties have witnessed tremendous growth in all sectors of Hong Kong's economy. There were also significant developments on the cultural front. As for HK Phil, there had been a list of new initiatives, including the establishment of the HK Phil Chorus, the launching of the subscription series, the setting up of HK Phil's Friends Club, the presentation of Pops concerts in the HK Coliseum and outdoor concert Symphony under the Stars, as well as the first tour to the mainland, etc. I worked hand in hand with the General Manager at the time, John Duffus, in making all these initiatives come into being. I have found my career with HK Phil very exciting and fulfilling. In 1994, after HK Phil celebrated its 20th anniversary, I resigned from my position as Assistant General Manager (Finance & Administration) and moved to Toronto, Canada, with my family. After a few years, I moved back to Hong Kong and joined the Hong Kong Consumer Council in 1998. I first took up a contract position in the External Affairs Department with a major role in helping organise the Council's 25th-anniversary programmes.

Interestingly, the Consumer Council was established in the same year when HK Phil turned professional. I was with the Consumer Council for 12 years, where I was in charge of the 6 core functions of the Council, namely: (1) Human Resources, (2) Finance & Accounting, (3) Information Technologies, (4) Council Secretariat, (5) General Administration and, (6) Events and External Affairs when I resigned as their Head of Administration and External Affairs in 2010. In November 2010, I joined the HK Phil again as the Head of Administration and Finance, subsequently promoted as the Executive Director of the HK Phil.

I served on the Board of the Hong Kong Arts Administrators Association and was elected Chairman of the Board in 2019. In the same year, I was also elected Vice-chair of the Board of Chairs of the League of China Orchestras. In charity, I am the Founding Chairman of Corners Field Social Service (HK, China) Ltd. I was also an active member of the Lions Club of Victoria Hong Kong, acting as the 3rd Vice-President in 2009-2010 and Honorary Secretary in 2010-2011.

Prior to re-joining the HK Phil, you served as the Head of Administration and External Affairs at the Hong Kong Consumer Council. How does your previous experience at the Hong Kong Consumer Council contribute to your current work in arts and cultural management?

During my 12-year tenure with the Consumer Council, I was tasked with multiple roles, from managing internal to external affairs. Internally, I had to ensure the smooth operation and effective support of the administration office. The Council at that time had a staff of over 200 members, with some working outside the headquarters at Consumer Complaint Centres in different districts. Effective communication among the staff was important. Externally, I worked with regional and international consumer bodies on various exchange programmes, including conferences and symposia. Through these programmes, I have developed expertise in organising mega-events. Moreover, the Hong Kong Consumer Council is a public organisation funded by the government, with policies and guidelines that closely follow government practices. At the same time, I was engaged in many governance exercises, reviewing internal control measures and supervising audits. So, all these exposures have equipped me with the fundamentals and core skills that have proved valuable experiences for my career.

As the Executive Director of HK Phil, could you describe your typical day at work?

Back-to-back meetings are not unusual on a normal work day, and I always have to find time to answer messages / emails and to attend to colleagues' questions and needs. During the concert season, I will be on duty on weekends whenever a performance occurs. At times, this could be relaxing and enjoyable when I have the chance to enjoy music. The applause and overwhelming response from the audience can always cheer me up. My fingers are crossed that everything is running smoothly and that I don't have to deal with unforeseen problems or emergencies! During the summer when the orchestra is on vacation, there goes the time for preparation of annual audits, year-end reports and staff appraisals as well as various marketing and subscription campaigns. In the HK Phil Office, there is never a boring day. We always have something exciting to look forward to.

As the Executive Director of HK Phil, can you describe your main role and areas of responsibilities?

My main role as Executive Director is to work closely with the Chief Executive in creating and maintaining an effective management team to support the overall operations of the orchestra. I oversee all financial matters to ensure the financial sustainability of the Orchestra, keeping proper books of accounts and maintaining good public governance. I assist the Chief Executive in developing and managing new projects, and act on his behalf when he is not in Hong Kong.

As the Executive Director of the HK Phil, do you need to work with the Orchestra players and the Music Director directly on a daily basis?

In the early days, when the management office was located backstage at the City Hall Concert Hall, our players often visited the office during rehearsal breaks. Before the auto-pay system was introduced, players actually had to come to me every month to pick up their salary cheques. I worked closely with one of the players who was tasked with taking attendance records to deal with all personnel matters of the orchestra. I have worked with a number of Music Directors in the past, including Lim Kek-tjiang, Hans Gunter Mommer, Ling Tung, Kenneth Schermerhorn, David Altherton, and now, Jaap van Zweden. With different personalities and leadership styles, their interactions with the Management Office were not the same. I worked more closely with Maestro David Altherton during his tenure as Music Director. He had his office in the Management Office and liked to spend time with us, advising on computerisation and discussing orchestral personnel and touring plans. With a more established staff structure now, the Music Director and players would not come directly to me unless their issues could be resolved with other colleagues.

Could you describe the staffing structure of the HK Phil?

The office has expanded from three departments in the 90s to a total of five now. The Administration & Finance Department is responsible for financial and accounting management, human resources, information technologies, governance and internal controls, Board Secretariat, general administration, and special projects. The Marketing Department covers concert promotions, publicity and media relations, ticketing and customer service. The Orchestral Operations Department is responsible for venue bookings and orchestra schedules, musicians' contracts and personnel matters, as well as logistic arrangements and concert productions. The Artistic Planning Department prepares programmes and activities of the orchestra, including education and outreach activities, and engages guest artists to be featured in our programmes. The Development Department is responsible for fundraising from the private sector.

Can you describe your management and leadership style? Would you describe yourself as a servant or participative type?

I see HK Phil as my family and my colleagues as my children. I would be protective and caring for my staff, mostly of the young generation. However, I would try to identify the strengths, weaknesses and aspirations of individuals and would trust them to perform their duties with minimum direction when I think they are capable of finishing the tasks on their own. This is what a typical mother would do in raising their kids.

Profit-making organisations versus performing arts organisations - what are the major differences in terms of managing their marketing, finances and human resources?

Obviously, profits always come first in a business or any profit-making organisations. Marketing strategies, budgeting and employees' remunerations are therefore geared towards how more profits can be generated. In managing the finance of a non-profit organisation, it is important to set a realistically achievable income target that is sufficient to cover the forecast expenditure. Rewards to staff are not based on monetary terms, as is the case in a profit-making setting. Although financial rewards are not the norm for non-profit organisations like the HK Phil, we do recognise the outstanding performance of our staff members and ample opportunities are available for career advancement.

What are the current challenges and difficulties you have been facing in terms of human resources management in the context of HK Phil?

The top and foremost of the challenges stems from the fact that HK Phil does not have its own home, making it very hard for us to plan long-term. Difficulties in securing rehearsal and performance venues have been an ongoing problem. The COVID-related quarantine measures have added difficulties in securing world-famous guest conductors and soloists to come to Hong Kong for performances. Meanwhile, many of our touring plans have been cancelled in the last two years or so. Another challenge that also affects the other sectors in HK as a whole is the brain drain situation, which has been more or less aggravated by the recent wave of overseas migration. There are a lot of opportunities in the local job market with more attractive salaries and a faster path for career advancement. It is not uncommon for young marketing professionals to leave the field of arts management for a more "money-making" career in other profit-making organisations. Overall, attracting, nurturing and retaining talents in arts administration has been very challenging.

Which parts of your job do you find most rewarding?

Over these years, I have witnessed HK Phil's achievements, from an amateur orchestra in the 70s to an award-winning world-class orchestra. I am very proud to be part of this fine orchestra of Hong Kong which makes me feel that I have done my little part in Hong Kong's cultural development. On the other hand, I enjoy meeting and making friends with musicians from various parts of the world. I get to know the stories about them and their culture. Of course, I enjoy going to concerts and being able to accompany the orchestra on its overseas tours.

When people talk about the HK Phil, what is the first image that comes to mind? Thirty years ago versus now, have you witnessed any major changes in how the general public views this local Orchestra?

When I first joined the HK Phil, few people knew that Hong Kong had its own orchestra. Today, the name "HK Phil" is widely known not only to the people in Hong Kong but also to people of other nationalities in many parts of the world. In the past, HK Phil was seen as exclusive to only the elites and did not form any part of the daily life of the general public. However, this notion has been gradually changing, albeit slowly, with our free and accessible outreach programmes to engage different local communities on a regular basis. We have also been launching the 'denim concert series' where the musicians perform in casual attire. The idea is to reach out to the grassroots and the younger generation in the community.

Regarding sponsorship, there is always a misconception that the Government fully funds the HK Phil. The truth is about 60 percent of our income comes from public funds, 20 percent from ticket sales, while the remaining portion relies on sponsorship and private donations.

How does HK Phil build its brand in the current digital era?

In the current digital era, we spend far less money and staffing on billboard-type advertisements or printed brochures or pamphlets. Instead, the focus is put on digital marketing for the following reasons:

- it is more flexible and allows for last-minute programme confirmation and changes;
- the costs are much lower;
- allows and enhances social media engagement;
- allows for niche targeting and more personalised information to be delivered.

At the same time, we produce a lot of online content and programmes for branding exposure and audience engagement. Some of these programmes were shared by other organisations, such as the HKETOs, to maximise the reach. This year, we have revamped the "Watch and Listen" programme, providing a wide selection of music content on our website.

COVID-19 has turned the world upside down. How have the HK Phil and you been coping with COVID-19?

It has certainly been very taxing and challenging for the management of any business and all kinds of corporations with the pandemic in recent years. The situation is so volatile and uncertain that literally no solid planning can be done. Therefore, we must adopt a more flexible approach to our programme and ticket sale mechanism. The temporary closure of performance venues from time to time has interrupted the orchestra's rehearsals and concert schedules, while quarantine requirements have posed limitations on the engagement of international guest artists. Our Music Director, Jaap van Zweden, who resides in the Netherlands and also serves as the Music Director for the New York Philharmonic is well sought after by other orchestras all over the world. It is very difficult for us to schedule his visits to Hong Kong to work with the Orchestra due to the ongoing quarantine requirements.

In 2020, we appointed Macao-born and Hong Kong-educated conductor Lio Kuokman as the Resident Conductor, who has led a number of important performances during the pandemic years. More local musicians were featured as guest artists in our main stage performances. We also introduced a number of online programmes and creative collaborations to keep our audience engaged when live performances were not allowed.

Do you have any other interesting or inspiring stories regarding the HK Phil that you would like to share with the readers?

In the 2023-24 season, the HK Phil is going to reach another milestone when it celebrates its 50th anniversary. A series of celebrations will include a major anniversary concert and other activities for the Hong Kong community as a whole. During my years with the HK Phil, I have witnessed not only the tremendous achievements of the orchestra but also the growth in the size of the HK Phil big family. Over the years, a number of our musicians have started dating and eventually tied the knot or even had children of their own. If I am correct, there are now at least 11 happily married couples in the Orchestra, and most of their children have turned out to be music lovers. Music really brings people together!

In what ways would you like the HK Phil to develop over the next five or ten years?

I very much hope that the HK Phil has its own permanent home like many other top-level orchestras in other parts of the world and that we shall eventually become one of the top orchestras in the world. Of course, we will continue to be the cultural ambassador of China, thereby helping to make Hong Kong the East meets West Centre of international cultural exchange.

What would be the ideal home for your orchestra? What kind of facilities would you like besides the most beautiful acoustics?

Ideally, a world-class concert hall should have the best acoustics for a symphony orchestra while providing office space for the management as well as sufficient spaces for the orchestra's regular rehearsals and storage of large instruments. Also, it should have the most up-to-date facilities for digital technologies to be embraced in presenting performances in order to enhance the audience experience. In the long term, a recording studio and a music education centre should be built as integral parts of this permanent home to cater to audience development programmes. Other features, such as food and beverages outlets, car parks, spaces for VIP and patron events, washrooms, etc., will help make going to a concert an enjoyable social event.

What would you like to be remembered for when you retire?

Frankly speaking, I would never dream that people would remember me for anything. For my part, I feel that I am just doing my job. However, I hope my colleagues or successor would share and feel my love for the orchestra. On the other hand, when I walk down my memory lane with the orchestra, completing Wagner's *Ring Cycle* is certainly one of the most important projects in my mind. In 2019, HK Phil was awarded Gramophone Orchestra of the Year, the first orchestra in Asia to receive the accolade. I look forward to creating more fond memories with the celebrations of the 50th anniversary in the next season.

Photo 1. Vennie Ho, Executive Director of the Hong Kong Philharmonic Orchestra.

Photo 2. In 2019, the Hong Kong Philharmonic Orchestra received the prestigious Gramophone Orchestra of the Year Award.

Photo 3. The Hong Kong Philharmonic Orchestra during a performance with Music Director Jaap van Zweden.

Chapter 13

Anders Hui, Second Associate Concertmaster of the Hong Kong Philharmonic Orchestra, Part-Time Lecturer, School of Humanities & Social Science, Hong Kong University of Science & Technology

Co-authored with:
Ziyan Ai
Phillip Deng
Kwan-Yi
Cactus Mao
Zhuoran Ma
Wang Jiaming

Introduction

Hong Kong-Canadian violinist Anders Hui first joined the Hong Kong Philharmonic Orchestra (HK Phil) in 2010 and is currently the Second Associate Concertmaster of the Orchestra. His accomplishments as a professional musician include being invited in 2007 by Christoph Eschenbach to be the Assistant Concertmaster for the Schleswig Holstein Music Festival Orchestra, performing with soloist Lang Lang in a month-long 23-concert tour across North America. In this position, he did tours around Hungary, Denmark, Brazil, and extensively in Germany. With this orchestra, he also worked with other world-renowned conductors, including Herbert Blomstedt, Mikhail Pletnev, Christopher Hogwood, and Ivan Fischer.

An active chamber musician and dedicated educator, Anders Hui is also serving as an adjunct faculty member at the Music Department of Hong Kong

Baptist University, and **Part-Time Lecturer** at the School of Humanities & Social Science, Hong Kong University of Science & Technology, and the Orchestra Academy Programme at the Hong Kong Academy for Performing Arts. In the following interview, Andres discusses the unique art of chamber music, as well as how young people of other academic disciplines can learn to explore the essence of collaborative learning through chamber music.

Can we begin this interview by first introducing yourself to your educational background and professional training?

I was born in Hong Kong but grew up in Canada. At a very young age, I was lucky to be introduced to music by my parents. I started learning the violin when I was five. I had a very good violin teacher, and the whole music-learning experience I received as a young boy was very inspirational. My violin teacher was also a conductor. In addition to teaching the violin, he conducted many youth orchestras and participated in community music outreach programmes. Following my violin teacher around as a young boy, under his tutelage, I was always given the opportunity to play the violin as a section lead, through which I gradually developed extensive and valuable knowledge of the orchestral repertoire, as well as how an orchestra is arranged and operates.

At a young age, I developed the understanding that playing in an orchestra is very different from playing as a soloist or in a chamber group. Playing in an orchestra at a young age taught me that all orchestra players must listen closely and work together to find cohesion and balance within the larger group. In short, one has to constantly find ways to work as a team, to listen not just to yourself, but also actively listen to and follow other instrument sections to respond to the changing dynamics, phrasing, melodic line, and more – which I think is one of the hardest things to master when playing in an orchestra.

I was very fortunate to have this kind of exposure at a very young age, a skill that has been very beneficial throughout my life as a professional orchestral player.

How did you learn to manage your time so well, and participate in so many music-related activities outside of school when you were growing up as a teenager?

I grew up just before the Internet era; hence, I did not spend much time watching YouTube or playing video games. I also had very devoted parents who would drive me around to my music lessons, and travel to different places for my performances. Meanwhile, they never forced me to practice my violin.

At what stage did you decide to pursue a career as a professional musician?

I did not decide to pursue a career as a professional musician until quite late in my schooling. At age 17, I won my first major music competition, the National Canadian Music Competition. My music teacher helped me a great deal in preparing for this competition. We spent much time working together after school for this 'life-changing' event. After winning this competition, I had the confidence that a successful experience gave me. Then it got me thinking, "Maybe I could actually do this for a living? Should I become a professional musician?"

After winning the Canadian Music Competition in Canada, I went to the U.S. to pursue my Bachelor's and Master's degrees at Indiana University, Jacob School of Music, studying with Mauricio Fuks and Nelli Shkolnikova. At the start, I had no personal connections in America, but my music teacher (in Canada) helped me start to network. I am so grateful to my music teachers in Canada; they came with me from Toronto to Indiana to audition for the Jacob School of Music. While studying at Indiana University, I won the Brahms Violin Concerto Competition and performed with the Indiana University Philharmonic Orchestra.

Since you already decided to pursue a career as a professional musician, what are the advantages of studying music full-time at a university compared to pursuing your studies at a music conservatory/music college?

At Indiana University, in addition to Music, I minored in Business Studies. In fact, the Kelley School of Business at Indiana University is one of the top business schools in the world. I think all young people should be diverse in their learning and exposure to adopt different approaches to problem-solving when they leave university and enter the world of work. The university environment is very valuable in providing countless and varying learning opportunities that allow young people to reach their full potential.

Before returning to Hong Kong to join the HK Phil, I understand you also spent time working in America, as well as spending two years in Germany -- studying under Kolja Blacher and Michael Vogler at the Hanns Eisler School of Music in Berlin. Kolja Blacher was the first concertmaster of the Berlin Philharmonic under Claudio Abbado from 1993 to 1999. What was the most valuable lesson you learnt from them?

When I was in America, I was the Assistant Concertmaster and Interim Concertmaster for Terre Haute Symphony Orchestra, as well as Guest Concertmaster for Carmel (IN) Symphony Orchestra. I was also Tutti Violin of the Columbus Indiana Philharmonic.

Before returning to Hong Kong and joining the HK Phil, I undertook further studies in Germany with Michael Vogler and Kolja Blacher, professors at the Hanns Eisler School of Music in Berlin. One of my violin teachers in Berlin (Michael Vogler), who was from the older generation of German music schools, taught me in my first lesson: "when you play, the sound and energy should point directly towards the audience. In other words, you should focus on producing a sound that can travel high and far – in a direction that would go straight and upwards in the air – in a notion similar to air circulation." He kept emphasising that as a violinist, you should fill the room (concert hall) with sound circulation. Since I received most of my training in North America, this concept of sound projection with the violin was totally new to me.

You are currently serving as the Second Associate Concertmaster of the Hong Kong Philharmonic Orchestra (HK Phil). What exactly does a concertmaster do?

In an orchestra, the concertmaster leads the first violin section. The concertmaster always plays any violin solo in an orchestral work. The concertmaster also leads the orchestra in tuning before each concert and rehearsal. In addition, the concertmaster also serves as a messenger between the conductor and the principal players of different orchestral sections. If the conductor has certain interpretive wishes or demands (e.g., decisions on bowing and/or other technical details of violin playing, and sometimes all of the string players, etc.) – they will be passed down to the concertmaster, and he/she will then relay them to the leaders of the respective orchestral sections. In short, the concertmaster functions as the 'bridge' or 'diplomat' between the conductor and orchestra and is accountable to both parties. The concertmaster also leads the string section through gestures (e.g., facial expressions, hand or body gestures, etc.) to communicate musical intents.

I understand you also work as the Orchestra Executive for Opera Hong Kong. Would you say that the roles and responsibilities of an Orchestra Executive are similar to those of a CEO of a major corporation?

In many ways, they are very similar to each other. Because both positions involve managing people, i.e., managing people of diversity; managing cultural diversity; setting morale for your colleagues; enhancing staff motivation; building working relationships amongst team members; developing a vision and strategy for your team to work towards; knowing what to expect at the end, results, etc. In orchestral playing, you have to anticipate what the music should sound like and the kinds of musical sensation it would bring to the audience. That's why not only the rehearsals are important; concert programming is equally important.

You are currently serving as a part-time lecturer at the Division of Humanities (HUMA), School of Humanities & Social Science Division of Humanities (SHSS) at the Hong Kong University of Science & Technology (HKUST). Could you provide a brief introduction to the HUMA, as well as the missions and philosophy behind their music programmes?

Maestro Bright Sheng invited me to teach Chamber Music at HUMA at SHSS. The SHSS offers various music and creative writing courses via the HUMA. All programmes are taught and led by professional artists and musicians like me, in which students learn the value of creativity and the essence of collaboration, as well as its practical applications in other fields of study. The students at HKUST are taught to understand the arts from the perspective of creators and producers rather than consumers and critics. The courses in Music offered at the HUMA include the following:

- HUMA1100: Music of the World
- HUMA1102: Enjoyment of Classical Music
- HUMA2103: Introduction to Music Composition
- HUMA2104: Music Theory I
- HUMA2105: Music, Drama, and Theatre
- HUMA2106: A New Approach to Music Making

- HUMA3101: Western, Opera, and Literature
- HUMA3102: Making Chamber Music A
- HUMA3103: Making Chamber Music B
- HUMA3105: Making Choral Music

Since students at HKUST are mostly business, science or engineering majors, what kinds of positive learning experiences would these students gain from taking part in such music appreciation, music creation, and music performance programmes offered at the HUMA?

Although most students are science, engineering and business majors and do not wish to become professional musicians in the future, they still learn the skills and values behind team building and collaboration via the chamber music programmes offered at HUMA. Recently, there has been a growing emphasis on collaborative learning implementation amongst higher education institutions worldwide. Based on our experience, students (regardless of their backgrounds or academic disciplines) can learn something meaningful, positive and practical through creating chamber music – since it is an art form built entirely upon active, engaging and collaborative learning. Within the framework of chamber music ensembles, students can learn innovative problem-solving skills as a team via positive social interactions and the development of creative rehearsal strategies. As such, students learn to identify artistic and technical problems and develop rehearsal strategies to solve them.

Dr. Amy Sze is a professional instructor (specialising in piano) at HKUST. She and I work together to audition the students, via which we try to identify the most talented musician students to be accepted in our chamber music programmes. There is a great variety of chamber music available. After the students have been selected, we ask them to form standard chamber ensembles comprising different instruments (piano, violin, viola, cello, etc.). After the student chamber ensembles are formed, we (as teachers) then assign them the appropriate pieces/repertoire to perform. Since these students are not professionally trained musicians, they are bound to have technical limitations. For example, you may have a very strong pianist within an ensemble group, while the string players might not be equally competent, showing technical flaws during a performance.

What kinds of chamber music pieces/repertoire would you usually assign your student chamber ensembles to learn and master?

It really all depends on their technique, i.e., technical competence. I usually suggest they focus more on the Classical and Baroque repertoire, e.g., Vivaldi, Bach, Mozart, Beethoven, Haydn, etc. Technically speaking, they are easier to play (though artistically & musically, they are not necessarily easier). Nevertheless, we all have to master all the technical aspects before we can move on to doing anything artistically, not to mention expressing emotions or ourselves. As part of their student project / assignment, the student chamber ensembles perform at the Shaw Auditorium at HKUST at the end of the academic year. Such student concerts are open to students, teaching staff, faculties and members of the HKUST community.

What is the key to successful chamber music?

The key to successful chamber music is collaboration, i.e., all the musicians on stage have equal importance in the piece, and all the instruments should be featured equally. In other words, all musicians should be working closely together, sharing opinions and striving to make something beautiful and meaningful. The skills required for chamber music are distinctively different from that of playing solo or symphonic works. In short, chamber music is a very delicate art form. Hence, it requires great precision and communication amongst a small number of players.

Although we use our instruments to express ourselves, we must first understand the composer's intentions when it comes to chamber music. Musicians are interpreters of the music they play. You have to interpret the composer's thoughts, intentions, and philosophy behind the piece to best captivate the listeners with the performance. Although you have very clear and accurate musical notations before you, it would only allow you to scratch the surface of the composer's intentions. As musicians, it is our job to dig deep into the artistic, spiritual, and philosophical territories and beyond to come out with music that will transcend and create meaning. When playing in an orchestra, the orchestral players' priority is to follow the conductor and/or stay with their section. Whereas for chamber music, every single musician onstage is equal, and we are all given a voice to express ourselves artistically while playing in collaboration with other musicians.

Could you list activities or programme highlights you and your chamber music students initiated at the HUMA?

In one year (2019, before the COVID-19 crisis), the HUMA students gave an outstanding recital performing the following chamber music pieces:

- Brahms Piano Quartet Op.25
- Schumann Piano Quartet Op.47
- Mendelssohn Piano Trio Op.49
- Prokoviev Cello Sonata
- Moszkowski Piano Duet

Despite these chamber music pieces' artistic and technical challenges, this recital went really well.

The HKUST students were also invited to apply for the Takako Nishizaki Student Performer Scholarships, an initiative of HKUST - HKUST Division of Humanities, supported by Naxos. The winning student will receive one term to the whole academic year of private (one-to-one) instruction on their major instrument with an instructor appointed by the HUMA. One year, the Scholarship winner was a violin student. This student was so technically competent that they could basically play anything and possessed the full potential to become a professional musician. However, she decided to do something other than music after graduating from HKUST. But having a chance to teach a student possessing this level of talent and technical skill was also a lot of fun for me. I want to say that there are quite a few unexpected talents on the HKUST campus. I, therefore, always encourage universities and other higher education institutions in Hong Kong to create more opportunities for nurturing such young and hidden musical talents.

If you were to be cast away on a desert island, what music scores or CD recordings would you bring with you?

There is so much music out there to choose from. As a professional musician, who loves his job, I could never bring enough with me. However, in a desert-island situation like that – when one really needs spiritual support and guidance from a higher power, Johann Sebastian Bach is one composer that really comes to mind, because Bach's music is so spiritual and nourishing for the soul. Even daily, when I get too busy and stressed out, I always go back to playing music by Bach – it has a sort of out-of-this-world, spiritual-cleansing quality – to cleanse away all the negativity, as well as any bad energy inside my mind and body. As such, Bach would be the ultimate composer I would take to work on, no matter where I go.

Before we conclude this interview, would you like to say something inspiring to our young readers considering pursuing a career as a professional musician?

Music is a powerful and universal language. Some even say that "music is the universal language of mankind" and "music is food for the human soul." Free from any cultural and language barriers, music is the language that communicates our innermost thoughts and most intimate feelings. In addition to creativity, aesthetic sensitivity and arts-appraising ability, through music learning, one could also develop self-discipline, self-confidence, patience, as well as innovative problem-solving and collaborative learning skills – these are all the critical skills and attributes that young people need (regardless the field you are in: the arts, science and technology, business, or sports, etc.) to succeed in any century. We must not forget that during the darkest hours, music can give mankind strength and hope, and it reminds us that love is worth fighting for.

Photo 1. Anders Hui performs in a recital at HKUST.

Photo 2. Anders Hui performs in a recital at HKUST.

School of Humanities and Social Science

Check out the Music Courses offered in Fall 2018 !

HUMA1100	Music of the World
HUMA1102	Enjoyment of Classical Music
HUMA2103	Introduction to Music Composition
HUMA2104	Music Theory I
HUMA3101	Enjoyment of Western Opera
HUMA3102	Making Chamber Music A*
HUMA3150	Independent Study in Creative Arts *

* Contact instructor directly to petition for enrollment

* Instructor consent required to enroll
  Contact Roderick Yu (roderickyu@ust.hk) to schedule an audition

Photo 3. Music Courses offered at the School of Humanities and Social Science, HKUST.

Photo 4. *Takako Nishizaki* (西崎崇子) Student Performer Scholarships (2018-19).

Photo 5. HKUST students perform in the HUMA Music Course Showcase Concert.

Photo 6. HUMA3103: Making Chamber Music B: Announcing Auditions (HKUST Division of Humanities).

Photo 7. Spring 2023 HUMA Music Course Showcase Concert @ HKUST – featuring students of: HUMA 3102 Making Chamber Music A.

Photo 8. Intimacy of Creativity 2010 Concert - The Bright Sheng Partnership: Composers Meet Performers in Hong Kong.

Chapter 14

Cho-Liang Lin, Music Director, Hong Kong International Chamber Music Festival

Introduction

Taiwanese-American virtuoso violinist Cho-Liang Lin is renowned for the longevity of his career, as well as his appearances as a soloist with every major orchestra in the world, including the Boston Symphony Orchestra, Cleveland Orchestra, Royal Concertgebouw Orchestra, London Symphony Orchestra, Philadelphia Orchestra and New York Philharmonic, etc. In addition to releasing over 20 recordings, Cho-Liang Lin is also the founder of several international music festivals. Currently, Cho-Liang Lin serves as the Artistic Director of Premiere Performances (formerly Hong Kong International Chamber Music Festival), and Music Director of La Jolla Summer Fest. "Musical America" named him its "Instrumentalist of the Year" in 2000.

In addition to discussing the missions behind his music festivals, in the following interview, Cho-Liang Lin shares his unique insights on the art of chamber music and ensemble playing with the readers.

Could we begin this interview by first introducing yourself, e.g., your early training in music back in Taiwan and the USA? Do you come from a family of musicians or performing artists?

As far as I know, my family has never produced a professional musician; my father was a nuclear physicist. I developed an interest in Western classical music, because my next-door neighbour was playing the violin, and so I wanted to learn the violin too. I aged 5, immediately dropped my toy and ran next door to watch. I remember sitting by my neighbour's music stand --- just watching him play his instrument. Apparently, I did that every day.

I started my first violin lesson with a quarter-sized fiddle, and my whole musical education went from there. At the age of 12, I moved from Taiwan to Sydney to further my studies with Robert Pikler (a student of Jenő Hubay).

At what stage did you decide to pursue a career as a concert violinist?

I grew up during the 1960s in Taiwan, so being a professional musician did not appear economically viable then. I also thought of becoming a scientist or an engineer, but I was not very good at mathematics.

When I left Taiwan for Australia (at about 11 or 12), I began to feel that I could make something out of my musical talents. At age 15, I moved to New York to further my music education at the Juilliard School. By age 16 or 17, I began to receive invitations to perform with some major orchestras here and there during their summer seasons – i.e., to perform in their popular concerts. Even though they were summer pop concerts, it was a big deal for a 17-year-old to stand on stage and play together with the St. Louis Symphony Orchestra (SLSO). That was when I began to feel being a violinist could be a viable career choice. When I attended the Juilliard School as a teenager, I thought if I could one day become a member of the New York Philharmonic, I would be totally happy.

In 1979, I made my début at Lincoln Center's Mostly Mozart Festival at 19, playing Mozart's Violin Concerto No. 3. At age 20, I made my début with the New York Philharmonic playing the Mendelssohn Concerto under the direction of Zubin Mehta in 1980.

When you were still a teenager trying to make a career as a concert violinist, how would the music critics describe your playing style as well as your artistic talent?

The game of writing reviews for performing arts seems to have undergone major changes over the past few decades. The newspaper business used to play a crucial role in building a musician's career. When I look at my earliest reviews from 1979 about my debuts, most of them were rave reviews. One year later, I made my debut with the Philadelphia Orchestra, and the *Philadelphia Inquirer* gave me one of the best reviews; it was as if my mother herself had written it.

Nowadays, we all know that it is really hard to get a proper review out of any newspaper. The industry has moved towards social media and other online outlets rather than paper reviews. When I look at these old reviews, I feel very grateful that they allowed me to be noticed in the world of classical music. It also gave me a sense of direction to keep growing and expanding my repertoire and knowledge in music, etc. The learning process for me, as a musician, has never really stopped.

When you were still a teenager, you were allowed to play with some of the major orchestras around the world. What was it like working side-by-side with many conductors of legendary stature? What have been the most valuable lessons learned from them?

I learned so much from watching these great conductors onstage and in rehearsals. When I was in my early 20s (no longer a teenager), I also had to learn how to express myself "ethically," "artistically," "musically," and "verbally," the conductors had a big part to play in this development.

For example, I had to learn how to artistically give and take. If the maestro wanted a certain passage to go slower or faster, and asked me to have a go, I learnt to say, "Yeah, let's give it a try." I would then have to trust the conductor with his knowledge and wisdom, and we would share the 'glove' onstage all after. Setting my professional boundaries has been important, and I was learning to stand up for what I need out of the rehearsal as a performer. Because, after all, I am the soloist. If I am pushed into a situation where I am playing a certain passage uncomfortably, it is going to affect my overall performance. The early days of learning are now long gone, however.

To me, music-making is always a collaborative effort because when I was very young, my teachers taught me unequivocally about working with others, particularly when playing in ensembles. I also realised that this 'collaborative' approach and attitude should remain the same when you are playing as a soloist (under the spotlight) in the concerto situation. My upbringing and education have taught me to be "humble" away -- this has become an essential trait for me, particularly if a fantastic conductor I admire wants to try something different.

I once performed the Beethoven concerto at a blazingly fast speed, because the conductor David Zinman (1936-), said he wanted to try this performance in a different style. Although I loved the end results, it took me a couple of rehearsals to feel comfortable because the pace and the man were much faster than I was used to. Artistically speaking, I gained a lot from the experience. Two weeks later, I was in Japan, playing the same concerto with the old grandmaster, Takashi Asahina (1908-2001) (from that old Germanic school), and he wanted a really slow tempo --- and suddenly, I had to put the brakes on my performance. I could not, in good standing, become egocentric and say, "Okay, I'm going to be the boss; you're 85 years old – so listen to me instead!"

Being a child prodigy, appearing on the stages of great concert halls around the world from an early age, do you feel you have missed a normal childhood and teenage life?

In my early teens, in Taiwan, I wanted to be a baseball player. I even organised my little league team. I even played catcher – i.e., putting myself in a dangerous situation where my hands would sometimes get injured. During my time in Australia, my parents would ensure that I had plenty of balance in my schedule, with enough time to play basketball, ride my bicycle, and play with my dog. These things were really fun and important, and to this day, I still enjoy the time away from the violin. It is important to remember performers are also normal people with normal lives outside the concert hall.

Could you describe Taiwan's overall arts and cultural scene, especially Western classical music, during the 1960s and 70s?

The classical music scene was not very strong in those days, since Taiwan was not an economic power then. Finding a classical musician of international star calibre to stop by in Taiwan for a recital or concerto was very rare indeed. In fact, my very first time attending a first-rate live orchestral performance was in Australia (just before I left Sydney -- to go to study at Julliard in New York); it was Leonard Bernstein was leading the New York Philharmonic on tour in Australia and New Zealand.

In terms of Western classical music, there was really not much going on in Taiwan during the 1960s and 70s. When I returned to Taiwan in the late 1970s, the overall performing arts scenes and acoustics of the concert halls were in very poor condition. The Taiwanese people would bring their portable cassette players to record my concerts illegally, and radio stations would set up their gigantic reel-to-reel machines right in front of my face to record my live performances.

What is the most important or valuable thing a music student can learn from other professional musicians when playing side-by-side in an orchestra or a chamber group?

Technically speaking, I think knowing that music does not exist in solitude is very important. Music needs to be played in the company of others, i.e., in a situation that requires a sense of communication and the ability to listen to others. For example -- when you are playing a symphony – every orchestral player has to play in tune -- this is a challenge that every musician faces. However, the Asian concept of ensembles is not as strong as their American or European counterparts, because everybody's initial focus in Asia is to 'outshine' – to become a big-shot soloist -- the next Lang Lang or Yo-yo Ma. But even young Lang Lang and Yo-yo Ma had to listen to what the other orchestra players did.

For example, if you are in the first violin section and have the first line of this overtone. If you play even too loudly as a collective, the melodic element in the oboe section will get lost or jammed out. You cannot just sit and play passively with your fingers as if you were detached from the whole music-making process. As an orchestral player, you must add meaning to your playing/phrasing – i.e., to participate sincerely and actively in the music-making with others sharing the same stage. In other words, you have to listen to what the other musicians try to do and actively participate and respond artistically. At the same time, you have to watch what the concertmaster is actually doing while waiting for the other players and the conductor's signals. That is a lot of information going into a musician's mind concurrently -- not an easy task. Being an orchestral player requires 100% participation and concentration.

The same also goes for chamber music. Once a year, students are invited to participate in the Taiwan Music Festival, which lasts for two weeks, and the students are given daily immersion in playing alongside the faculty. The experience is meant to upskill the students' listening ability to figure out their role in that particular music-making moment as a valued ensemble member. Rehearsals are so important for developing and honing these skills.

When I support the students who are participating in our music festival, I constantly remind the violinists sitting near me, "Please pay attention, listen to this, and why are we doing this. When we are playing side-by-side with them at that particular juncture – we would constantly be sending them gentle reminders of what they should be doing – reminding them, "Can you make something meaningful out of those two notes?" It is a rather complex process, and nothing is straightforward.

We use our Taipei Festival to find ways to best cultivate these students' sensitivity and activate their curiosity in listening when playing in ensembles. The student applicants have to go through a very rigorous audition process. Out of all the student applicants, we only picked 47 or 48 people each time. During the audition process, we listen to these student-applicants' musical sense and maturity to find the ones who would benefit the most from the experience and best fit into our Festival. In other words, we are always looking for the participatory type of musician – i.e., open-minded and willing to listen to others – someone who can and is willing to become a soul partner in music making. Under this context, we might not necessarily choose someone who can give the greatest performance as a soloist – but instead, a musician who can give a really beautiful and yet meaningful interpretation of some excerpts of orchestral music.

Could you briefly introduce Beare's Premiere Music Festival and describe the missions, visions, and philosophy behind the Festival's programming and operations?

Andrea Fessler founded Premiere Performances (formerly Hong Kong International Chamber Music Festival) as a registered charity in March 2007. Having lived in Hong Kong since 2004, Andrea Fessler perceived a strong demand for classical music concerts, but there were very limited choices for solo recitals, and even less for chamber music. As such, Andrea Fessler decided to found Premiere Performances to fill that cultural gap.

Premiere Performances launched its first Hong Kong International Chamber Music Festival in June 2009. Premiere Performances' annual event features concerts led by world-class chamber artists, plus dozens of free workshops, lectures, master classes and concerts around the city. The entire Festival aims to bring Hong Kong audiences the richness of chamber music and its endless variety of instrumental combinations performed at the highest international level. In fact, Premiere Performances celebrated its 10th Anniversary in 2017 – the Festival is recognised as the presenter of the world's best classical and chamber music performers in Hong Kong.

How did you become the Artistic Director of Beare's Premiere Music Festival?

Andrea Fessler is the Founder of the Festival, and we made contact while I was in Hong Kong and discussed whether I would like to take over the Festival as the Artistic Director. She explained to me what the Festival was all about. I thought about it and realised that I really liked the concept and values, as well as the challenges that came along with the Festival. I thought it to be very important work and an opportunity not to be missed working with somebody like Andrea Fessler, who has the vision and the drive, so I said "YES."

The Festival has been operating in Hong Kong for over a decade. Have you witnessed any major changes in audience participation over the years?

The festival audience grows each year, and we are also trying to find more diverse venues for our performances. Hong Kong does not have a large selection of suitable venues for chamber music performances. There are always some advantages and disadvantages when planning chamber music performances in Hong Kong. Our Festival's ticketing system is not part of the central ticketing system in Hong Kong, as it is an independent system; this is problematic as concertgoers are not familiar with the software. Although there are many music halls in Hong Kong, for the most part, they are unsuitable due to their large size. As such, we are always looking for small to medium-sized concert halls in Hong Kong. The ideal venue should seat an audience of approximately 600.

You have performed in some of the greatest music halls around the world. Would you say that the quality of acoustics of music halls tends to vary from country to country?

I think one can consistently find great-sounding halls in Japan; they seem to have a special talent for acoustic design. The UK has a large array of concert venues, but the quality of the acoustics differs dramatically despite being the capital for Western classical music. The music halls in Vienna all sound fantastic. The concert halls in Taiwan and Mainland China (Shanghai and Beijing) are too large or too small for chamber music. Both locations would benefit from medium-sized halls that could seat about 600 audience members.

As a soloist and as a member of an ensemble group, what is it like to perform in an 'acoustically perfect' concert hall?

It is a beautiful experience! After 40-plus years on the circuit, I have performed in an array of quality, both good and bad concert halls; you just have to make the best out of every situation. The deal space has a 'sense of feedback and flow' from the acoustics. For example, after playing a note, you can hear the sound travel out and gradually return to you; it is a lovely sensation, a velvety-quality sound. I dislike when the acoustic is 'dry' and 'rough.' As a musician, it is always a very inspiring experience when you can actually enjoy the venue you are performing in.

During a performance, when everything is going right on stage, can you feel the energy from the audience?

Normally, that has nothing to do with the beauty of the acoustics in the music hall. I can do that independently. However, when the concert hall and the audience perfectly come together, the audience and musicians on stage have a truly memorable experience. I will take the energy from the audience anytime and any day. You can feel the energy from an audience highly concentrated on your performance.

There are also cultural differences in terms of how audiences around the world express approval of performing artists. When performing in Western countries, typically, you play the first piece, and people would show they love it within the first 15 minutes. As a performing artist, it is really delightful and encouraging as it energises you for the rest of the concert. However, in Asia, typically, people are more reserved. You may feel the first piece went well, but there may be no applause or only short applause. If you don't know the audience from your previous experience – such a lack of enthusiasm from the audience could easily make you feel distracted or discouraged. But in fact, they reserve the most vociferous applause for the second half of your concert; they often are saving it until the very end.

Throughout your life as a successful concert violinist, do you have any regrets? If given a second chance, would you choose to do certain things differently again?

No, I don't have any regrets. When my daughter was born, I just wanted to spend a few more days with her and my wife. I have never regretted the decision to go down the musical path. I am very happy with what I have chosen, i.e., my life and career as a professional musician. I know that regardless of the instrument I play, music is and will be a lifelong passion. I feel that as I age, my passion for music grows stronger each year.

As a violinist, do you see yourself as the musical servant of the composer? Do you think good musicians should be faithful servants of the composers?

I really believe in historically informed interpretation of the works of musical giants. Unfortunately, none of us knew Beethoven or Mozart in person; however, I think I represent their music faithfully. Meanwhile, I am against this very dogmatic approach, i.e., you must play exactly as the music says. I really hate that sort of authoritarian approach where there is no leeway at all. I guess musicians are similar to actors – we get provided with a script and learn and rehearse our lines, but each actor must find their own way to deliver the same part. As a musician, you have to say something musically that touches not only the audience, but also yourself in an intuitive way. As great as music making can be, it has to be rooted in a solid knowledge base of understanding your instrument, the style of the music and the historical and performative norms of the era it was composed in.

Photo 1. At age 5 in Hsinchu, Taiwan. Just a beginner.

Photo 2. In Taipei National Concert Hall. It was 2020. The world had shut down and concert halls went dark as the pandemic raged. Yet, Taiwan was a relatively Covid-free place and concerts actually took place. I was so moved by a hall full of music loving audience when the world didn't have live concerts, I took a selfie to remember this happy evening.

Photo 3. In a recent concert in Bogotá, Colombia.

Photo 4. A reflective moment in a concerto.

Photo 5. Concert poster.

Photo 6. Concert poster.

Photo 7. Concert poster.

Photo 8. Concert poster.

Photo 9. Looking to a good future.

Chapter 15

Dr. Celina Chin, Executive Director, Hong Kong Chinese Orchestra

Introduction

Founded in 1977 by the Urban Council, the Hong Kong Chinese Orchestra (HKCO) has won many accolades, including: "leader in Chinese ethnic music" and "cultural ambassador of Hong Kong." In October 2002, HKCO was awarded "The Most Outstanding Achievement in Advancing Contemporary Chinese Music" by the International Society of Contemporary Music. Dr. Celina Chin is the current Executive Director of HKCO. Dr Celina Chin holds a doctorate in Professional Studies from Middlesex University, a Master of Arts degree in Strategic Management for Non-Distributing Organisation, a Diploma in Company Direction and a Professional Diploma in Corporate Governance & Directorship from The Hong Kong Institute of Directors. She also completed the Professional Programme in Arts Administration organised by UCLA and the former Urban Services Department.

In the following interview, Dr. Celine Chin discusses the unique role that HKCO plays in shaping the overall cultural landscape of Hong Kong, as well as the signature repertoire of the Orchestra.

Could we begin this interview by first introducing yourself, for example, your professional training and educational background? For instance, what did you study at the university? Do you come from a family of musicians? Are you also a trained musician yourself?

I hold a doctorate in Professional Studies from Middlesex University, a Master of Arts degree in Strategic Management for Non-Distributing Organisation, a Diploma in Company Direction and a Professional Diploma in Corporate Governance & Directorship from The Hong Kong Institute of Directors.

I enjoy music, but I am not a musician myself. I am privileged to have worked alongside many great talents in the performing arts industry for over 30 years. Understanding their priorities and concerns enables me to work towards building an effective environment for their creativity to thrive. It is most satisfying when the various groups I work for grow both artistically and organisationally.

Could you briefly introduce the Hong Kong Chinese Orchestra (HKCO)?

HKCO was set up by the government in 1977 and was incorporated in 2001. It is an establishment of 91 artists and comprises four sections: bowed strings, plucked strings, wind and percussion. It remains to date the only professional Chinese orchestra of this scale in Hong Kong.

The primary mission of HKCO is to serve the people of Hong Kong with quality Chinese music. It shares its music with the public in major venues, in the community and online. It also initiates instrumental festivals for the public to enjoy. For example, the Hong Kong Drum Festival was launched in 2003 and has become a popular annual event.

Going hand in hand with the above mission is HKCO's commitment to nurturing local musical talents and cultivating a new audience generation. A major and ongoing effort is to support and recognise new compositional talents by actively commissioning them for original compositions and new arrangements and performing their works in HKCO's concerts.

To groom and nurture the young generation of musicians, HKCO holds instrumental classes and collaborates with the Hong Kong Academy of Performing Arts (HKAPA) on workshops such as Master Classes on Chinese Music Conducting. HKCO expanded to provide opportunities for young musicians by establishing the Hong Kong Young Chinese Orchestra.

To grow the audience for Chinese music, HKCO reaches out to the mass public through projects and events held in conjunction with television, radio stations and other partners. We teamed up with the Hong Kong public to play together, citywide, the *erhu*, the drum and the *dizi*. This resulted in a Guinness World Records award for having the largest number of people playing these musical instruments simultaneously across the city.

A third important mission that HKCO takes on is the research and production of musical instruments to elevate their sound quality and sustainability. This is an endeavour not commonly found among orchestras worldwide. It is a huge undertaking to revamp and restore bowed-string instruments into *Eco-Huqins* as a game changer. The sound quality of the new

Huqins was so much improved that it gave HKCO an enviable orchestral sound that attracted Chinese orchestras in the Mainland and Taiwan to purchase the new instruments. HKCO also won various green/innovation awards for its efforts.

Last but not least, HKCO acts as a cultural ambassador to perform on the Mainland and overseas to promote Hong Kong and Chinese music.

What is the signature repertoire of HKCO?

Instead of focusing on a signature piece, I'd like to take the opportunity to highlight a special characteristic of our music that shapes HKCO.

While paying homage to classical works forms an integral part of its programme, HKCO sees driving the creation of a contemporary sound and building a repertoire unique to the orchestra as essential for both HKCO and the continuous development of Chinese music. Over the years, HKCO has actively commissioned over 2,400 new compositions and arrangements of diverse types and styles. This voluminous and highly original oeuvre makes HKCO stand out among other orchestras. Its broad repertoire ranges from traditional to contemporary, ethnic to experimental.

Music From The Heart exemplifies HKCO's unflagging pursuit of high-quality new creations. Launched in 1999, this long-running annual programme invites local composers to submit new works. HKCO then premieres selected works at its concert. The programme has since recognised the talents of more than forty composers and their one hundred compositions.

HKCO further promotes the exploration of new frontiers in music by bringing efforts to the international arena. These events include the International Composition Prize 2013, which HKCO co-organised with the Luxembourg Society for Contemporary Music, and Chinese Music Without Bounds - International Composition Competition in 2017, which were acclaimed as platforms for composers to publish new works and for musical exchange.

How did HKCO become the Cultural Ambassador of Hong Kong? In what capacity is HKCO representing Hong Kong?

It has been a core role of HKCO since its inception in 1977 to bring 21st-century orchestral Chinese music to a global audience. In addition, HKCO supports the government in promoting Hong Kong as an international and culturally diverse city by performing at government events on the Mainland and overseas.

The orchestra has been invited to perform at Carnegie Hall in New York, the "Golden Hall" in the Musikverein concert hall in Vienna, and other major concert halls worldwide. The orchestra has also participated in cultural festivals, including Festival de Saint-Denis in France and Festival van Contrasten in Amsterdam. Furthermore, HKCO collaborates with local musicians when visiting overseas to promote an in-depth understanding of Chinese music.

Over the years, HKCO has toured 103 cities in 26 countries as far north as Tromsø in Norway, within 400 miles of the Arctic Circle, and played Chinese music to audiences from vastly different cultures, such as Russia and the Middle East.

Performing and conducting musical exchanges with musicians in Mainland China is equally important. HKCO has toured many cities in Mainland China. The high respect for HKCO is reflected in its being the only ethnic orchestra invited to perform in the inaugural season of the National Centre for the Performing Arts in Beijing. HKCO was also the sole performing group from Hong Kong.

The HKCO participates in overseas events organised by the government and its Hong Kong Economic and Trade Offices worldwide to promote Hong Kong. HKCO was a member of the delegation led by the Chief Executive of Hong Kong to London for the relaunch of the Hong Kong campaign following the city's recovery from SARS (severe acute respiratory syndrome) in 2003.

What is the average age and gender distribution of HKCO?

For the 2021/2022 fiscal year, our artist's average age was 40. The share of female and male artists is 51% to 49%, respectively.

Could you describe your career path to becoming the Executive Director, HKCO? To join HKCO, you also served for the Hong Kong Repertory Theatre, Festival of Asian Arts, Chinese Music Festival, Hong Kong International Film Festival, Hong Kong International Arts Carnival, etc. How do such professional experiences contribute to your work as the Executive Director, HKCO?

I was an Immigration Officer in the Hong Kong Immigration Department for six years before joining the then Urban Services Department (USD) as a

Cultural Manager. In the twelve years that followed, I served at the Hong Kong Repertory Theatre, Asian Arts Festival, Hong Kong International Film Festival, International Arts Carnival and lastly, HKCO in 1996. When HKCO was incorporated in 2001, I was seconded there to head the transition and was later appointed as its inaugural Executive Director.

The various postings in the USD provided excellent opportunities for me not only in organisational management, but also in planning and executing large-scale performances as well as international festivals and events, working with local and foreign media, hosting overseas arts groups, etc. Working with artists gives me a front-row seat to their artistry and an understanding of their considerations and concerns. All of these helped build a solid foundation for my work in HKCO.

I would also add that my experience in the Immigration Department contributed to my striving for effective corporate governance for HKCO. The discipline of law enforcement agencies provides a good perspective on the prudent use of discretion in the decision-making of performing arts organisations and the development and regular review of administrative guidelines and sound financial practice.

The Immigration Department's emphasis on teamwork also impacted me as an art administrator. One incident particularly left a lasting impression on me. A teammate stepped on me from behind when we were practising marching. Not wanting to disrupt the march, I stepped out from the formation to fix my shoe. I later learned from the commanding officer that despite my good intention, my leaving the formation had actually broken up the teamwork. Instead, I should have continued marching and left the decision to pause the march to the commanding officer. HKCO comprises individuals, each gifted with their own artistic flair. Unison cannot be more important than in the context of an orchestra. I see managing and communicating this balance and team building as crucial aspects of my work for the orchestra's success.

HKCO is the "only Chinese orchestra to research and use their own instruments, which they sell to other orchestras in China and Taiwan." – could you elaborate on this?

This function of researching and developing musical instruments distinguishes HKCO from orchestras in general.

Chinese musical instruments had long been used for solo or small ensemble performances, which emphasised the "personality" of individual instruments. Only in the last century did Chinese music orchestras come into being; this is when variation in tonal quality among the same type of musical instruments became an issue. The main determinant for the lack of uniformity was the use of python skin, a common material for mounting on the sound box of *huqin*. Its uneven thickness causes "noise" and results in tonal variations among instruments. This needed to be addressed if HKCO could attain a top-quality orchestral sound. Practical concerns further hastened HKCO to redesign the instruments. Python skin is sensitive to changes in temperature and humidity. For HKCO, which planned to embark on concert tours worldwide, fluctuations in tonal quality would be unacceptable. Moreover, environmental protection regulations in some countries banned the import of instruments bearing python skins. The material had to be replaced for HKCO to perform internationally.

After extensive research, starting in 2003, HKCO identified PET polyester film, which excels in uniform thickness, high vibration and strong elasticity, to replace python skin. HKCO also investigated modifying the curvature of the sound box interior and the thickness of the wall of *huqins* to further improve sound quality. The first product of the revamp was the *eco-gaohu* in December 2005. Work on the bass instruments ensued, with the bass *gehu* debuted in February 2009. By the 2010 season, over forty *Eco-Huqins* had been produced and were featured in HKCO's performances. The entire bowed-string section of the orchestra switched to using the new instruments afterwards. Research on improving other musical instruments is an ongoing endeavour and continues to date.

Eco-Huqins revolutionise the orchestral sound. They give HKCO a signature sound that is cohesive and expressive, with full and rounded tonal effects for both high-pitch and bass instruments. A strong testimony to the success of *Eco-Huqins* comes from peer organisations in the Mainland and Taiwan. Orchestras there were attracted to the improved sound of the new instruments and purchased them from HKCO. The Music Office of the Hong Kong government also procured them for use by its students. HKCO's innovation has also earned various environmental protection awards, including the 4th Ministry of Culture Innovation Award in the Mainland in 2012 and the Hong Kong government awards.

You also hold a doctorate in Professional Studies from Middlesex University. How do your academic and research writing skills contribute to your current work as the Executive Director, HKCO?

The rigorous process of research, such as methodology review, critical examination of hypotheses and findings, and the structured presentation of arguments and results, has helped strengthen the leadership skills that my work calls for.

Entitled "The Value of Art," my doctoral thesis explores how to measure the performance of performing arts organisations. It examines the nature of these organisations in which intangible values may take precedence over monetary gains. For example, box office sales may not be suitable as a major key performance indicator (KPI) because it is unlikely to fully reflect the significance of the works performed or their benefits to individuals and society. The thesis reviews value-for-money audit as a tool for addressing such challenges and discusses its strengths and shortcomings. It concludes by putting forward critical success factors for such approaches to be effective.

The subject is highly pertinent to my work. I am pleased that I garnered many insights from working on the doctoral thesis.

As the Executive Director, HKCO, could you describe your main roles and areas of responsibility? Could you describe your typical day at work? Is there ever a typical day at work?

If I may describe my job scope in a broadly simplified way: anything other than conducting and performing on stage falls under my responsibility. There really is no "typical day" because of our daily challenges.

The main areas of my work include fostering an environment conducive to creativity for our artists, detailed planning and liaison work for overseas concert tours, brand building and marketing, and communicating with stakeholders and the public. I am glad I have the strong support of a professional team to execute the many demanding projects and day-to-day work. One of the challenges HKCO faces in the future is that while Chinese music has been a long-established cultural heritage, it remains a niche form of art/leisure activity in Hong Kong. Factors impeding its growth in popularity include misconceptions that Chinese music equates to Cantonese opera and preconceptions that it is old-fashioned and an outdated form/style of music. These views of Chinese music are hardly what the music of HKCO is about. The orchestra redefined the experience of listening to classical Chinese music with its rich orchestral sound. Its contemporary and experimental performances make Chinese music relevant to modern-day life and sustainable as an art form. It is no easy task to cultivate public understanding and develop an interest in HKCO's music. For this, my team and I work continuously on branding to persuade and engage the public.

A large part of this is in encouraging the young generation to learn Chinese musical instruments; HKCO organises orientation sessions in addition to music classes. We observe that parents usually select the *erhu*, the most widely known Chinese musical instrument, for their children to learn. While it is most encouraging that parents arrange for their children to learn Chinese music, we want to connect them with a broader range of musical instruments. Through our "Choose Your Own Chinese Musical Instruments" project, parents and their children attend sessions and get hands-on experience trying them out. This enables families to find an instrument that suits their child's temperament, which may make learning more enjoyable and lasting.

As the Executive Director, HKCO, could you describe your working relationships with the orchestra players and the Music Director of HKCO? Could you describe your management and leadership style? Would you describe yourself as a servant leader or a participative leader? What type of idea leadership style is best suited for a performing arts organisation like HKCO?

I see myself as a participative leader. I value partnerships for creating and achieving things together, which applies to my relationships with both the artists and the administration teams.

I aim to partner with the artists to help actualise their artistic visions and talents. To use musical instrument research as an example, I ensured that HKCO assigned appropriate resources and had an effective infrastructure to support the huge endeavour. We first created a dedicated position, Research Development Officer (Musical Instrument), under the Education and Research Department in 2003. We facilitated the transfer of Mr. Yuen Shi-chun, who was previously the Principal of Liuqin and had the expertise and commitment to modernising Chinese musical instruments, to the position. We enabled further support by setting up a Research and Development Department with Mr. Yuen as its director in 2004. We also placed the Instrument Reform Project under HKCO's regular establishment to obtain a stable stream of resources. HKCO's Artistic Director, Mr. Yan Huichang, also became the head of the Instrument Study Group, and Mr. Yuen was among the deputy heads. The strong leadership added weight to the project and affirmed HKCO's commitment.

An interesting episode on partnership is the *Erhu* Festival in 2001. We were to assemble 900+ *erhu* players at the Tsimshatsui waterfront to perform together to promote Chinese music to the public. We worked on the daunting logistics of how the large group was to actually perform. For example, there was insufficient space to put hundreds of musical stands. We brainstormed many ideas, including desperate but creative ones, such as attaching the scores onto the back of every musician so that the person behind can read and play accordingly. Finally, we came up with a small but innovative idea: to use the *erhu* itself as the stand. I sought help from the Hong Kong Repertory Theatre with their mastery of props to custom-make a tiny clip-on device for holding musical scores that could be placed unobtrusively onto the *erhu* of each musician. The event was a big success, attracting a lot of media attention. It was a great experience in which I, my team and orchestra members worked together for solutions.

Profit-making organisations versus performing arts organisations (like HKCO) – what are the major differences in managing the finances and the human resources between these two types of organisations? What is the definition of effective financial and human resources management in a performing arts organisation like HKCO?

Profit-making is a core KPI for commercial organisations. Their main outcomes, such as volume of goods produced and sold, are tangible and can be expressed as figures for evaluation.

HKCO, too, generates income. However, as discussed in my doctoral thesis, relying on revenues or other standard KPIs as the determining parameters for measuring performing arts organisations may eclipse or distort the intangible but important outputs of such organisations. The Hong Kong government recognises the special nature of arts organisations. It adopts a value-for-money audit to examine the economy, efficiency and effectiveness of their activities. For such an approach to be effective, more thoughts need to be invested into deciphering the intangible values. Understanding auditors and the nature of arts groups and the industry is also essential to adequately measure their effectiveness.

Let me give some examples to illustrate the intangible values of HKCO's activities.

HKCO's mission is to strive for artistic excellence and develop Chinese music. While its repertoire includes well-known and popular works, it also commissions and performs contemporary and experimental pieces that may only appeal to a niche audience but are artistic milestones in the development of Chinese music. These high-quality avant-garde works are indispensable in HKCO's contribution to propelling the development of contemporary Chinese music and in HKCO's rise to international status as a leading Chinese orchestra. If we were to use box office sales or social media *likes* alone to measure the effectiveness of such works, we would be missing out on their critical values. Similarly, the value of HKCO's work in nurturing young artists and composers may surpass their immediate results, such as the number of classes held or new compositions produced. Concert tours and participation in government overseas promotions help elevate the status of Chinese music and the image of Hong Kong, which cannot be fully expressed in figures. Just as importantly, the mental pleasure of music and the contribution of such to society are essential outputs of HKCO.

Regarding your human resources question, I work with our HR team to provide a supportive environment that encourages our artists and administrative staff to reach their artistic potential/goals. Self-actualisation brings fulfilment. This utmost form of satisfaction is fuel for motivation for the individual artist. The concerted efforts of artists to excel will enable HKCO to attain peak after peak of artistic achievements.

What are the current difficulties and challenges in financial management faced by a majority of arts and cultural administrators in Hong Kong?

Close to eighty percent of HKCO's funding is from the government. Box office and sponsorship contribute the remaining twenty percent in approximately equal proportion. While HKCO can increase its revenue by simply raising the price of tickets, we are cautious about this approach as higher prices may deter concertgoers, which will do a disservice to HKCO's goal of sharing music with the public.

HKCO is among the nine designated performing arts groups that receive government support. We are very appreciative of the funding from the government for HKCO, and this has been steady over the years. Our challenge, as discussed previously, is more about finding a performance evaluation approach that considers the intangible values generated by performing arts organisations.

What are the current difficulties and challenges in human resources management faced by a majority of arts and cultural administrators in Hong Kong?

I cannot speak for other organisations, as the issue HKCO has may not be common among other arts groups. Specifically, HKCO is finding it difficult to attract artists from the Mainland.

We work hard to groom local musicians, but the Mainland remains the chief source of talent for HKCO. We find it is becoming increasingly difficult to recruit artists from there.

Hong Kong used to be the desired destination for Mainland artists. Its appeal has diminished in recent years as orchestras in Mainland China become more established. They can now offer overseas performances and other opportunities similar to those offered by HKCO. As such, Mainland artists may choose to remain there to pursue their careers. Moreover, the relatively high cost of living in Hong Kong acts as a disincentive to them. Aggravating the situation is that HKCO has lost a few artists during COVID-19 as they resigned to reunite with their families in the Mainland. We hope to be able to solicit more sponsorships so we can improve the remuneration package for artists.

What parts of your job as the Executive Director of HKCO do you find most rewarding? And which do you find most frustrating?

It is most gratifying to see HKCO being recognised as the foremost Chinese orchestra globally. I am also very much moved by the appreciation our listeners show and also the impact of a constructive social role played by HKCO. I can't thank the local audience enough for their unfailing support throughout the years. When an overseas audience applauds our performance with standing ovations, it always gives me goosebumps because they tell us that, despite being unfamiliar with Chinese music, HKCO's performance has such a moving quality they find strong resonance in. I am also pleased that our branding efforts are seeing results. With the support given to our annual Hong Kong Drum Festival since 2003, the number of participants in the Hong Kong Young Chinese Orchestra and music classes continues to increase.

Even so, I would like to see Chinese music further grow in popularity. Currently, the ratio of learning Chinese and Western musical instruments, as well as the audience for Chinese and Western music concerts, in Hong Kong is approximately 1:3. HKCO will continue to work hard towards popularising Chinese music.

COVID-19 has turned the world upside down. How have HKCO and you (as the Executive Director) been coping with COVID-19?

COVID-19 forced HKCO to cancel its concerts inside and outside Hong Kong. It also deprived us of face-to-face interaction with the public as our community programmes and fan meetings had to be cancelled.

However, thanks to the dedication of our artists and administrative staff, HKCO was quick to turn the crisis into an opportunity.

HKCO had a strong online presence and upped its online engagement with the public. We showed solidarity with Hong Kong through the #DrumChallenge social media campaign. Our percussion artists cheered Hong Kong with uplifting drum beats on HKCO's YouTube channel. Public members got creative in response to our open invitation and submitted videos of their drum sessions using pots and pans in the kitchen or anything they could tap on. HKCO also supported the performing arts industry by organising the Hong Kong Net Festival to feature works and performances by composers and musicians. The event provided financial support to industry members as their work opportunities dwindled during the pandemic.

HKCO further engaged the public with its music by working with 3HK to produce a "5G. Syncs with the Power of Drums" online concert in June 2020. This marked HKCO as the first performing arts group in Hong Kong to adopt 5G technology to live stream outdoor concerts. It was available for viewing on the official websites and social media channels of both HKCO and 3HK. The concert was also streamed live by Metro Broadcast, KKBOX, hmvod and JOOX. A month after the success of this event, HKCO hosted another online event by transforming the 2020 edition of Music From The Heart into an online concert. In addition, HKCO enriched the contents of its YouTube channel by producing music videos (MVs) and uploading videos of past performances. The MVs were a hit on the Internet and social media, with over 10 million views. HKCO was invited by renowned cultural platforms such as Nowness to feature the MVs there, a recognition of both HKCO's music and the quality of its MVs. On an individual level, our artists took turns appearing online to engage with viewers.

Looking back, HKCO was quick to venture beyond the established means of delivering Chinese music, such as concert performances and music recordings. Our experience has shown that Chinese music can achieve great results by leveraging state-of-the-art 5G technology and the consumer trend of video watching. Our MVs' cinematic renditions of Chinese music elevate the appeal of this traditional art form to the contemporary viewer. These originally ad hoc activities in response to venue closure and social distancing protocols have broadened HKCO's performance formats and audience reach. Many of them have since been incorporated into HKCO's regular programmes.

What percentage of your revenue comes from box office sales? To what extent has COVID-19 affected the annual revenue of HKCO?

As mentioned earlier, box office sales contribute around 10% of our revenue. While concert cancellation did mean a loss of income, it created opportunities for HKCO to redeploy resources originally assigned for concert staging to support the production of new online programmes such as MVs and the Net Festival. It also made the refurbishment of the HKCO studio possible to support 5G broadcasting capabilities so we can have the economy of hosting 5G live stream events in our own venue in the future.

HKCO "attained many awards including 'The Most Outstanding Achievement in Advancing Contemporary Chinese Music' by the ISCM World Music Days 2002 Hong Kong and a new Guinness World Record for the highest number of erhu players performing at the same time" - what do such accolades mean to you (as the Executive Director) and HKCO musicians on both a professional and personal level?

The many awards are affirmations of HKCO as a world-class Chinese orchestra, in particular HKCO's contribution to the advancement of contemporary Chinese music. To use HKCO's commissioned work, Jing-Qi-Shen (《精．氣．神》), as an example, the piece is recognised as the epitome of contemporary Chinese music, albeit it was deemed too abstract for the general audience when it premiered in 1998. It won second place in the International Contemporary Music Exchange Concert organised by the International Music Council of UNESCO in 2001. Despite its success, I was still worried when HKCO included Jing-Qi-Shen in its programme for its Russian tour in 2013, having been told that Russian audiences were upfront and they would boo or even walk out if they didn't find a performance to their liking. It turned out that my worry was unnecessary. Jing-Qi-Shen sent the audience into a rapture, and they started shouting "encore" immediately after the piece ended. The orchestra was certainly surprised by the encore in the middle of the concert, but we were all elated! Even today, jing-Qi-Shen is well received by local and overseas audiences, demonstrating its powerful language, universality and timelessness. We last performed this great piece in February 2020 at the Müpa Budapest in Hungary before the global lockdown pandemic. Readers are welcome to experience performances at the HKCO Net Concert Hall (See: www.hkconetconcerthall.com).

HKCO attained three Guinness World Records for having the most people playing the *erhu*, the drum and the *dizi,* respectively. These events represent our large-scale efforts in promoting Chinese music. Also, as illustrated previously, their success resulted from the seamless partnership between the artists and the administration team.

Any other interesting and inspiring stories regarding HKCO that you wish to share with the readers?

HKCO has been on an amazing journey since its inception. I would very much like to invite the readers to learn more about our music by watching our YouTube channel, attending our concerts, classes, and community activities.

Photo Credit: HKCO

Photo 1. Dr Celina Chin, Executive Director of Hong Kong Chinese Orchestra.

Photo Credit: HKCO

Photo 2. HKCO attained three Guinness World Records for having the most people playing the erhu (2001), the drum (2003) and the dizi (2005), respectively. The Hong Kong Drum Festival organized after the SARs outbreak in 2003 has now become an annual mega event that includes community drum classes, professional concerts and the Hong Kong Synergy 24 Drum Competition since then.

Photo Credit: HKCO

Photo 3. Under the baton of Yan Huichang, HKCO Artistic Director cum Conductor for Life, the Orchestra gave a concert at the Carnegie Hall in 2009 as part of the "Ancient Paths, Modern Voices: Celebrating Chinese Culture" Festival presented by the Carnegie Hall. Leading by Maestro Yan, audience performed with the Orchestra with the rattle drum during the piece "The Yellow River Capriccio" and the concert ended with enthusiastic standing ovation from capacity audience.

Photo Credit: HKCO

Photo 4. HKCO toured in Switzerland, Germany, Belgium, Austria and Hungary in January 2020. The concert at Hungary was live broadcast to the world via the renowned classical music broadcast platform, Medici TV.

Photo Credit: HKCO

Photo 5. 'Victoria Harbour at Night – Inaugural Cruise from the Home Port' – To celebrate the inaugural cruise from the home port Hong Kong after three-year suspension during the Covid-19 pandemic (March 10, 2023). Supported by cutting-edge technology, the concert conducted by Maestro Yan Huichang, featured an uplifting musical programme showcasing Victoria Harbour in all its glory and provided a spectacular 5G audio-visual experience for viewers in Hong Kong and overseas.

Photo Credit: HKCO

Photo 6. 'Ji' – The performance has music as the overall vehicle of expression, and blends other forms of performing arts, such as modern dance, movement, Taichi Wushu Dance and children's choral singing. The result was an insightful showcase of traditional Chinese cultural thinking of tai chi. (July 15-16, 2022 at the Grand Theatre of Hong Kong Cultural Centre)

Photo Credit: HKCO

Photo 7. HKCO took the audience on an unforgettable journey through time with a combination of traditional and futuristic works from Western and Chinese genres, featuring Cantonese opera and cutting-edge arts and stage technology at "Hong Kong Arts Festival – The Stage Door on Mars" concert on March 17-18, 2023 at the Concert Hall of Hong Kong City Hall.

Photo Credit: HKCO

Photo 8. 環保胡琴 Eco-huqin series_左起 from left_ 高胡 Gaohu、 中胡 Zhonghu
、 二胡 Erhu、低音革胡 Bass Gehu、革胡 Gehu. The Eco-Huqin series which the
Orchestra developed has won not only the 4th Ministry of Culture Innovation Award
in 2012, but also many other awards presented by various institutions for its green
and innovative concepts.

Chapter 16

Colin Touchin, Presenter, RTHK Radio 4

Introduction

Colin Touchin is a British conductor, composer, clarinettist, recorder player, festival adjudicator and broadcaster. His distinguished career includes fifteen years as Director of Music at the University of Warwick, and conductor of award-winning ensembles, including the University of Warwick Chamber Choir, Warwickshire County Youth Orchestra and Birmingham Schools' Wind Orchestra. He has conducted the National Youth Wind Orchestras of Great Britain, Wales, Luxembourg and Hong Kong and has founded several ensembles in the UK, notably the Spires Philharmonic Orchestra, Chorus and Youth Orchestra in Coventry and the National Youth Recorder Orchestra.

Currently based in Hong Kong, he is the Musical Director of the Hong Kong Welsh Male Voice Choir, Grace Notes, an acapella female choir and guest conductor of the Tak-Ming Philharmonic Winds. He hosts a weekly programme on Saturday mornings for RTHK Radio 4. He has guest conducted the Hong Kong Police Band, City Chamber Orchestra of Hong Kong in concert with singing star Hayley Westenra, and numerous performances of The Snowman & The Bear since 2011. In the following interview, Colin Touchin discusses his experiences leading the Lufthansa Orchestra in Frankfurt as the Chief Conductor, as well as his path to becoming the presenter of the RTHK Radio 4 classical music programme.

Could we begin this interview by first introducing yourself, for example, your professional training and educational background? For instance, what did you study at the university or music college? Do you come from a family of musicians or performing artists?

My name is Colin Touchin, and I've been in Hong Kong on and off since 1996. At home in Manchester, in the UK, we had an upright piano, and my older brother and I started piano lessons before we were ten years old. My father had played the piano for his father, a bass singer, in oratorio performances in Bristol, and he had a good record collection. We would listen together and chatted about music often when he would drive me to the local amateur orchestras, where he was both a librarian and timpanist, and I was a clarinettist. After school in Manchester, where I studied clarinet with Graham Turner of the Halle Orchestra, I gained a diploma on the recorder at the age of 16 and conducted it for the first time around the same period. I went on to read music at Keble College, Oxford [University], where I carried on playing and singing in some 500 performances in 3 years ranging from the 12th-century Play of Daniel to world premieres, composing and conducting. There was also family talk of earlier ancestors being in the Bournemouth Symphony Orchestra at the turn of the 19th to the 20th century and also a leader of the first all-woman mandolin band, but I've never been able to confirm these stories!

What motivated you to leave your home country (UK) to set up a base for your 'show business' career in Hong Kong?

I was one of three music staff members at the University of Warwick (where I was Director of Music from 1989 to 2003) chosen to spend a week in Hong Kong in the 1990's to spread the word about our university and encourage applications. While I went to ESF schools, the Hong Kong Youth Arts Festival, and Music Office ensembles, I was encouraged to consider moving to Hong Kong. Twenty years later, after my first visit, I made the move. However, I have returned regularly to Hong Kong since that first awe-inspiring visit, sometimes five times in one year and once for five consecutive weeks. My now wife Alicia had also made contacts in Hong Kong, and we felt we could contribute to the development of artistic and cultural ideas by moving here, so we decided in 2015 that we would make a permanent move from our Coventry home, and indeed we've continued to develop our business interests and enjoyment of the artistic community (she is involved in excellent new jewellery design using amber).

Could you describe your experience as the Chief Conductor of the Lufthansa Orchestra in Frankfurt?

This heart-warming opportunity developed from another contact at the University of Warwick: a postgraduate violinist there became a flight attendant for Lufthansa, and the airline established its own Symphony Orchestra. She remembered my work conducting the university orchestra and asked if I might be interested in attending Frankfurt and conducting one of their concerts. After the first 2 hours of rehearsal, the committee drew me to one side for a private chat. I thought I'd done something terribly wrong, but they simply wanted to offer me a permanent position as their chief conductor. We've worked together for several years and hope conditions will allow us to meet again to celebrate the orchestra's 10th anniversary in November 2021. As you might expect, they are very well organised and determined to play well and always improve – it is an excellent and friendly working arrangement, and I'm apparently the only one who can ever get away with telling the pilots what to do! The players come from many areas of the airline – flight crew, ground crew, technical, research and hospitality, etc. It includes some ex-professional musicians, so there is a very high standard of playing and commitment. This is one of those serendipitous 213elationshipps, from the first moment we hit it off, the goal being to make great music together. The company regards our work highly and has invited us to perform in Puerto Rico and Sofia at Lufthansa Technik facilities as a flagship cultural ambassador, we have hopes to appear in Manila, and if that comes off, we hope to drop in on Hong Kong, too!

Could you describe your experience as the Musical Director of the Hong Kong Welsh Male Voice Choir and the Founder/Conductor of the British Brass Company of Hong Kong?

I have conducted the City Chamber Orchestra of Hong Kong in the (almost) annual *Snowman and The Bear* programmes, except one year where we replaced this with a solo soprano Hayley Westenra concert. Also, the Hong Kong Welsh Male Voice Choir was invited to participate. While rehearsing with them, we seemed to get on well, so when I was more permanently based here, and their conductor was due to return to Wales, I took the opportunity to put my name forward, and they invited me to become their Musical Director. In 2019 we celebrated the choir's 40th anniversary by releasing a CD (A Welsh Fortyssimo) and by going to the great Llangollen International Eisteddfod, the first time the choir had actually sung in Wales; we sang ten performances in six days. After one, a regular local listener at the festival addressed me: "You can't be from Hong Kong! Only voices from the valleys can sing like that!" – a great compliment and an example of the immediately warm and impressed response the choir generates in Hong Kong, thailand, the Philippines, London's Royal Albert Hall, and elsewhere. Again, this is a very well-organised, deeply committed ensemble of enthusiastic music-makers, and we have some very enjoyable rehearsals and performances sharing traditional Welsh and international music with loyal and new audiences.

About three years ago, some local brass players approached me with the notion of forming a UK-style Brass Band, so we set up the BBC-HK – the British Brass Company of Hong Kong. One of our first performances was with the HK Welsh Male Voice Choir on St. David's Day (1st March) that year, and we immediately impacted the musical community. Although it will be a while before such a wind-based ensemble can meet safely and regularly again post-COVID, we are planning new events and look forward to becoming a regular event in the HK music calendar.

Could you describe your path to becoming an RTHK Radio 4 classical music programme presenter?

Five years ago, I was invited to present a Saturday morning music programme standing in for another presenter. After a couple of months, the proposal came from Jimmy Shiu that we re-name and re-style the programme along the lines of what is now In Touch With Music – one hour each of chamber, choral and wind band music. I draw the selections from my own CD collection (to which I'm frequently adding new titles!), and we aim to provide some recognised composers and performers, but also many less-well-known or completely new names to vary the repertoire and hopefully maintain a good level of interest in what we broadcast each week. It also makes me listen to and learn about composers and music I've never encountered, so it's part of my ongoing musical education.

From this opportunity, I have also been invited to present further series of programmes about musical terminology, the orchestra's history, music for recorders, Songs of the Earth and introduced Live on four concerts, including one or two live events.

RTHK Radio presenters versus producers – what are the major differences in their functional roles and areas of responsibilities?

Broadly speaking, the presenter is the voice you hear introducing and linking the performances, while the producer is monitoring and sometimes controlling the style, duration, intensity and communicative delivery of the person in the studio behind the voice, and also ensuring that the final recording is of appropriate and consistent quality in technical terms. Many of the presenters are also occasional producers, and some of the producers are occasional presenters. It helps each know the work of the other and enables sympathetic and effective cooperation and artistic collaboration.

DJ (disc jockey) versus presenters versus broadcaster – what are the major differences in their functional roles and areas of responsibilities?

The broadcaster is often taken to mean the organisation as a whole and might be regarded as an almost impersonal administrative system. But the people within the system value their personal skills and development highly, motivating them to continue to contribute effectively to the output broadcast on radio or tv. A DJ is commonly thought to be someone who spins discs for light entertainment, but this is, at its height, one of the most difficult and skilful jobs in presenting. DJ's know the tempos, keys and sonority of each track well, so they can be blended together into a seamless patchwork of stylishly consistent music. A presenter can rise to a similar level, but the role sometimes is seen to be rather like a living library index card system: providing some brief programme notes about the composer or the music or the performers, or all three elements required to make a successful and memorable listening experience. We've all heard enthusiastic presenters who draw us into the listening experience, we eagerly share the music they introduce, and perhaps we've also heard some less immediately engaging deliveries which, however knowledgeably constructed, don't quite grab our attention the same way. In each instance, there may be a happy ideal of inviting and engaging with the listener in a manner appropriate to the material. It is important to avoid coming across as more important or more memorable than the created work itself.

Could you describe your working relationships with Stacey Rodda (RTHK Radio 4 Producer) and Jimmy Shiu (Director, RTHK Radio)?

Excellent.

What makes a good and popular classical music radio presenter?

In the UK, I've admired those voices that make you feel genuinely at home, wherever you're listening; I respect those who share facts with a natural sense of revealing things known and unknown without making me feel I'm out of my depth or ignorant of too much that is about to be performed; and I love presenters who unashamedly share their passion and knowledge just as if they were your favourite university lecturer at home having a coffee together. So, solid information, passion for the subject, and a genuinely warm-hearted character are the qualities we might recall similar to your best and favourite school teachers!

Given the overwhelming amount of classical music performances freely available on YouTube and other online platforms, why do/should people still listen to classical music presented by professionally trained musicians as presenters on the radio?

An online platform can provide the musical performance itself, but it usually doesn't offer much background information about the people who made it, why it was written, or the circumstances during which the artist struggled to make it come to life. Sure, one can do additional online research in/on one's own time, but it's never as personal as the human voice presenting, and these days I sense more people value this human element, even more now than maybe 10 or 20 years ago. We are indeed traversing an evolution by media of what we appreciate in our local and more distant culture, but we are also beginning to realise that we have become more distanced from much of what we value through the very technology which otherwise has made that resource more immediately available. There will always be a demand for the human element, and we must aim to keep it human, too!

Do you consider Hong Kong a "cultural desert"?

No. In every country I've been fortunate to visit, many things work well or not so well. Hong Kong is no different in having some very successful and well-established cultural programmes, while also missing out on some helpful infrastructure. On my first visit, I noticed that each musical organisation wants to go on its own, is reluctant to collaborate with others, and is almost afraid to share in case someone might steal their ideas or place them in the artistic hierarchy. This is the main negative of Hong Kong's musical life, as I see it – the unwillingness to share artists, projects and members – although there are exceptions to this observation, as in every other place. For example, in the UK, we have effective organisations advising and helping small concert promoters, music teachers, composers, performers, administrators, etc.; these have not taken hold in Hong Kong to any significant degree. Maybe there is a general reluctance to want to belong to any organising body. But there is much to be gained from combining the time and effort expended by one group to promote a visiting performer or educator that other groups could share. It would be good to reduce the suspicion between apparently competing ensembles and increase the genuine respect for each other's aims and achievements.

That said, I see in Hong Kong (pre-Covid, and now re-emerging) a vibrant and varied cultural programme encompassing music, art, drama, sculpture, architecture, photography, film and design, which is rich, entertaining, intriguing, sometimes daring, sometimes innovative, and often keenly passionate. The level of culture required to lift a city or country out of the "desert" description is easily surpassed by what happens here, even when compared with other great arts and music capitals worldwide. Hong Kong cannot have everything, and neither can New York, Vienna, or London – what each has is fascinatingly diverse and committed to engaging their communities as deeply and fully as possible.

You have conducted and led workshops for students and teachers in 20 countries, including Taiwan and China. Could you describe the overall arts and cultural scene in Hong Kong – in particular, the concert-goers and opera-goers in Hong Kong- their appreciation and appetite for Western classical music – compared to China and Taiwan?

When I first attended serious concerts in Hong Kong in the late 1990's, there might be some distracting noise from the audience, as not everybody seemed prepared to sit silently to listen with complete concentration. Restlessness can be caused by the quality of what's happening on the stage, of course, but this behaviour often occurs despite the high level of entertainment. Recent years have witnessed a real change in this respect. Although music can often be maltreated as a mere backdrop at social functions, the artists receiving limited attention or respect.

In China, I have conducted several concerts in large halls where the listeners seemed very diligent and attentive and gave lectures with equivalent concentration. Taiwan's audiences are also very eager to listen and learn: I would say that the young people there (school-age) show more willingness to sit patiently while the music is performed, whatever their feelings about their situation or the quality of the programme.

However, one of the worst audiences I conducted before was in Vienna in the 80's, at a high school, where we performed some Mozart – the standard of behaviour was typified by the school's music teacher talking loudly to her students while we played, and not about the music. One of our hopes with music education is to encourage respectful behaviour by all listeners. They can hear and learn, and so can those sitting next to them, if everyone sits still while the music develops and wraps them in its magic. From mere passive hearing, we also must encourage active listening; this is a very specific and vital distinction.

What parts of your job as a presenter of RTHK Radio 4 do you find most rewarding, and which do you find most frustrating?

Fortunately, very little frustration enters my life as I am naturally a patient character, and I realise we all fall short of ideals requiring us to be sympathetic towards and accepting of each other when things don't go exactly according to plan. The moral is to make flexible plans, not to expect or insist on every detail working out perfectly every time. I would love to know more about the audience listening when I'm talking about the music. I would be interested to know if they would like to know more about a composer's life story or the titles of the music we perform. It is gratifying that acquaintances and strangers have approached me from time to time to thank me for including such-and-such a piece in a programme, or to enquire for further information about a less familiar work. One big reward, therefore, is confirmation that we are providing something useful and desirable in the selection and variety of the playlists. And, as I indicated above, the opportunity for me to listen to and learn about new people and music in this huge field of "classical" music is always a source of delight and inspiration.

As a conductor and radio programme presenter, were there any situations in the past where you had to rely on your own skills and experiences to find solutions to a problem at the last moment to keep the show running?

Indeed, as a conductor, I lived through several unexpected moments in concerts: a soloist stopping mid-way through the third movement of the Beethoven Piano Concerto No. 4 saying: "I'm sorry, I've forgotten what comes next" (after a brief conversation we re-started successfully and as undemonstratively as possible; at the interval, one listener said they were enjoying it very much, so I asked "what about the concerto?" and she had apparently not noticed the break or the chat or the re-start at all!). On another occasion, a couple of minutes into the overture, the orchestra leader lay down his violin, and then lay himself down next to his chair. He told us all he was about to suffer an epileptic fit, so we stopped playing, and called to our 2nd bassoonist, who was a practising physician and dealt with the patient efficiently and quietly; the leader's desk partner took his chair, the rest of the violins re-seated themselves, and we began the concert again. After the interval, the leader was able to re-join us.

Another soloist, at the organ this time, and therefore quite far away from the orchestra as he was in the organ loft, managed to lose his way in each of the three movements of a Handel Organ Concerto. These sections were unaccompanied, but he omitted many bars in regaining his pathway, causing me to give a few eager gestures at the orchestra to be ready to come in sooner than they had expected while counting their many bars' rest.

Most memorable, perhaps, was an amateur orchestra playing Brahms' 1st Symphony. A strong principal oboist lost half a bar in the allegro 6/8 and tried to correct herself by dropping another half-bar. Unfortunately, she had chosen the wrong half to drop, and so was now one whole bar out with the orchestra. Because she was a strong player, she took the whole wind section with her, so I now had the strings and wind playing together when they should be answering each other. I gestured, I waved, I looked pleadingly in each direction where there might be some recognition of the problem and its potential solution, but well, when the players know something is wrong, they often put their heads further down into their music, rather than looking up to the one person who might just be able to help them! (Nowadays, I always say the musical part is a question paper with no answers on it – players have to look up and listen out to find the answers around them.) Eventually, we reached the recapitulation, at last, a well-known landmark in the music, and everyone was once again on the same bar at the same time. Listening to the recording, the music is wrong for 106 bars, and one of the trumpeters, who has only a little to do in that movement, somewhat quizzically looked me in the eye as we reached the double bar of that first movement and gave a little handclap and head-nod, as much to say, "Well done, mate, you got through that, just, by the skin of your teeth"!

What would you like to be remembered for when you retire?

I have no intention of retiring: I'll keep sharing music and my love of music with all who want to make it and listen to it as long as I can. But if there is one thing, we might all aim to put on our epitaph, it could be: "He made a difference".

Why do we turn to music in times of crisis?

Music exists because it expresses feelings that we have decided cannot be suitably or sufficiently expressed in any other way or through other media, i.e., words, paintings, architecture, sculpture, etc. Some music has indeed the potential to soothe unhappy, disturbed or grieving souls on a temporary or regular basis, while some inspire action, positive and constructive, as well as negative, violent and destructive.

All composers have responded to their surroundings and circumstances to different degrees, sometimes creating long-lasting works of inspired comfort (settings of the Requiem, for example) and sometimes depicting the pains and horrors of war alongside the peace and release following such conflicts.

There are cases, too, of music adopted for such a purpose; for example, Nimrod from Elgar's Enigma Variations has been played very often for funerals, yet it was originally a depiction by the composer of an intimate, friendly dialogue about Beethoven's late quartets; and equally famously, Barber's Adagio for strings was originally the slow second movement of a string quartet, which he arranged the same year (1936) for string orchestra. It became the go-to music for lamenting once it was broadcast in America in 1945, commemorating the death of President Roosevelt.

Why do we turn to music? We can cry or laugh along with music, allowing the vibrations to stimulate our physiological reactions, leading to our belief that we are being relieved. Some years ago, I did some research with a psychologist in the UK using two compilations of either upbeat or calming music recordings to investigate if specific music chords generally affected diverse members of the public, whether they originally knew the music or not. It was inconclusive! But we did find a partial correlation between certain composers' creations and some predictable emotional responses. This field of research is ongoing in several countries and was first reported to me when I was a student at Oxford in the early 1970's.

It is interesting to note that, even today, we often choose our new friends by their taste in music: look at the newspaper dating adverts, and one of the most frequent indicators for potential love matches is shared musical preferences. From this basic level, we can all count our close friends by the times we attend concerts, films or stage plays together, it is good to have some endorsement for our own likes, and so we gravitate towards those with similar taste in musical sound, cinematic art and theatrical drama.

At a deep level, our bodies react to the vibration of sound for many timbre of the cello is particularly emotional, while quite a proportion cringes slightly when the highest piccolo or violin harmonics can be heard too clearly. Our hearing systems vary so much, and our life experiences prepare us to accept, tolerate or reject specific sound worlds through training or merely regular exposure. To endure painful moments in life, we find it simplest to be still, without words, and surround ourselves with a sound that allows us to feel, to think, to remember, timelessly and without any coercion to feel some specific response, until we feel ready again to re-enter reality.

In such times, this process can both endorse and encourage our feelings, releasing what might otherwise have been locked inside; music acts as an ointment to draw out the poison and begin the healing.

Beyond this, of course, maybe we just like the sound it makes?!

Photo 1. Colin Touchin.

Photo 2. Combined Lufthansa KonzertChor, Lufthansa Sinfonisches Orchester and Spires Philharmonic Choir from Coventry, Brahms *Requiem* in Frankfurt 2019.

Photo 3. Hong Kong Welsh Male Voice Choir on main stage, Llangollen Eisteddfod, 2019.

Photo 4. Lufthansa Sinfonisches Orchester, Frankfurt Airport, 2017.

Chapter 17

Dr. Winton Au, Founder, One Month One Art

Introduction

Funded by the Chinese University of Hong Kong, One Month, One Art (OMOA) is set up with the mission to develop attending art performances as a habit amongst young university students that integrates into their daily lives. Founded by Dr. Winton Au in 2020, OMOA. Dr. Winton is currently an Associate Professor in the Psychology Department, The Chinese University of Hong Kong (CUHK). In the following interview, Winton talks about the motivation that led him to found OMOA at CUHK, as well as the immeasurable psychological benefits that arts participation could bring to young people and society at large.

Could we begin this interview by first introducing yourself, for example, your professional training and educational background? For instance, what did you study at the university? Do you come from a family of artists, musicians, performing artists or creative people?

I received this training in psychology in the USA. I got this undergraduate degree at the University of Wisconsin in Madison, and my PhD degree at the University of Illinois in Urbana-Champaign. After graduating, I returned to Hong Kong to teach Psychology and have been at The Chinese University of Hong Kong ever since. There is nothing related to arts in my family upbringing. My copywriter sister is the closest thing to a creative person. When I was young, I had limited piano lessons up to Grade 5, the most "formal" performing arts training I have ever received.

I did not encounter performing arts again until 2006, when I was simply looking for some leisure activities. My criterion was to do something that was not work-related. I thought about ceramics or making glasses, but then I did not want to get my hands dirty. Somehow, I came across short-term drama acting classes offered by HKAPA EXCEL (The Hong Kong Academy for Performing Arts Extension and Continuing Education for Life). The first lesson was quite an unusual experience for me. I had to take off my shoes, and there were no desks or chairs, standing almost the whole time and not taking any notes. The drama teacher was CHAN Wing Chuen, the first batch of graduates in HKAPA drama school. Soon I was taking many more drama classes offered by him and also other drama courses offered by other teachers. Very much a drama enthusiast, I even took a one-month course over the summer to study clown and bouffon under Philip Gaultier, and another one-month in summer to study masks in the USA.

Could you briefly introduce One Month One Art (OMOA), including its mission, philosophy behind its operations, and funding sources?

OMOA's visions, missions, and goals are as follows:

- 願景　Vision:　建立欣賞表演藝術的習慣，讓藝術融入生活，變成一種生活態度。To develop attending art performances as a habit that integrates into daily life
- 使命　　　Mission:　　　建立以觀眾爲本的藝術平台，令香港成為藝術最普及的城市，凝聚熱愛藝術的觀衆。To develop an audience centric platform making Hong Kong the city with the most art lovers
- 目標 Goal: 培養一月一次欣賞藝術表演的習慣。To cultivate a habit to enjoy an art event every month

For physical health, we are advised to drink 8 glasses of water a day, do 30 minutes of exercise, and sleep 8 hours a day. For our arts and cultural health, perhaps we attend one art event a month. Among people who attend art events, it is about two times a year that people go to some kind of performing arts. The name of the organisation and its motto is to develop a mindset that encourages people to be regular patrons of arts activities. Perhaps we may never achieve the goal of attending an art event once a month, but knowing that we are not reaching this goal is a step forward to drive us to engage in arts more. This organisation has only been established for one year. The first project received funding from a social impact fund provided by The Chinese University of Hong Kong to support a theatre docent scheme. We are gathering theatre enthusiasts to provide them with training to prepare theatre appreciation guides for the audience. The major project we are still seeking funding is to develop an app as a performing arts marketing platform. We aim to implement a loyalty scheme as a marketing tactic to encourage more arts participation. The app shall also be able to provide more targeted information to bring the "right" arts to the "right" people.

What motivated you to set up OMOA?

My original interest is in psychology research to understand audience experience. However, I soon realised that art groups are not quite interested in audience experience; they are more interested in bringing in an audience. Over 4-5 years, I talked to 20+ theatre professionals to understand what they thought the industry lacked. I gathered from these interviews that the industry lacked an audience development platform to promote theatre as a whole. Each theatre group promotes its own production; but hardly anyone promotes theatre as a whole. The initial goal is to promote theatre; however, some people suggested that perhaps promoting performing arts, in general, should be a more encompassing mission.

You are currently serving as an Associate Professor in the Psychology Department, The Chinese University of Hong Kong. How do your teaching and research experiences as a psychology professor contribute to your current work as the Founder of OMOA?

I want to believe that my training in psychology gives me an insightful understanding of audience psychology. My research background allows me to conduct various audience experience projects with different art groups both large and small, which I think have helped me understand the motivations and barriers to arts engagement. One concrete application of psychology research is developing a feedback scheme in the app that OMOA is developing. Instead of the typical "like" button that people use to give their feedback, we ask the audience to give feedback on a show with buttons of "intellectually stimulating," "emotional contagion," and "sensational," which are the key attributes research has found in audience experience.

I think my being an academic in a university and NOT a theatre practitioner puts me in a nice neutral position to promote arts. What I am promoting about arts is definitely not out of self-interest to get more audience to have a bigger box office. I guess the neutral academic position has this advantage. Instead of how my university work adds to OMOA, I would say it is actually the work in OMOA that adds to my university work. While reaching out to different performing arts people, I expanded much of my network and connections, which have facilitated me in developing research opportunities to get access to data.

OMOA aims to "offer a fresh perspective into art performances via a guided experience" – why is it so important to offer a fresh perspective to art performances? In addition, via what channels and platforms does OMOA aim to achieve that?

I guess this quote is about the theatre docent scheme that OMOA is doing right now. The emphasis on "guided experience" is simply that survey over survey has shown that one of the top barriers to engaging in arts is not understanding what art is. The docent scheme is about providing more background information and pointers on how to appreciate the artwork. Reader's response theory would say that an artwork is what a viewer sees. We are not imposing what we or the artists think of the artwork onto the viewer. However, artists should also not be adamant about telling the viewers if the viewers want to know. To novices, literally, they have no clue even where to begin to make sense of an artwork. The idea of guided experience is to provide them with a perspective on how to look at things. This is all part of arts education to help viewers develop their own tastes and confidence to interpret independently.

According to the OMOA Homepage, "Does it surprise you that for every $10 of salary paid by the arts and culture industry, an additional $20 is generated in the wider economy through indirect and induced multiplier impact?" Could you provide examples to illustrate your point?

I don't have examples to prove this point; I simply "believe" the report making this assertion. Perhaps this is not vigorous enough on my part to blindly believe what this report says. However, for return-on-investment calculation, quite a bit of guesswork goes into the equation, as I have also learnt from personnel assessment, supposedly my area of expertise, when computing the savings of using good employee selection tools. There are vigorous equations, but some numbers put into the equations could, at best, be educated guesses.

Could you provide a list of exhibition and cultural programme highlights developed/initiated by OMOA?

Currently, we are in the middle of running the docent programmes. The theatre productions we have developed appreciation guides are shown on this page (www.1m1a.org/appreciation/). More shall be forthcoming.

What is the average age of the audience attending the OMOA exhibitions and cultural programmes?

For the docent training scheme, we have admitted 25 participants, mainly young people about 20 to 30 years old. Unfortunately, the docent materials have only been distributed online, given the COVID-19 situation, and we do not have any information on their profiles.

Young people and students in Hong Kong versus their counterparts in Taiwan, Mainland China, Singapore, and Japan – could you describe the major differences in their self-motivations and attitudes towards arts participation among the four regions?

I do not have data on their motivations. However, regarding arts participation in general, arts participation rates in Hong Kong are lower than those in other developed regions. According to HKADC (2018), 55% of Hong Kong people have participated in at least one art form in the past 12 months. In USA and UK, however, arts participation rates are 72% (Americans for the Arts, 2018) and 64% (Department for Digital, Culture, Media and Sport, 2018), and they are over 80% in other European Union countries like Denmark, Netherlands, Finland, Sweden, Iceland, Norway, and Switzerland (Eurostat, 2017). In Singapore and Taiwan, they are 78% (National Arts Council of Singapore, 2015) and 87% (Ministry of Culture of the Republic of China, 2018).

What are the current difficulties and challenges faced by OMOA in terms of audience development?

We have yet to launch the app as the primary project of OMOA in audience development. Perhaps the first challenge is finding funding to support the development and operation of the app. Some private funding provides seed money for app development. The next challenge is securing arts organisations to support the app. I see a lot of potential for art groups to put concerted effort into promoting arts in general. Being able to connect art groups to support a joint initiative is one major challenge.

In what directions do you want the OMOA to develop in the next three to five years?

The prime objective of OMOA is to develop the audience development app. The docent scheme is a side initiative that we got started. For the app, I will not underestimate its difficulty in staying afloat. Especially since LCSD has commissioned a formidable ticketing platform to replace URBTIX, we are hoping that the 1M1A app will still exist in three to five years.

Given the recent M+ Museum controversy after the introduction of Hong Kong's national security law, how do you think this would affect Hong Kong's cultural tourism industry and arts participation among young people in Hong Kong?

While definitely an embarrassment for M+ management, it is good publicity for M+, making it relevant to people here and abroad. I anticipate it will become an Easter egg treasure hunt activity for people to scrutinise what gets in there and guess what could have been left out. Sincerely, I think the whole ordeal is way overblown. But people will be ever more sensitive in putting a political spin on the selection and deselection of any artwork to be displayed.

What parts of your job as the Founder of OMOA do you find most rewarding? And which do you find most frustrating?

Most rewarding is finding a way to contribute to arts that I love as a passion and as a leisure activity into "work" that I feel like I am not "wasting time" just pursuing a hobby. As someone without any formal training or professional experience in arts, OMOA gives me the opportunity to make a possible contribution as practitioners do. Getting funding is perhaps frustrating; failing to get funding only means I am not doing it as well as others - just have to try harder and smarter.

How do you constantly find new ideas and inspiration for developing exhibition themes and performing arts programmes to engage the general public? Based on your experiences, what is the best way to reach out to untapped audiences in Hong Kong?

I have no new ideas or inspiration as we are still implementing the app idea and trying out the loyalty scheme idea to make art relevant and enhance interest. We have to work with their friends who are art lovers to bring in a new audience. I think LCSD has been doing well in audience development for schoolers to bring in shows or students out to see shows. For 'adults', reaching them is hard. Unless the artwork is so famous that people feel a "need" to see it simply not to miss out on a conversational topic, friends are required to bring these untapped audiences into the art venue. Earlier, I mentioned a lack of knowledge as a barrier. Having friends who know about arts gives these new audiences the necessary knowledge. To reach out to an untapped audience, we need to provide motivations and incentives for their friends to bring them in.

What are your views on the potential for the development of cultural tourism in Hong Kong? In your opinion, what are the best ways to enhance public participation in the arts in the context of Hong Kong?

Perhaps there are organic ways and inorganic ways to do so. Inorganically, it could be some government subsidy or giveaways for each citizen to see one free performance a year. This is a very far-fetched idea, but it is a matter of whether we think arts are important enough to have "mandated." If it is too much once a year, perhaps ten shows in a lifetime like the continuous education fund? Or perhaps simply allowing people to allot that $10,000 CEF for arts participation expenditure will do it already?

And then, now that we have this imagery demand, we immediately see that we perhaps do not have a sufficient supply of shows. Organically, it is about drawing the audience into the arts purely because of the intrinsic interest in enjoying them. Bringing in or nurturing top-notch productions and exhibits is one way; the Hong Kong Arts Festival has many sold-out performances that get attention in the public media. Would it be possible for these performances to have an extended performance period to draw in untapped audiences, even simply to clock in?

Hong Kong itself lacks any long-running shows. It is definitely not a matter of lack of creativity or quality that these shows do not exist. It is more like a lack of venue than good shows without a venue to create a following or a sensation.

I do believe in the idea of the Greater Bay that with the express rail, there could be a one-hour travel circle bringing in many more untapped audiences outside of Hong Kong. Providing a potentially wider audience pool could perhaps ignite the vitality of the art scenes. But of course, the animosity against mainland visitors will be a hindrance. It is a "problem" of artists too; I will blame them for not creating more enticing art for the public. I feel that artists are too much into producing high arts and despising the entertainment value of arts.

Recently, I have conducted a study showing experimentally that celebrities could indeed enhance the motivation of nonfans to see a drama. So indeed, a good way to bring in a new audience is to utilise the star power of celebrities that the public knows very well.

Why do people turn to art and music in times of crisis?

I do not know if this is indeed the case. But I can see that turning to art and music could help. One explanation is about escapism; those arts could supposedly draw a person away into another world. But so can a good book or a video game.

Music could indeed regulate emotions. People use music to set the right mood (positive mood management), as a diversion (like escapism mentioned), and to make themselves feel better (negative mood management). But there is medical evidence showing how music can increase relaxation and reduce stress through restoring homoeostasis and music increases dopamine which leads to reduced blood pressure.

Sir Roger Scruton says, "Beauty is a value, as important as truth and goodness… The beautiful work of art brings consolation in sorrow and affirmation in joy. It shows human life to be worthwhile." As a psychology professor, what do you think of the above statement and belief towards art?

There are perhaps different ways to approach this statement. Beauty is not much in the eyes of the beholder. I am no expert on aesthetics. However, regarding physical attractiveness, there is strong agreement on what features are attractive and what are not. And in terms of sound perception, people dislike dissonance sounds. I cannot name other modalities, but I understand there is a general consensus on what is beautiful and what is not.

And do people generally prefer beautiful things? And I think it is also yes. But could people develop an acquired taste for things not generally beautiful? Also yes. Repeated exposure enhances our liking. What is beautiful is good is a strong phenomenon in human perception and social psychology. Beautiful things enhance our interest towards that object. From a psychological perspective, liking something beautiful is natural, not shallow or something. This is human nature, and perhaps it has a survival value too.

But in terms of art, this is interesting. My very little knowledge is that aesthetics is not a necessary element in contemporary art. The shocking value and grotesque façade perhaps stimulate intellectual and emotional reflection, bringing out the appreciation at a different level. So it is perfectly understandable that art could still be art even if it is not 'externally' beautiful; its beauty could touch our hearts and minds.

Typically, we think of beauty as the form but not the content; thinking about beauty as both an external and internal attribute could broaden our understanding and appreciation of art.

Photo 1. Winton Yu.

Photo 2. Poster.

Photo 3. Poster.

Photo 4. Poster.

Photo 5. Poster.

Photo 6. Poster.

Photo 7. Poster.

Chapter 18

Michelle Kim, Founder & Artistic Director, Hong Kong Generation Next Arts

Co-authored with:
Wong Sze-Wing (Mila)
Li Shanghao (Cara)
Xu Rui (Ryn)
Gao Xiang (Chris)
Fu Jingying (Roxanne)
Zhang Zhaowei (Sandy)

Introduction

Founded in 2009, Hong Kong Generation Next Arts Limited (HKGNA) is a Hong Kong Charity whose mission is to inspire and nurture artistic excellence and personal success in our next generation of young artists and transform lives through music.

A concert pianist Michelle Kim is the Founder & Artistic Director of the HKGNA. In the past decade, via HKGNA, Michelle Kim has created countless opportunities for nurturing talented young musicians, as well as disadvantaged and underprivileged youths, to perform in prestigious concert halls, including Carnegie Hall. In the following interview, Michelle Kim discusses the missions and philosophy behind the operations of HKGNA, as well as the power of music in changing hearts, minds, and the world around us.

Can we begin this interview by first introducing yourself, for example, your professional training and educational background?

My name is Michelle Kim. I am Korean-American; I am a Hongkonger. I am the Founder and Artistic Director of the Hong Kong Generation Next Arts (HKGNA). I am a music advocate and a pianist who graduated from the Juilliard School of Music with a bachelor's and master's degree in piano performance.

Do you come from a family of musicians or performing artists?

I was born in Seoul, Korea. I do not come from a family of professional musicians, but my father would often sing at home. He was a business major but also studied composition on the side. My father would sing German opera arias as a tenor as a serious hobby. He would also play and sing along with the music he composed himself. My mother was equally passionate about ballet and classical music; there was always music at home as a child. Actually, my life in music began with my mother, because she is the ultimate 'tiger mother.' It was her (my mother's) mission in life to make me a concert pianist. I began my musical training at age four. I literally had to practice 8 to 10 hours every day before and after school.

I gave my first concert at the age of 5. At age 10, I made my orchestral debut with the Seoul Philharmonic Orchestra. I then graduated from The Juilliard School, earning both a Bachelor's and Master's in Music. I also received the prestigious Arthur Rubinstein Award and garnered top prizes in numerous international competitions, including the Bartok-Kabalevsky-Prokofiev International Piano Competition and the Vincenzo Bellini International Piano Competition. I was featured as one of the "Inspiring Women of Hong Kong" in the October 2013 Anniversary Issue of Marie Claire for her charity work in Hong Kong. I made my home in New York and Hong Kong with my husband and son. Hong Kong is also where the HKGNA is based. I was awarded the 'Hong Kong & Shenzhen Lifestyle Award' by the Southern Metropolis Daily for being an ambassador for culture and performing arts and promoting youth development in Hong Kong in 2011.

I was honoured to be featured as one of the "Inspiring Women of Hong Kong" in the October 2013 Anniversary Issue of Marie Claire for my charity work in Hong Kong and also received the Ministry of Culture, Sports and Tourism Award from the South Korean Government for the dedication and contribution to Korean classical music abroad and enhancement of the reputation of Korea In2020. I made my home in Hong Kong with my husband and son. Hong Kong is also where HKGNA is based.

Can you provide a brief introduction to the Hong Kong Generation Next Arts (HKGNA)?

HKGNA is a non-profit organisation founded in 2009 with the mission to inspire and nurture artistic excellence, and personal success in our next generation of young artists and transform lives through music. The programmes of HKGNA include the Music Angel Programme, which provides music development programmes for disadvantaged youths who have experienced difficulties in life and aims to transform their lives through music. To achieve our mission, HKGNA has set out to pursue the following:

- To create exciting opportunities for talented young artists to perform in the world's most prestigious concert halls;
- To provide gifted young musicians with an opportunity to study with world-class artists from all over the world at HKGNA Music Festivals;
- To develop and promote excellence in the performing arts in Hong Kong and provide audiences with classical music of the highest standards;
- To establish an HKGNA fellowship and mentorship programme dedicated to developing and improving the lives of young people;
- To design and offer other music and educational programmes for disadvantaged and underprivileged youth to nurture their creative talent and empower them to fulfil their dreams and aspirations.

Under HKGNA, we have created the following programmes, competitions, and fellowships:

- *Musical Angel Programme* – it is considered the absolute core of the HKGNA. With the unshakeable belief that music can change lives and move hearts, the Musical Angel Programme (under HKGNA) is devoted to offering music education to disadvantaged youths in Hong Kong, who are struggling with various difficulties in their lives. The HKGNA has been serving organisations such as St. Stephen's Society and Operation Dawn, rehab centres for disadvantaged youth, as well as Arts with the Disabled Association HK, in which we also provide music training and development to visually-impaired young artists. With the Musical Angel Programme, we presented visually impaired pianist Lee Shing at Carnegie Hall, and last year, we presented a blind violinist Jisun Kim at the HKGNA Music Festival 2021.

- *HKGNA Fellowship* – this Fellowship programme aims to facilitate the development of young performing artists and gives them the opportunity and challenge to assist economically disadvantaged youth with music development and mentorship. Working with community organisations or directly with youth, our Fellows participate in youth outreach activities specific to the needs of young kids who have a genuine passion for music and develop leadership and mentoring skills. The HKGNA Fellowship activities include hands-on engagement and interaction with underprivileged youth in teaching instrumental lessons, performing together on stage, and leading or participating in music education development programmes. Our Fellows are included as featured performers in recitals and chamber concerts and provide other performance opportunities for advancing the mission of HKGNA.

- *HKGNA International Music Competition* - is open to youths of all sorts of family and social backgrounds. HKGNA offers the winners of our Music Competition the chance to perform locally and on world-renowned stages, such as Carnegie Hall. Being able to perform on the stage of Carnegie Hall is like a dream come true for any young artist. We are very proud that HKGNA awarded and presented our past Competition Grand Prize winners with concert performances at our HKGNA Music Festival and at Carnegie Hall in 2010, 2015 and 2017. In 2017, our grand prize winner performed to a sold-out concert audience at Carnegie Hall in our 20th Anniversary of HKSAR celebratory concert supported by the Hong Kong Economic and Trade Office New York. Our Competition winners are also awarded cash prizes from our title sponsor Yang Won Sun Foundation. The Hong Kong winners were also given the opportunity to perform with other overseas and international winners in a Hong Kong Debut Concert.

- *"Music Heals!"* is a program that was initiated by HKGNA in 2015, offering free music therapy workshops and events in Hong Kong. In response to the COVID-19 pandemic, we launched a series of online and offline workshops with different topics through "Music Heals!" in 2020 and 2021, such as autism, ADHD, dementia, depression and hospice care to the global audience with renowned guest speakers, educators, and music therapists from around the world. Through "Music Heals!", beneficiaries will have the opportunity to experience the therapeutic benefits of music and improve their emotional, cognitive, and social well-being. The program serves as a platform that connects selected individuals with certified music therapists in a safe and supportive environment, providing a unique and meaningful experience for all involved.

In short, HKGNA is dedicated to inspiring and nurturing artistic excellence and personal success in our next generation of young artists and transforming lives through music.

What motivated you to come to Hong Kong, since this city is not exactly a cultural capital for classical music?

I first came to Hong Kong to perform for my teacher, Pianist Yin Cheng-Zong. We fell in love with the place immediately, which led to my husband's job offer as an expat in finance.

Shortly after I arrived in Hong Kong, I had a very traumatic experience when I gave birth to my son; I almost died. Because of that, I began to ask myself what I could do with my talent (as a musician) that would benefit the community. The birth of my son has also inspired me to build something inspiring, long-lasting, and, most importantly, meaningful for the next generation of young people, especially serving underprivileged youth. The desire to do something good for the community (and not just for myself) motivated me to found the HKGNA. Through HKGNA, I found my passion and purpose to help the next generation of youths pursue their musical aspirations and dreams.

According to your online biography, you have initiated many projects to advocate for young artists and disadvantaged youths. All these are motivated by a profound belief in music's power to transform lives. Could you tell us more about your advocacy projects for young music talents?

I think it is very important to advocate for young artists, because I know how difficult it was for me when I was just starting out as a young musician. To become a professional concert pianist, unique talent is only the beginning, and far too many young talents are fighting to be discovered. For example, there are just so many amazing young musicians worldwide, but we will never get to know them because no one has given them a chance to shine.

As a young struggling musician (regardless of how talented you are), you need maximum support in training, education, and professional connections. You need emotional and psychological support in so many different ways, because the life of a concert pianist is unbelievably competitive, very single-minded: full of solitary and unexpected twists and turns. It is much more than just practicing at the piano. Musicians are also perfectionists, very emotional, and sometimes hypersensitive. We can easily get discouraged or obsessive or get our self-confidence crushed. You cannot just have outstanding technical skills to be a good musician. On top of all these, you also need to be smart to solve the intellectual riddles or puzzles of the music you are playing. As such, one cannot simply expect us (musicians) to lead a normal person's life.

The story of the HKGNA actually began with Jackie Pullinger, a British Protestant Christian missionary to Hong Kong and founder of the St. Stephen's Society. Jackie is also a professionally trained musician who graduated from the Royal College of Music in London and specialised in the oboe. She came to Hong Kong in the 1960s, and she speaks Cantonese fluently. In 1981, she started a charity called St. Stephen's Society, which provided rehabilitation homes for recovering drug addicts, prostitutes, and gang members. By December 2007, it housed 200 people. The work carried out by St. Stephen's Society was recognised by the local Hong Kong Government, which donated the land for the rehabilitation homes. The work carried out by St. Stephen's Society continues.

I met these disadvantaged youth when I was serving with Jackie Pullinger. Jackie said to me, "Perhaps you could teach boys music?" My initial response was, "No, I don't teach beginners! Besides, I was still recovering from the traumatic birth of my son." But I later decided to give it a try. None of these boys (from St. Stephen's Society) had any music background. Most of them had never even touched the piano. Some of the boys were terrible with me initially, e.g., giving me hostile and dirty looks. So, I had to start with the very basics, e.g., where to find the C note and how to put the fingers on the keyboard. A few months went by, and we gradually began to connect. When you teach music, you cannot just teach people how to play an instrument; you also need to teach them how to open up their emotions and listen with their hearts. Gradually, I saw them changing through the power of music. I witnessed the actual transformation in these boys' lives through music.

Towards the end, one of the boys (with a big dragon tattoo who used to scare me) actually became the hardest-working and most loving person. In fact, he became my favourite student. On the day of the concert, when he began to perform onstage, his parents were crying – I believe it was their proudest moment. Although none of these boys would become professional musicians, I actually saw and witnessed how music had a profound positive impact on young people's lives – i.e., instilling discipline and goodness in them.

What are the funding sources for HKGNA?

In addition to delivering performances of classical music of the highest standards, HKGNA's mission is to create exciting opportunities for young musicians to learn from, as well as to perform side-by-side with world-class artists from all over the world. Through HKGNA, we have already created many valuable opportunities for young musicians from the Hong Kong Government, different local and foreign consulates in Hong Kong, corporate and individual support and sponsorships..

Do you know any other non-profit or performing arts organisations carrying out similar charity projects (supporting underprivileged youths interested in music) like the HKGNA?

I would like to think HKGNA is one of a kind and a unique music charity that serves both excellent artists and also disadvantaged & under-privileged youths. HKGNA stands for "Excellence, Community & Inspiration." So, I am proud to say that the HKGNA is a pioneer in performing arts charities that advocates and nurtures both excellent young artists and underprivileged & disadvantaged youths who are passionate about music.

As the Founder & Artistic Director of HKGNA, could you describe your typical day at work? Is there ever a typical day at work?

When we are running the HKGNA Music Festival, I would be literally working 24/7 non-stop. I feel blessed to have our team at HKGNA who are dedicated and incredibly passionate about our missions and initiatives. During a music festival, anything could happen. As the Artistic Director of the HKGNA, I have to handle everything that comes my way. When it comes to concert programming, I have to take all these elements into consideration:

- Selection of pieces based on the overall theme of the festival, or a particular concert under the festival;
- Selection of piece to be performed based on the availability of the invited artists, and their specialties, repertoires, and interests;
- Ordering of pieces to be performed based on allowable time;
- Even distribution of both local rising stars (including the Hong Kong Academy for Performing Arts) and artists of international calibre.

What kind of music do you enjoy listening to as a professional musician during your free time?

I like to listen to Bach in the morning; it helps to clear my mind – the simplicity, purity, and every work Bach wrote was for God. So it really speaks to my heart and mind. I love to listen to all genres of music including jazz, rock, hiphop, rap, pop and classical, of course! Because HKGNA also presents different genres of music, I love to broaden my horizons to new and different types of music and artists.

Do you think becoming a better person helps you be a better musician?

Absolutely. My faith is very important to me, and it has made me a better person. And that in turn made me a better artist. Through my faith, I was able to love myself, find joy and gratitude, which comes through in my music. It has also allowed my music to become more profound, more sincere and more heartfelt.

What would you like HKGNA to be remembered for?

I would love HKGNA to be remembered as the vessel and the special force to uplift our community and let our community around us experience the true power of music!

What would you like to be remembered as a musician and as a human being?

I would like to be remembered as a musician who passionately advocates and champions for our youth and the true power of music. I would love to be remembered as a mom who tried her best and gave the best of myself to my husband and my son.

What would you like to be remembered for when you retire?

I don't want to consider retirement as I will never really retire. I have to let my life speak for itself when I am gone. :)

Photo 1. Michelle Kim.

Photo 2. HKGNA musical angels in the past at Central Harbourfront in 2013.

Photo 3. HKGNA musical angel performing in outdoor concert at Central Harbour front in 2013.

Photo 4. HKGNA musical angel, a visually impaired pianist Lee Shing making Carnegie Hall Debut.

Photo 5. Michelle Kim performing with SAR Philharmonic at the Hong Kong Cultural Centre.

Photo 6. Canto Pop Star P1X3L performing at the HKGNA Music Festival 2022.

Photo 7. Michelle Kim making opening remark at the HKGNA Music Festival 2022.

Photo 8. Musical Comedy Duo Igudesman & Joo performing at the HKGNA Music Festival 2022.

Photo 9. Soprano Sumi Jo performing at the HKGNA Music Festival 2022.

Photo 10. Soprano Sumi Jo performing at the HKGNA Music Festival 2022.

Photo 11. The Spectacular view of the HKGNA Music Festival 2022 at the West Kowloon Artpark.

Photo 12. HKGNA musical angel, a visually impaired pianist Lee Shing making the Carnegie Hall Debut.

Chapter 19

Lindsey McAlister, Founder of Hong Kong Youth Arts Foundation and Wendy Tsang, Director of Hong Kong Youth Arts Foundation

Introduction

Established in 1993 by Lindsey McAlister OBE, JP, Hong Kong Youth Arts Foundation (HKYAF) organises inclusive and inspirational projects that reach out to youngsters of all cultures, backgrounds, languages, and abilities, and actively creates opportunities for those who are disadvantaged and underprivileged. Each year, HKYAF reaches over 800,000 people through its projects, exhibitions and performances. McAlister was recognised in the New Year Honours List 2006 as an Officer of the Order of the British Empire (OBE). She received this in recognition of her commitment to education and for her contribution to UK arts overseas. In 2014, she was appointed to become a Justice of the Peace (JP).

In the following interview, Lindsey McAlister and Wendy Tsang share with the readers the mission and philosophy behind the HKYAF, as well as their endless creative strategies in encouraging the young generation in Hong Kong to participate in the arts.

Could we begin this interview by first introducing yourself, for example, your educational and professional background? Do you come from a family of artists and arts administrators?

I was born in the Northwest of the UK. I did my A levels, majoring in Fine Arts and Photography at Southport College of Art & Design, and later earned my BA (Hons) in Creative Arts (specialising in Theatre, Visual Arts & Dance) from Manchester Metropolitan University (Cheshire campus). Upon graduation, I was able to put my studies in Creative Arts to work at the Arts Council of Great Britain and the Gulbenkian Foundation, implementing the

"Arts in Schools Report." Before coming to Hong Kong, I served as Artist in Residence at Quarry Bay School, English Schools Foundation (1989–1991) and Founder/Artistic Director for Scrambled Legs Youth Dance Company (1991–1993). As you can see, all my work has focused on young people. I was drawn to theatre early in my childhood in the United Kingdom. I love creating something from nothing. Initially, I wanted to be a performer, but early on, I realised I was rubbish and found that directing was my forte—to suit my bossy personality.

Before joining the Hong Kong Youth Arts Foundation (HKYAF), I was an outreach social worker helping at-risk youngsters. I felt a bit frustrated then because the resources we could provide weren't always exactly what the youngsters needed. One of my duties was to help teenagers join a street dance performance organised by the Hong Kong Youth Arts Festival (which would later become HKYAF). As they danced, I saw young people with low self-esteem and little self-confidence magically transform into stars. At that moment, I realised art is a great medium for helping young people to think for themselves, explore their strengths and resolve problems. Later, I joined HKYAF and continued to help youngsters from another perspective—the arts!

What made you decide to come to Hong Kong?

Twenty-three years ago, I left the UK to travel for a year before arriving in Hong Kong. The plan was to travel for a bit, run out of money, and then return to my job with the Arts Council back in the UK. I ended up having an amazing time in Southeast Asia, and it just so happened I had a friend living in Hong Kong, so I stayed with her. I remember vividly it was in Kowloon Tong Station—when I put my foot on Hong Kong's soil, I knew I would be brought here to do something really special. I am not terribly religious but quite spiritual, impetuous, and intuitive. You could say that I am not a big thinker, but a big heart and gut person. So, within 2 hours, I gave up my UK job. I started in Hong Kong doing jobs like teaching English in kindergartens and choreographing fashion shows. But after a short time, I knew I wanted to create something more. I soon started working in English Schools Foundation and as an artist-in-residence for a year in Hong Kong and realised I didn't want to get stuck with expat kids. I definitely wanted to do something with the Hong Kong community, which very much motivated me to establish the Hong Kong Youth Arts Foundation.

Could you describe the mission and philosophy behind HKYAF?

Established in 1993, HKYAF is a charity that aims to provide access to high-quality, non-competitive, free-of-charge arts experiences for all young people aged 5 to 25. HKYAF organises regularly inclusive and inspirational projects that reach out to youngsters of all cultures, backgrounds, languages and abilities, and actively creates opportunities for those who are disadvantaged and underprivileged. Each year, HKYAF reaches over 800,000 people through its projects, exhibitions and performances, etc. In terms of HKYAF's philosophy—we believe that quality art experiences can enrich the learning process by offering new ways of channelling energy and looking at the world. Amongst the multitude of crucial benefits that arts opportunities create are increased creativity, self-expression and self-esteem, plus problem-solving, communication, leadership and teambuilding skills. In fact, HKYAF's mission statement hasn't changed since we started 30 years ago (i.e., to empower young people through the arts).

When HKYAF was first established, what were the initial responses from the local children and schools towards its arts programmes?

Schools were quite slow on the uptake. During the first couple of years, most of the HKYAF programme participants were international schools—just because that was where I had many of my professional contacts. In other words, during the first two years, there were many expats from many elite schools. Then, all of a sudden, in the subsequent years, things just kicked off, and we got a lot more features in the local media. Surprisingly, many local schools participate in our HKYAF programmes in the third year.

What have been the major difficulties and challenges during the initial period when HKYAF was first established?

We don't use the words "challenge" or "problem" because we would reframe those two words as "opportunities." So, the "opportunities" were definitely the fact that I had to work with local people, and my lack of Chinese language ability was a real issue. In addition to the language barrier, things like finding space and money were another problem. So, in the early days, I hadn't a clue about how to raise money—so I had my Yellow Pages, and I was calling companies one by one, which obviously didn't work. Eventually, I started going around and meeting and talking to people.

On that same day, three people suggested that I talk to Po Chung, founder of DHL International, the Chairman Emeritus of DHL Express (HK) Ltd, and the Chairman of The Hong Kong Institute of Service Leadership & Management of The Good Life Initiative Limited.

So, I contacted Mr. Chung's office assistant, and he said, "Your timing is amazing, because Mr. Chung has actually just started this organisation where he's giving funding to seeding projects. Your idea is very attractive. Why don't you send in a proposal?" And I was thinking, well, I don't even know what a proposal is.

I wrote what I *thought* was a proposal and sent it in. His assistant rang me back and said, "Mr. Chung has read your proposal and really likes your idea. Can you come in and do a presentation?" I don't know what a presentation is. Is that like a one-woman show?

So, I did the "Lindsey McAlister one-woman show," and it was to this bank of men in suits—it was a very intimidating experience. At the end of my presentation, they said, "We love your idea, but you've got no track record. You have been in Hong Kong for three years, you don't really know the culture, and you don't speak Cantonese..." So, when I left the office, I was very disheartened because I thought this would be the big thing.

I decided that nobody was going to give me money because of all those things, so what I had to do was to *make* this event happen. I thought, well, what do you do when you've got no money? You go to the bank and take out an overdraft.

So, I went to Standard Chartered—which is so ironic because they are now one of our big partners. I sat down in front of the bank manager and said, "Hey, I've got a really great idea for a project; I need to borrow some money." They thought I had a lot because I was an expat, but I had actually only had HKD$500 in my bank account. So, they said I was way too high risk—no way they were giving me any money.

And I said, "I'm afraid I'm not going anywhere until you give me HKD$200,000." The whole day passed, I sat in the bank manager's office, and he kept coming and going, and I thought he was going to get the police. I'm going to get arrested and thrown on the street. Around 4 o'clock, he sat down and said, "You promise you're going to pay this money back?" I said, "I absolutely promise," not knowing how I would do this. He tells me the money's been put in my account.

This was 30 years ago and obviously would not happen today. So I went out, bought theatres, got the artists, created the program, and sent everything out to everyone I've met in the interim. And Po Chung rang me and said, "I'm actually impressed, because you've proved me wrong. How have you done it? I'm looking at your programme, and I don't see any sponsor logos." So, I told him about the bank manager, and he thought it was absolutely hysterically funny.

He asked if I could go to his office the next day at 2 o'clock. I arrived, and he was this tiny little man sitting at this massive desk with his pen poised over a checkbook. When I walked in, he asked, "How much is your overdraft?" He gives me a check for HKD$200,000. Then he asked, "How much for your whole first year?" And I think *a million dollars*? He wrote me a check for a million dollars. That was the point where I thought Hong Kong really needed this project because if *he* believed I could do it, then I could definitely do it. It's a good story, because if you get off your bum and make something happen, you can do anything! It's very empowering.

How does HKYAF further enrich the lives of the children and young people in Hong Kong?

HKYAF is not just about teaching and training them. We are about utilising what they already know. Obviously, through being involved in our projects, they will grow artistically, creatively and intellectually, etc. We are not just training them how to dance; it is about giving them the multidimensional experience of performing arts, like choreography, creating new work for an exhibition, etc.

After being involved in an art project, they would usually come out super confident about who they are. They can stand in front of a room full of people and say or do whatever. They develop their creative thinking skills, problem-solving skills, and also empathy. There are also other valuable experiences that these young participants could gain from our programmes (e.g., collaborative learning, developing resilience, learning commitment, etc.).

My experience in working with young people from different schools is that there is a massive difference between the local and international schools, definitely in confidence. Just the ability to walk into a room and have a conversation—to form a statement—to tell people what you believe in. But it doesn't take too long for a local school kid to work in our environment and develop the same qualities. They reinvent and recreate themselves by being involved, particularly if they are working on the big show with me, where they have around 50 to 60 kids from different backgrounds participating simultaneously.

Could you describe the staffing structure of HKYAF?

Our structure's quite simple. HKYAF is made up of a total of 13 staff members. Meanwhile, Lindsey is our Founder, and I am the Director. Under HKYAF, we have the Visual Arts, Performing Arts and Communication Teams. About three to five people are under each team, and all 13 of us are women.

What kind of personalities are you looking for in joining HKYAF?

We look for people who fit into our culture, and that is "passion over everything." Under HKYAF, everyone is working in a very relaxed, trusting style. We don't have office hours or how many days of the week to come into the office. We have only ever done one single performance appraisal. As long as the work gets done, I don't care. In fact, we have employed people who are so fabulous, so why would we bother micromanaging them, since they already exhibit high professionalism?

At HKYAF, we are quite a small team, so if you join the Performing Arts Team, you know we do a big show at the end of the year, but that is just one of the gazillion things that we do. So, everyone at HKYAF is expected to be multitasking. Even our HKYAF board members don't fully understand everything that we do. When we were actually looking for someone to join our Communications Team, I wrote down a list of traits: (1) bubbly, (2) bright, (3) brave, and (4) creative. Since I am a risk taker myself, I want people around me willing to put themselves on the line. I don't want people to just be, "Yes Women!" Because I have such a strong vision, I want people who could actually put in ideas. For example, 1.5 years ago, Cristie Lam came to HKYAF with a music background (which is one of our weaker areas). Since then, we have managed to launch a new singer-songwriter programme, and another music initiative. In short, I want people who can bring their passion and leave their mark on what they are doing at HKYAF.

When hiring new people to join HKYAF, what kinds of technical skills or professional knowledge do you look for among the recruits?

This person must be able to communicate in both English and Chinese, although the initial interview will take place in Cantonese. Good and effective presentation skills are also essential, as certain roles require more than others. If you are heading a team, you also need practical leadership skills. We will give the heads (team leaders) a "big picture" direction, but it's up to them to decide how to deliver it.

For visual arts programmes, we have a strong mission of what we want to achieve but don't limit our team on how to do it. There are 10,000 different ways to do it, so we don't restrict them to using old methods. For example, we try to observe what it is that young people need in Hong Kong, and what kinds of artists we can work with to achieve that. HKYAF encourages them to explore different opportunities because it is not rocket science but art.

We take people of all ages, but the heads (team leaders) tend to be a little bit older and have a lot more experience and background in their own areas of expertise. Having said that, we will let the younger members become project managers because they won't be assistants forever, so we'll take steps to train the younger members. In short, it is about incrementally building them and confidence building. At the end of the day, anybody can do anything if they put their mind to it. So, it's about how much passion they want to exhibit. I want the team to feel that they can try different and new things.

As the Founder of HKYAF, could you describe your leadership and management style?

At HKYAF, I manage a small visionary team of 12. We (Wendy and I) are responsible for the creative vision, promotion and management of the artists, schools, teachers, and young people involved, event management, and publicity of the projects that we create.

In terms of leadership style, I am to lead by example. I wouldn't ask the team members to do anything I wouldn't do myself. In terms of my management style, I'm very trusting and open with my colleagues. In short, I am a very hands-on leader. My team and people outside of HKYAF can see that I am very passionate and inspired by the work we do. Everything we do at HKYAF is interactive. If you are able to actively create and get involved in something, you could undoubtedly empower young people to have a voice through the arts. In terms of my work ethic, values, and principles, very early on, I was mentored by one of the professors from the college who saw something in me and got me involved in projects. I suppose she gave me the confidence to go, "I can do anything!"—so that has been my philosophy ever since.

How does HKYAF get the young generation in Hong Kong involved in the arts?

Different projects have different aims. Some projects use really specific groups of young people in mind, while some other programmes aim to involve the general public to participate (e.g., Standard Chartered Arts in the Park 2018 managed to attract over 180,000 visitors).

Many of our HKYAF projects are quite issue-based, so we encouraged young people to create art with recyclable materials for one project. We also used art to make the audience more aware of social issues—so they learn by participation. One of the things we always say is, "What I hear, I forget. What I see, I remember. What I do, I understand!"

Being involved breaks down preconceptions. My latest project is called "Only A Girl." It's an LGBTQ+ project. At the audition, one of the things they discussed was why they wanted to be involved, and out of hundreds of kids, a very high percentage identified with the LGBTQ+ community. They felt it was a very unusual project for people to do in Hong Kong. Many of the kids did identify as part of the community and others are allies. Hopefully, people will be a bit more accommodating and open and curious. We want to create a dialogue and communication between kids who are gay and kids who aren't.

The intention behind this programme was to create a piece that could educate, but also entertain people. So, the performance quality will be extremely high, but you will go away having learnt a bit about LGBTQ+. It was a massive thing for young people who identify with different pronouns. The time was right for HKYAF kids to actually have a voice. I simply couldn't believe how many local kids came.

The Jockey Club also sponsors a community project called "The Hong Kong Jockey Club Community Project Grant: stART Up Community Arts Project" Each year, we look for an area we want to explore. In the past, we did cyberbullying; this year, we focused on climate change, and in the coming two years, we're focused on racial harmony. We do it through language and culture; art is a perfect platform. We also have a project called "Jockey Club "Project Silver" Intergenerational Arts Project." We noticed that there were very few art activities for elders in Hong Kong, and many of the existing ones are quite low-level. So, we wanted to bring exhibits and inspire the arts in them, so we do a programme every year for the older generation too. We are quite good at looking for the needs in Hong Kong, as we want to be the trendsetters rather than the trend followers.

How does HKYAF find inspiration and new ideas to continue launching new programmes to engage the existing audience and reach out to new target audiences?

We are never short of ideas. We can never actually do everything we want because we don't have all the resources. The programmes that get funding are obviously of interest to our sponsors and/or local communities. Fortunately, our sponsor's work is not just reliant on one person in the organisation, as we have had very different handlers in companies (e.g., Standard Chartered and SWIRE) over the years.

For example, Standard Chartered Arts in the Park, organised by HKYAF, has been Hong Kong's largest and much-anticipated outdoor youth art event. Via the Standard Chartered Arts in the Park 2022, HKYAF presented two days of outdoor showcases and performances, all inspired by four wonderful works by British writer Charles Dickens: *Oliver Twist*, *A Christmas Carol*, *David Copperfield*, and *Great Expectations*. As well as fun outdoor events, it also includes a week-long programme of online activities.

The COVID-19 crisis has turned the world upside-down. How has HKYAF coped with the difficulties and challenges of the COVID-19 pandemic?

During the COVID-19 crisis, we needed to figure out how to recreate certain projects online instead of relying on actual face-to-face interactions and engagements with the audience. Because if we don't produce anything, we don't earn any income. We have been very lucky that our partners and sponsors have been very supportive and understanding in these tricky times. In fact, the HKYAF learning curve in virtual has been enormous. Our team has been incredibly resilient and adaptable throughout the COVID-19 crisis, despite the challenges of changing working and audience-engaging practices in addressing the COVID-19 pandemic.

In the post-COVID era, what is the future of HKYAF?

In these exceptional times, the arts have become more vital than ever to help people heal and feel empowered. So, we will adapt and redesign projects to inspire young people to stay creatively connected. We don't see challenges at HKYAF, fuelled by our imagination and creativity, just opportunities!

Why would people turn to art and music in times of crisis?

We use the tagline "Stay creatively connected!" Through difficult times, the arts are a wonderful way of connecting people spiritually, emotionally, physically, and more. We were surprised at the popularity of the projects we launched online because we expected the number of participants would be drastically reduced. On the contrary, the actual number of participants was far more reaching than we originally thought. For one of the HKYAF dance projects, we had different people from different countries also participating. To our surprise, the Standard Chartered Arts in the Park 2022 online programmes were enjoyed by over 80,000 people.

In what ways does HKYAF contribute to the overall arts and cultural scene in Hong Kong?

One of the most basic things would be to create a passion amongst the young people in Hong Kong—to support their art projects, as well as create new audience groups for the arts of the future. Via HKYAF, we aim to encourage young people to consider the arts and/or other related creative industries as possible career paths. As such, we are creating the artists, designers, and teachers of the future of the arts in Hong Kong.

Via HKYAF, we also bring arts to the local schools. Most of the time, the local schools don't have the resources to bring in high-quality artists. Together with HKYAF via partnerships, we are also doing exhibits and public spaces (e.g., PMQ and Tai Kwun, etc.) and raising the profile of individual local schools.

Thirty years ago versus now—could you describe the evolution of programmes (e.g., format, style and content) developed by HKYAF?

Young people in Hong Kong are very good at desktop-sized artwork and drawings, because the schools train them in that area. So for HKYAF, we encourage them to do group projects and giant pieces like four meters high. We want to push them out of what they usually know.

We always have our artists work with the staff and teachers. HKYAF would provide them with the training. We want to break the conception of what "art" is or should be, because it changes and develops with time. Traditional art used to be drawing and painting, but many different art styles exist. We send lots of different, non-traditional materials to create opportunities for them, to exhibit their art in cool, unusual spaces, etc. Many of our visual art pieces are transient, as some might go up in a shopping centre or other public places. We do a project called "HK Urban Canvas"—about getting emerging artists to work with community members, as well as creating a visual representation that goes on a shutter. We have also created these "Art Packs," which are activity-based packs. It is an opportunity for people who are stuck at home to have activities for their kids to do. The Art Packs provided QR codes linked to online videos, storytelling, performances, etc. We gave away 30,000 of those QR codes. Such online programmes have enabled us to become more adaptable for the future and also allowed us to become far more hybrid in how we do things.

What would you like to be remembered for when you retire?

I wanted to be remembered for making a positive difference in the arts and cultural scene in Hong Kong. With my work with HKYAF, I get to be physically engaging with these young people every day, so I never questioned the value of art. My husband is a surgeon who gets to heal people, cure diseases, and keep people alive in his everyday work. What we do with HKYAF is not just entertainment; it is also about changing the lives of children and young people involved in our projects—thereby developing totally different perspectives of their own futures. Via HKYAF, I think we can change lives for the better! Hence, I would like to be known for benefiting and serving the community—that is already enough for me.

One of the things I am often asked is if I have had any kids that have gone on to do spectacular things. It has been quite interesting because we have a girl who starred in the next Marvel movie, *Black Widow*, featuring Scarlett Johansson. We also have a kid in Berlin filming a Netflix series, and another starring in a Mainland Chinese film. So, we've got kids that have gone further in the creative industries. I have been mentored and inspired by some amazing people; hence, I hope I have mentored and inspired the children and young people whom I work with.

What is your most memorable HKYAF project?

Standard Chartered Arts in the Park. Since joining HKYAF twenty years ago, I've been learning how to adapt and adjust to different challenges, like how to engage a large number of visitors—up to 190,000 people! But each time I saw the happy faces of the participants and visitors, it was all worthwhile and hugely rewarding.

What advice can you give to fresh graduates?

If you don't understand, don't be shy to ask! There are so many different ways to work things out; you need to be creative and put in 100% to get the best results. Don't be quick to criticise someone else's way of dealing with problems—see things from their perspective, understand their intentions and learn from experience. And always show your passion!

Photo 1. Lindsey McAlister.

Photo 2. Wendy Tsang.

Photo 3. Hong Kong Urban Canvas 2019.

Photo 4. Miller Performing Arts: Only a Girl.

Photo 5. Jockey Club "Project Silver" Intergenerational Arts Project (1).

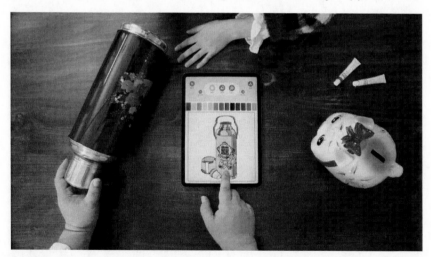

Photo 6. Jockey Club "Project Silver" Intergenerational Arts Project (2).

Photo 7. Standard Chartered Arts in the Park 2022.

Photo 8. The Hong Kong Jockey Club Community Project Grant: stART Up Community Arts Project 2021.

Chapter 20

Dr. Mui Kwong-chiu, Chairman of Hong Kong Composers' Guild

Introduction

Founded in 1983, the Hong Kong Composers' Guild (HKCG) is a professional association of serious composers with objectives to promote and cultivate music composition in Hong Kong. Apart from organising concerts, publishing scores and producing recordings of works by Hong Kong composers, HKCG also takes an active part in inspiring interest in composition, especially amongst youths and in developing music as a vital creative art form in Hong Kong.

Dr. Mui Kwong-chiu is the current Chairman of HKCG, the Director of Composers and Authors Society of Hong Kong (CASH), a member of the Chinese Musicians' Association, the Artistic Director of the World Dulcimer Orchestra and Honorary Advisor of the NEXUS Ensemble based in Hong Kong. In 2020, he was awarded 'The 14th Hong Kong Arts Development Award Artist of the Year (Music)' by the Hong Kong Arts Development Council. For his achievements in music and contribution to Hong Kong society, he was awarded the Hong Kong Baptist University (HKBU) Distinguished Communication Alumni Award, celebrating the 50th anniversary of the HKBU Communication Department in 2018.

Dr. Mui's works include Shakuhachi for the Crane Dance Suite for the Hong Kong Cultural Festival, The composer/director of the Cross Media Beach Concert for the Hong Kong Youth Festival in 2018, Composer of Cross Media Chinese Music Theatre Intoxicating Nature and Ode to Water for the Hong Kong Chinese Orchestra; Double Concerto for Piano and Flute for The Great Earth; Reincarnation of the Prunus Mume for the Hong Kong Repertory Theatre; Spring Ritual and Eulogy for Hong Kong Dance Company and Symphonic Poem Genesis for orchestra. He represents HKCG to attend the International Society for Contemporary Music (ISCM) and composes many music themes for Radio Television Hong Kong TV programmes. In the following interview, Dr. Mui discusses the missions behind the HKCG and his career path to becoming the Chairman of the HKCG.

Could we begin this interview by first introducing yourself, such as your professional training and educational background? What did you study at the university? Did you come from a family of musicians or performing artists?

I was born into a musical family. My father was a Cantonese opera singer who played many musical instruments. As I was raised in a musical environment, creating music has naturally been my lifelong pursuit since childhood.

I sang in music concerts when I was in secondary school, and I won awards in the school singing contests. I completed my study of cinematography at Baptist University but later studied music and composition at the Hong Kong Music Institute as I love music. I later completed my MPhil and PhD in the University of Hong Kong while my research area is in music composition. My interest in both music composition and movies shaped the path of my music career as a music composer, with a particular interest in multimedia music works, film music and musicals, as well as a prolific repertoire.

Was it a calling for you to pursue a lifelong music career?

I think my music career is a calling for me, and music composition is indeed my lifelong career.

Could you provide a brief introduction and a history of the Hong Kong Composers Guild?

The Hong Kong Composers' Guild (HKCG) is an organisation for serious music and composers. It was founded in 1983 and has 150 music composers. We have three aims:

- Pursue excellence in musical creativity,
- Enhance the music education of the Hong Kong public as well as educational institutions, including primary schools, secondary schools, tertiary institutions, and kids in kindergarten.
- To connect with the global network of contemporary music organisations, including Rostrum (which is based in Paris under the

auspices of UNESCO), the ISCM (International Society of Contemporary Music) and ACL (Asian Composers League).

HKCG also collaborates with the Education Bureau of Hong Kong to foster interest in music compositions at schools and universities by supporting and presenting student music composition concerts. As an organisation, we have regular meetings of the Board of Council Directors to proceed with the Guild's music activities, and daily operations and to manage the grant and funding applications.

The HKCG Council has a committee of eleven council directors, a Chairman and two full-time staff. We employ additional freelancers to assist our operations when we stage musical festivals and music events. We have two sources of financial support: The Hong Kong Arts Development Council and the music fund from the Composers and Authors Society of Hong Kong (CASH). We present a music festival towards the latter months of each year. *Musicarama* has been a brand of HKCG over the past two decades and is now rebranded as the *Hong Kong Contemporary Music Festival* series. The latest ones include the *Hong Kong Contemporary Music Festival: Hong Kong Delights* in 2018; *Hong Kong Contemporary Music Festival: Asian Delights* in 2020, and *Hong Kong Contemporary Music Festival: Global Delights* in 2022. Between the festivals, we present another concert series with different themes to present different music colours for diverse music presentations. We are going to celebrate the 40th anniversary of HKCG with three concerts and an exhibition in 2023, and the first half of 2024.

Over the past forty years, we have presented numerous concerts and music projects with various music organisations, including the Hong Kong Education Department Bureau (EDB) and other cultural organisations. Just to introduce a few, namely: Match Making Concerts – When Emerging Performers meet Forerunner Composers (working with RTHK Radio 4); Quality Education Fund – Music Composition Training Programme with Cultural Exploration (2014 - 2016, collaborating with EDB); GalaMusica – School Creative Works/School Chamber Competition (2018 to present, also working with EDB) and ISCM - Musicarama 2015 (working with ISCM). We collaborate with prominent art forces, including the Hong Kong Chinese Orchestra, Hong Kong Philharmonic Orchestra, City Chamber Orchestra, Hong Kong Children's Choir, Windpipe Chinese Music Ensemble, and many other prominent artists. To connect with the rest of the world, we presented Japan-Hong Kong Exchange Concert (2018) and France-Hong Kong Exchange Concert (2019). We are a section of ISCM and participate in the

ISCM World Music Days every year. We submit scores and send delegations to ISCM to participate in such international exchanges. We are running an HKCG mentorship scheme to guide and train bright young local student composers to compose. Every year we work with RTHK Radio 4 to stage the New Generation concert to provide a platform for tertiary education student composers to compose and perform their works publicly, and most importantly, to broadcast the works on such fine music channels. We worked with enthusiastic donors to compose and promote Chinese choral music, borrowing Chinese Tang poems as lyrics. We presented concerts of such orientations, published scores and CDs for such meaningful music activities to blend music creativity with Tang poems. In the pandemic era, we switched to the online digital platform to sustain music creativity in Hong Kong. During such a difficult period, the venues were locked down, everyone was required to wear masks for pandemic prevention, and we continued online.

Could you describe your path to becoming a chairman of the Composers' Guild? What are your major roles and responsibilities?

I was the Vice Chairman before I became elected as the Chairman. We have AGM or general elections every two years. My role as Chairman is to guide HKCG with the three objectives I have just mentioned: collaborating with the Hong Kong Education Department Bureau (EDB) to foster music education at schools and universities, pursue excellence in music creativity, and maintain global networking to connect with the global music community including ISCM, ACL and Rostrum.

How does the Hong Kong Composers' Guild act to the music scene, particularly by creating new income and supporting contemporary music compositions?

Hong Kong Composers' Guild (HKCG) comprises high calibre professional composers. Many hold PhD or MPhil degrees, hold important teaching posts at music departments of well-known universities in Hong Kong, and are members of local professional music organisations. Their music works are of high artistic quality, many earning international acclaim and awards, and are often presented in world-class auditoriums and music festivals. HKCG also organises annual contemporary music festivals, collaborating with acclaimed local and overseas performance groups, including Hong Kong Children's Choir, Hong Kong Chinese Orchestra, City

Chamber Orchestra, Hong Kong Philharmonic Orchestra, Contemporary City Dance Company and many others. The concerts are not only well received in Hong Kong but also are regularly featured in the ISCM, ISCM Collaborative Series, Asian Composers League (ACL), receiving high acclaim. The composers receive commission fees for their music creativities.

Can you describe your style of composition and what your signature pieces are?

I have been receiving commissions to compose different genres of music for various purposes, including formats of multimedia, video, film music, orchestral, contemporary, Chinese traditional, modern music, cross-media, television, pop jazz and commercials. As a professional composer, I must meet the commission's requests. I cannot say there is a fixed style, but I do have my own music language, which I cannot describe in words. The two signature pieces are my cross-media Chinese music theatre, Intoxicating Nature, and Ode to Water, both collaborations with the Hong Kong Chinese Orchestra. It is an integration of various art forces with my original music as the primary and fused with dances, stage settings, props, lighting, theatre designs, video projections, poems and Chinese calligraphy.

What are your ideas and inspirations for your new compositions?

My new compositions are musical depictions of inspiration from nature, travels, poems, photographs, and paintings.

Regarding Hong Kong, Mainland China, Thailand, and Tokyo, what are the major differences in the environment for contemporary composers between these four regions?

Yes, there are differences in the environment for contemporary composers in these four regions. Hong Kong is very open to contemporary music compositions and enjoys a hybrid of the culture of the West and East due to its historical and cultural background. Mainland China is becoming more and more open to the West in terms of styles of composition while retaining a sophisticated, culturally rich root. Tokyo keeps a forerun position in the contemporary world music arena due to the exchanges with the world in the past decades, while retaining a strong Japanese tradition in its contemporary music creation. I have seen gradual progress in the contemporary music scene in Thailand in the recent decade.

But what is so unique? Can you describe this uniqueness?

Hong Kong composers enjoy a unique musical style with their own music languages reflecting their own cultural and historical environment. Hong Kong is lucky to have forerunners of contemporary music composers who have contributed much to local music creativity and music education for the past four decades. Composers like Doming Lam, Richard Tsang, Chan Wing Wah, Law Wing Fai, and many others have contributed a wealth of music works. Among them, Doming Lam's *Insects World* and *Autumn Execution* for Chinese orchestra are two masterpieces well recognised in Hong Kong, Asia and the West. Young active composers who graduated from the Hong Kong Academy for Performing Arts (APA), Hong Kong Chinese University (HKCU), University of Hong Kong (HKU) and many others can unfold their music creativity by taking part in various concerts tailor-made for them. For example, *'Music from the Heart'*, a music project launched since 1997 by the Hong Kong Chinese Orchestra (HKCO), provides a platform for professional musicians for young composers to write for Chinese music instrumentation. The project is presented in collaboration with HKCG and CASH with rewarding results as the artistic quality of pieces by young composers is very good. Meanwhile, the *New Generation* presented by HKCG with support from CASH and Radio Television Hong Kong are examples of other music platforms for young composers. They can submit their works, and professional musicians perform their pieces. These programmes are meant to nurture young composers, who can develop their skills and techniques by participating in these programmes.

Given the overwhelming amount of classical music performances freely available on YouTube and other online platforms, how does this new digital environment influence how contemporary composers approach new music composition, especially their creative process?

The new digital environment available on YouTube strongly influences musicians and composers. Through these online platforms, especially during COVID-19, easy access to music works performances surely benefits the creativity of composers and musicians, especially during these difficult pandemic eras. There is a general tendency to limit the number of sessions/instrumentations instead of a full orchestra during the pandemic. Brass or blown sections may be limited, but bowed strings, plucked strings, keyboard music and percussions are possible instrumentations. No doubt, large-scale works for the post-pandemic eras are coming.

What parts of your duty as the Hong Kong Composers' Guild chairman do you find most rewarding and frustrating?

The most rewarding is that after hard work, all the musical presentations are well brought out and attended by audiences and composers. The frustration is that many good works could not be presented because of the various constraints, including the lockdown during the pandemic. The regular RTHK (Radio Television Hong Kong) studio or public venues were closed, and concerts had to be postponed, affecting the art community, the performance, and the music development.

Are there any other inspiring stories in your role as the chairman that you like to share with the readers?

The digital online platform programme supported by ADC during the pandemic era is very inspiring and encouraging. I witnessed the premieres of seventeen new works by Hong Kong composers during such a difficult pandemic online. The composers have a music presentation and sessions to explain their works and creative process. I have physical attendance of all the seventeen world premieres during shooting. A three-fold interaction of musicians, composers and audience of the pieces or demonstrations of certain sections of the pieces are very interesting. It demonstrates how the music was given birth and how the three interacted online.

Photo 1. Dr. Mui Kwong Chiu, Chairman of the Hong Kong Composers' Guild and Director of Composers and Authors Society of Hong Kong.

Photo 2. Chairman Mui Kwong Chiu delivered the welcoming speech during the press conference of *Musicarama* music festival in 2016, which was presented by HKCG.

Photo 3. A snapshot of Dr. Mui working in his recording studio.

Photo 4. Dr. Mui's relaxing moment during the press conference of Hong Kong Composers' Guild in 2016.

Photo 5. Cross Media Chinese music theatre *'Ode to Water'* was rerun by Hong Kong Chinese Orchestra in 2017. The composer of this piece Dr. Mui Kwong Chiu posed in front of the concert banner outside the performing venue, Hong Kong Cultural Centre Concert Hall.

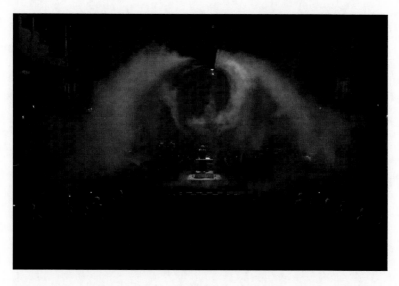

Photo 6. The opening scene of 'Ode to Water': The Dawn of Time. (Photo permission by Hong Kong Chinese Orchestra).

Photo 7. Dr. Mui's signature piece Cross Media Music Theatre *'Ode to Water'* employs his originally composed music as the primary art force, which is integrated with video projection. A huge white gauze is set up in the concert hall as the projection screen. (Photo permission by Hong Kong Chinese Orchestra).

Photo 8. Dance is also featured at Act 5 *'Drums that Drive up Waves'* of *'Ode to Water'*. (Photo permission by Hong Kong Chinese Orchestra).

Chapter 21

Levina Li-Cadman, Co-Founder, Art-Partners Hong Kong

Introduction

Established in 2016, Art-Partners Hong Kong is an independent art consultancy founded by Levina Li-Cadman and Sarah Pringle to conceptualise, develop and realise place-making art projects from Hong Kong across Asia. With over two decades of experience delivering engaging and memorable projects for world-renowned artists, Art-Partners Hong Kong aims to combine creativity with business acumen to add value through art and culture.

In addition to founding Art-Partners Hong Kong, Levina Li-Cadman is also the Co-Founder of Sassy Media Group (2011); White Cube Business Consultant – Contemporary Art Gallery (London, Hong Kong) (2010-). Levina Li-Cadman was also Development Consultant at the Royal Academy of Arts (2015-19). In the following interview, Levina Li-Cadman discusses in detail the business model of Art-Partners Hong Kong and the secrets behind the success of the art auction business in Hong Kong.

Self-introduction – could you introduce yourself and tell us about your professional training and educational background? What did you study at the university or art college? In addition, did you come from a family of artists, art historians, or art dealers, or are you also a practising artist yourself?

My mother was an amateur painter, so that was my first introduction to art. I went to a small liberal arts university in the US called Pepperdine University in Malibu and got a bachelor's degree in Business Administration. Going to a liberal arts college gave me an overview of art history, which made me realise that art reflects the geo-social-political moments over time; and gave me a lot of insight into art. I'm not from a traditional art background, and most art professionals come from a fine arts or art history background, so my route into the art industry was through business development.

After graduating, I focused mainly on business development in various industries, first in modelling and fashion and then in WarnerMedia (formerly Time Warner Inc.), entertainment, and licensing. I was always based in Hong Kong, covering about 11 countries in Asia, which gave me an in-depth knowledge of the APAC region. I then joined the Financial Times launch team in Hong Kong and was responsible for their Luxury Business and Partnerships sector. Through the Financial Times, I started working with Christie's, and I think that was when I really transitioned into the art world. So, I joined Christie's 16 years ago as the Business Development Director for the APAC region. That was my springboard into this career in the art world.

I also worked in business development across several auction categories. So not just Contemporary Art, Modern Art, Fine Wine, Jewellery, and Antiques. I always say it's a fantastic way to get into the industry to gain real insight into how the art deals are done behind the scenes in the secondary market. So it was really interesting. After working at Christie's for two years, I had to take a break from my career to start a family. I thought it would be great as a professional to understand more about the primary art market. The secondary market is when I buy an artwork and then resell it. The primary market is when the artist sells through a gallery. An artist who sells to the gallery on the primary market is a significant part of the market. There are different transaction rules and standard terms and conditions for primary acquisitions.

I joined White Cube as a Business Consultant. I wanted to understand how the primary art market works, and I think it was really important to understand it from the top of the market with an international gallery. So I started as a consultant to the founder of White Cube. The gallery has a roster of superstar artists, including Damien Hirst, Gilbert & George, Antony Gormley, and Tracey Emin, to name a few. I've learnt how the primary art market works, and it's much more interesting than the secondary market because, in the secondary market, you're mainly just reselling what someone else bought. Whereas in the primary market, you get to work directly with the artists as they create their artworks for the gallery exhibitions.

Can you provide a brief introduction to Art-Partners Hong Kong?

Art-Partners Hong Kong is an independent art consultancy established to conceptualise, develop and realise place-making art projects from Hong Kong throughout Asia. With over two decades of experience in delivering engaging and memorable projects for world-renowned artists, we combine creativity with business acumen to add value through art and culture. I was exposed to contemporary art early in my career because one of my very good university friends is a third-generation art dealer. He went to work for Larry Gagosian straight out of university in 1993, and I was spending a lot of time in New York for work then, so I was exposed to the contemporary art scene in New York in the 1990s through my art dealer friend. That experience sparked my interest in contemporary art.

In 2010, I joined the White Cube Gallery as a consultant, probably the second international gallery to open in Hong Kong after the Gagosian. Tim Marlow, who was working at White Cube, became the Artistic Director of the Royal Academy (RA), and he asked me to join and help him with the RA's Patron Development Programme in Hong Kong. I joined and worked for four or five years. The RA office has exhibitions and also educates the next generation of artists, so it was fascinating to understand how art institutions and museums work.

While at White Cube, I also started working on public art projects. I was asked to work on Antony Gormley's 'Event Horizon' project in Hong Kong. This was the most extensive public art installation ever staged in Hong Kong. There are 31 sculptures on the rooftops of buildings and at street level in the Central and Western districts. This project introduced me to the field of public art, which was still very new in its development in Hong Kong compared to the US and Europe. That was also when I met my business partner Sarah Pringle. We then decided to set up the Art-Partners Consultancy to fill this gap in the Hong Kong art scene, where clients such as corporates, companies, museums or institutions could hire us to create bespoke commission art projects.

Can you describe the staffing structure of Art-Partners Hong Kong?

Sarah and I are the co-founders of the company and focus on conceiving new ideas and art projects. We focus on building relationships with clients to ensure that we understand their needs and recommend the right artist for the commission art projects. We also have our Associate Director, Tania, who's been with us for five years; she came from an art-oriented high school in Hong Kong and graduated from university with a degree in Visual Art. Besides Tania, we have a project manager, a couple of junior project managers, and a financial administrator. When we take on large-scale public projects like 'Art for Everyone @HKMoA', where we installed artwork images to be displayed across 655 locations in Hong Kong, we shall hire more project staff to supplement the team's resources.

Can you list a few major clients that Art-Partners Hong Kong is currently representing in Hong Kong?

One of our key clients was The Friends of the Hong Kong Museum of Art. During COVID-19, we thought about what kind of public art programme we could do to fit in with the social distancing measures and inspiration the public positively. Because at that time, people were not allowed to go into the museums, and many exhibitions were cancelled or postponed due to severe restrictions. So I thought, wouldn't it be great to do a public art project where we just took the art to the streets? We were inspired by this public art project called 'Art Everywhere', in collaboration with the Tate, which took images from the museum's collection and displayed them on over 22,000 billboards around the UK. They called it Art Everywhere, and we thought, wow, why don't we do that in Hong Kong? This is the biggest public art project we've ever staged and the largest scale ever attempted in Hong Kong to date.

What are the other major projects that Art-Partners Hong Kong is currently working on?

With the reopening of the Hong Kong Museum of Art (HKMoA), the much-anticipated opening of the M+ Museum, and the Hong Kong Palace Museum, the governments are putting more effort and resources into making arts and culture as a key part of urban planning and development.

We also became the art consultant for the Peak Tram and were asked to work with female Chinese-Australian artist Lindy Lee to create a monumental sculpture for the reopening of the Peak Tram. The original plan was to fabricate and assemble the sculpture in mainland China. However, Lindy was unable to visit as she is based in Australia. The team had to move the entire production of the 10-tonne, 10-metre-high "Eye of Infinity" sculpture to Australia. It was completed and installed at the entrance to the Peak Tram Station in August 2022.

There are very few public art installations in Hong Kong's CBD, and the team is very proud of this project. We provided full service to the client, from research, artist selection, acquisition, installation and marketing. Lindy's beautiful creation greets every visitor to the Peak Tram Station. The sculpture has 33,000 perforated holes, which light shines through 24/7. Its long pillar shape looks like an eye, and it would light up at the highest frequency when a peak tram arrives at the station and dim when a peak tram departs.

How do all these different overseas and local professional experiences contribute to your current work as the co-founder of Art-Partners Hong Kong?

I think what's also contributing to our success is the ability to work in any country because I spent, you know, 13 years covering 12 countries in Asia and traveling extensively. So, whether the art project is in Singapore, China or Australia, the most important factor is that we know these markets. So, we're able to expand our business model on a regional basis. We bring to the table an understanding of the client's business and initiatives and then use art and culture to promote that. Of course, the regional knowledge and a network of contacts in each country to help us deliver these projects successfully is very important. It's really about teamwork. I think having regional experience in your career is great because it gives you many more opportunities to grow your business. Because I came out of business school, and my second job was already on a regional scale. It allowed me to work across the Asia Pacific and hit the ground running; I have contacts in all these countries I have worked in before.

As the Co-Founder of Art-Partners Hong Kong, could you describe your management and leadership style?

I'm a big believer in a management style called the One Minute Manager, which I highly recommend. It's a Harvard Business School textbook that you can read in half an hour. It says that as a manager, you have to tell your team what your goals are because they need to clearly understand the objectives of the business to help you as a team to achieve them. So, we like to set goals when a person is hired, and we have big-picture goals, such as the revenue target we need to achieve. Each of our employees understands these goals and how to achieve them. We would set three goals for each employee, SMART goals (specific, measurable, achievable, and trackable). We set and review these goals throughout the year, and the success of their performance is benchmarked against these goals, and these goals also have revenue numbers attached to them.

What are the secrets behind the success of the art auction business in Hong Kong?

Hong Kong is the third largest art market after New York and London. So, what makes Hong Kong's art auction business so successful? First, we have zero tax on art; it's not the same in mainland China, where you have to pay over 30% tax if you want to buy artwork from international artists. And because of its proximity to the rest of Asia, the big auctions take place in Hong Kong, and once the client buys the artwork, it is also delivered to them in Hong Kong. Clients can then choose to store it in Hong Kong, which is tax-free. Across the APAC region, Hong Kong has the best laissez-faire approach to art and taxation, which has fuelled the success of the art auction business.

In what directions do you want Art-Partners Hong Kong to develop in the next three to five years?

Continue to do what we're doing, grow our business, explore projects we haven't done before, reinvent ourselves, and be more sustainable. Everyone has a role to play in the world to be more environmentally conscious and sustainable. We always look at environmental factors and buy carbon credits to neutralise the carbon footprint in our projects. Our long-term horizon is to train a team to run a sustainable business, financially and environmentally.

Why do you think people turn to art in times of crisis?

It's simple: art makes people happy. There are many studies about art in hospitals, especially in the UK. If you look at a piece of art and like it, it creates endorphins and makes you happy. In times of crisis, people want to let themselves be distracted by art.

Laurence's 2022/23 research project "The Art of Creative Research" was funded by the Faculty of Liberal Arts and Social Sciences at the Education University of Hong Kong, and enabled via a collaboration with The National Institute of Education, Nanyang Technological University Singapore. It was part of an initiative to share the practice-based research work of creative arts educators with a wider international audience, both within and beyond the realm of academia. With an exciting and important international focus the exhibition at The Gallery, NIE Singapore (January 2023) showcased a range of works by fifteen staff from the Education University of Hong Kong, The National Institute of Education (NIE) Singapore, The Arts University Bournemouth UK, The Royal College of Art UK, Cambridge University UK, and University College London UK. A dedicated website and printed catalogue supported the physical exhibition, providing an informative collection of video interviews with the exhibitors, and other related project information and links.

https://www.theartofcreativeresearch.com
www.laurencewood.co.uk

Photo 1. Levina Li-Cadman.

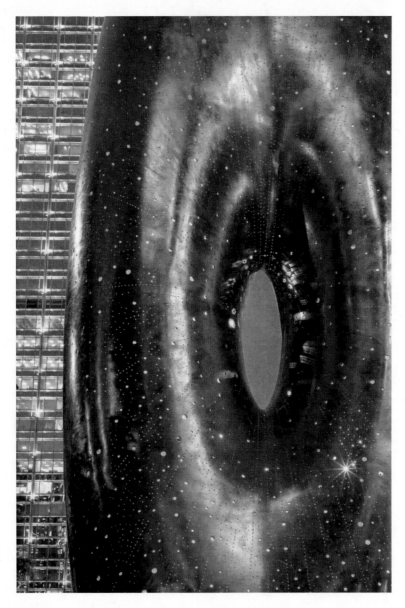

Photo 2. *Eye of Infinity* by Lindy Lee.

Photo 3. *Eye of Infinity* by Lindy Lee.

Photo 4. Art for Everyone @HKMOA.

Photo 5. Art for Everyone @HKMOA.

Photo 6. Art for Everyone @HKMOA.

Photo 7. *Event Horizon Hong Kong* (Photo Credit: Photography by Oak Taylor-Smith).

Chapter 22

Paul Tam, Executive Director, Performing Arts Division, West Kowloon Cultural District Authority

Introduction

With over 20 years of experience in performing arts management, Paul Tam has been serving as the Executive Director of the Performing Arts of West Kowloon Cultural District Authority (WKCDA) since 2020. At WKCDA, he is responsible for steering the strategic planning and sustainable development of these venues and oversees their business direction, artistic development, venue operations, technical and production, facilities planning and delivery. Before joining WKCDA, Paul Tam served as the Executive Director of Hong Kong Ballet (2014-20), General Manager of the Hong Kong International Literary Festival (2013-14) and Director of Marketing, Hong Kong Philharmonic Orchestra (2009-13). He is a Board Member of the Hong Kong Arts Administrators Association, a Governor of the Federation of Asian Cultural Promotion and a Board Member of the International Society for the Performing Arts. In the following interview, Paul discusses the strategic goals of the Performing Arts Division at WKCDA and his entrepreneurial leadership style that enables the balance between arts and business at WKCDA.

Could we begin this interview by first introducing yourself, for example, your professional training and educational background? What did you study at the university? Do you come from a family of musicians or performing artists? Are you also a trained musician yourself?

I am Paul Tam, Executive Director of Performing Arts at WKCDA. I received both my undergraduate degree in classical piano performance and composition and an MBA in Arts Administration from York University in Canada. My family is neither musical nor artistic – my dad was a businessman, and my mother was a housewife. Of their four children, only I chose the arts as a career.

Could you describe your career path to becoming the Executive Director of Performing Arts, West Kowloon Cultural District Authority (WKCD)?

I am truly blessed that I have worked across the spectrum of arts disciplines over the last two-plus decades, covering theatre in Canada, music, dance and even literature in Hong Kong, and a year of arts management fellowship in the US. Despite my training in classical music, my first job out of college was actually a short stint at the Professional Association of Canadian Theaters (PACT) in Toronto. For many reasons, I decided to repatriate to Hong Kong in the mid-90s and had my first break as the Audience Development Manager with the Hong Kong Philharmonic Orchestra (HK Phil), overseeing its learning and participation work. I was promoted after one year to be their Assistant General Manager in marketing, public relations, and education until 2003, when I won a one-year Vilar Fellowship at the Kennedy Centre in D.C., Washington.

Upon my return to Hong Kong, I did not immediately go back to the arts but dabbled in a range of non-arts jobs, including World Wildlife Fund, the Hong Kong Australian International School, Aedas and owning a bar and restaurant! I was out of the arts for almost five years before HKPhil beckoned again. I joined the orchestra again as their marketing chief for about four years until 2013 before moving on to a small Arts Development Council-funded organisation called Hong Kong International Literary Festival to be their General Manager, promoting English literature and book talks. Then the job of Executive Director for the Hong Kong Ballet came along, and I was there for six delightful years until March 2020. The rest is history. As you can see, it has been an interesting career, I must say.

What are your professional achievements and the unique skills you are best known for throughout the arts administrator community in Hong Kong that will add value to the WKCD?

My professional achievements? One of the earliest career highlights I remember with a lot of fondness is the HKPO x Hacken Lee LIVE at the Hong Kong Coliseum, a Hong Kong Philharmonic cantopop crossover concert at the Hong Kong Coliseum. It must have been the year 1998 or 99. Lee was in a bit of a professional rut then, so I was trying to find creative ways to fill up the two concerts with a combined audience of 16K. With few resources, my team and I went to great lengths to position the concerts, hunt for the target audiences, and put out a pretty smart marketing campaign. The end result? We had to open two extra concerts, and the recording went gold! But the ultimate reason it still holds dear to me is that the artistic product was fantastic. The chemistry between Lee and the conductor Wing-see Yip and the orchestra was simply perfect. It was an artistic and commercial success.

If I am to pick a highlight from my mid-career, it will have to be my time spent at the Hong Kong Ballet, being part of the driving force to rebrand, rebuild and revitalise the institution. When I joined the Hong Kong Ballet, it was just coming out of a public relations bend. And their audience-ship had been stagnant and branding dull. Upon my arrival, the Board and Management went through a lot of soul-searching to come up with a plan to rebuild and rebrand the organisation. Then Artistic Director Septime Webre was brought in to give the ensemble the creative fuel that he is so known for. Over the six years I was there, the audiences and revenues, including box office and sponsorship, went up dramatically. Looking at the organisation now, I am filled with pride and joy that it is one of the most exciting arts brands in Hong Kong.

That brings us to "now" - West Kowloon Cultural District, a truly game-changing cultural project that is gaining great momentum with the openings of the two museums in 2021 and 2022. The highlight for me here, which is ongoing, is the launch of the arts tech festival "Creative Tomorrow" at the time of writing this interview. A major, first-of-its-kind arts-tech festival by WKCD and exclusively sponsored by the Hong Kong Jockey Club, spanning from August 2022 to March 2023, it is curated along two programming strands: (1) traditional art forms such as Chinese opera, jazz, pop and theatre reimagined and retold digitally and (2) a collection of experiential installations and performances staged outdoors, indoors and locative media, in-game worlds, etc.

Could you describe the missions and visions of the Performing Arts Division, WKCD, and the philosophy behind its operations?

West Kowloon's vision is to develop an integrated arts and cultural district that will provide quality culture, entertainment and tourism programmes with a must-visit appeal to both residents and visitors from around the world; meet the long-term infrastructure needs of Hong Kong's arts and cultural development strategies and foster organic growth and development of culture and creative industries; and become a hub for attracting and nurturing creative talent, an impetus to improve quality of life, as well as a cultural gateway to the Greater Bay Area.

As for the Performing Arts Division, we further develop the WKCDA's vision into 5 strategic goals developed in 2020: the artistic, business and manning parameters within which our vision is met, programmes developed and produced, audiences engaged, financials reached (and hopefully exceeded) and staffing groomed to deliver all the strategies and action plans: (1) Artistic Excellence: To foster artistic excellence and innovation across the PA disciplines (2) The Art of Learning: To ensure lifelong arts learning for diverse communities throughout Hong Kong and beyond, (3) Audience & Visitors: To expand interfaces and deepen relationships with our audience, patrons and the general public; (4) Earning Our Way: To finance our ambitious plans for the next three years (5) People Power: To assemble and groom the best team to deliver these goals.

Could you describe the staffing structure of the Performing Arts Division, WKCD?

At WKCDA, we run a hybrid staffing model supported by permanent, contract and casual staff. We also have a centralised service model, providing back-office support services such as finance, human resources, legal, facilities management, security, fundraising, marketing, and public relations to artistic units such as Performing Arts Division, M+ and Palace. Under my direct authority, I oversee Artistic (Xiqu, contemporary performance, learning and participation), Technical & Production (back of house), Venue Operations (front of house), Administration and Planning.

As the Executive Director of the Performing Arts at WKCD, could you describe your typical day at work? Is there ever a typical day at work?

For me, a typical day involves a calendar that will instantly and constantly move due to unexpected changes. Taking away all the internal and external meetings, there may be an impromptu visit by a major patron. Or an artist just so happens to be coming to the district for rehearsal, and they want to chat. Or a crisis at one of our venues that needs my swift attention. There are constants too – attending my own shows, events or workshops and watching those of others.

As the Executive Director, Performing Arts, WKCD, could you describe your main roles and areas of responsibility?

I lead the Performing Arts Division to deliver world-class programmes in performing arts venues and facilities in the West Kowloon Cultural District. I am responsible for steering the strategic planning and sustainable development of these venues and oversee their business direction, artistic development, venue operations, technical and production, facilities planning and delivery.

Could you describe your management and leadership style? Would you describe yourself as a servant leader or a participative leader?

I believe I lead by vision. I am definitely not a micromanager, but I am pretty hands-on. I am also a fair boss and prize equity more than anything else. My leadership is also entrepreneurial, as I need to balance arts and business at WKCDA, which doesn't receive government funding for operations.

When designing new cultural programmes for the future seasons, how do you balance creating more opportunities for local and up-and-coming artists versus bringing overseas artists of international stardom to Hong Kong?

WKCDA is an international arts and cultural project, and the Performing Arts Division prides itself on presenting some of the best arts from Hong Kong and around the world. Due to COVID, we have relied almost solely on local talent for live performances for the last two years. If there is ever a silver lining to this pandemic, it would be the opportunity for the local audiences to come to appreciate the home-grown talents. That said, in our upcoming seasons, we cautiously anticipate (and pray) that international travel will gradually relax to bring mainland and international arts to the city once again. We have in our plans a platform called Young Creators Platform to nurture local upcoming talent. We have also been liaising with our various Mainland and international peers to form partnerships and collaborations in anticipation of the opening of the Lyric Theatre Complex. Very exciting stuff will be soon upon us.

How do you draw a balance between enhancing the local audience's taste and appreciation towards the arts by giving them somewhat less accessible programmes versus providing them with more popular programmes that could bring in good box office numbers? Given the convenience of Internet connectivity, mobile devices have increasingly dominated our lives. What are the new trends and opportunities in cultural programme marketing? Furthermore, what are the latest trends in facility management (particularly in performing arts venue management)?

Audience development is a key part of our work. And I believe that WKCDA and PA are for everyone. Our programming architecture builds upon it too. I have devised a model in which the performing arts season will be fronted by festivals and blockbusters such as the annual Freespace Jazz Festival, the inaugural West K-Pop Festival, Blackbox Xiqu Festival as well as the Freespace Dance. Blockbusters include both international and local major brand names to provide the best arts to the audiences. They are to be complimented by our research and development work driving innovations and pushing the artistic envelope. Finally, we will buttress these with strong public programmes such as The Dance We Made and The DH Chen Foundation – West Kowloon Tea House Student Matinee.

Over the last two decades, digital experiences have transformed how audiences engage with arts and culture and are driving new forms of cultural participation and practice. The COVID-19 pandemic has accelerated its growth. Technology also makes artistic and cultural experiences more accessible, tapping into previously untouched audiences. There have been many interesting and successful examples of how the arts use digital technology to engage with their audiences. The Sydney Opera House's digital season launched at the outset of COVID-19 or West Kowloon's Digital Stage; its Empty Theatre series and the Creative Tomorrow Festival, which runs from August 2022 to March 2023. Apart from maintaining the profiles of these institutions and expanding their reach beyond the in-person audience-ship, it also ensures that even those with disabilities, older people with accessibility issues, and those beyond the city's borders can access and benefit from cultural participation. However, this increased engagement through digital technology has ramifications – i.e., the line between artist and audience is increasingly blurred due to the interactive, participatory format. It's giving artists and arts organisations plenty to think about, particularly how they tailor their creative processes and products. Another thought is that when online performances are normally free or low in price, how will that impact the price sensitivity for live performances? These issues need to be analysed and strategised to support the growth of arts tech.

Artistic experiences aside, digital technology significantly impacts how the artistic contents are communicated with their intended recipients; the institutions are branded to how the venues are managed. On the marketing front, the buzz is about data-driven digital marketing – how to capture big data of the audiences or public so that arts organisations can be more effective with targeted marketing strategies and tactics. The other buzz is influencer / KOL (key opinion leaders) marketing which predominantly takes place online. Influencer Marketing is more important if the promotional campaign is for the Mainland market.

Technology has also increased the capabilities of theatre in many ways too, from LED and digital lighting that has drastically improved experiences over the traditional lighting system to the immersive sound system that greatly enhances the acoustic possibilities to automation in cable systems, motors, control boxes and software which allows more complex stage design and better transitions. Examples include Blacktrax (tracking system) and Meyer Sound Constellation Acoustic System.

Has mobile digital technology created new opportunities for audience building and outreach, enhancing public participation in the arts? What is the definition of effective and successful "Artistic Planning & Management" in Hong Kong?

To plan for and manage artistic growth and programming strategy well anywhere in the world, you have to deeply understand the local culture, its people and their social and artistic needs. What's a culturally relevant artistic season for a New York City institution differs from a culturally relevant artistic season in Hong Kong or Kuala Lumpur. Providing a platform for local artists (I define the word "local" not just by birth but also by the artists' base) to grow and shine should be the cornerstone of any successful artistic planning and management strategy. But all this will need to be supported by sustainable business planning and fundraising.

What are the current difficulties and challenges most arts and cultural administrators face in Hong Kong, particularly in business growth, sponsorship and donation?

COVID-19 has been incredibly challenging for artists and arts organisations. The uncertainties it brings have been extremely frustrating and discouraging, making long-term planning almost impossible. The exodus of talent from Hong Kong is another critical issue that the sector faces. From backstage technicians to programmers to marketers, the heavy turnover affects the quality of service (on stage and off) and morale.

At WKCD, how do you plan to create new fundraising and sponsorship opportunities for the performing arts? Is branding an important part of successful fundraising?

Branding is key and is one of the doctrines Michael Kaiser shared with us at the Kennedy Centre. He used the term Institutional Marketing to describe it versus Programmatic Marketing, which is what you do to promote each production. The better the shows you put on and promote them, the more brand equity will be accumulated over time. The better your institution is branded, the less you need to pay to promote each production which is very expensive. Pretty simple but very smart, right? So, to answer your question, branding is very important for the arts, especially because we are not armed with large promotional budgets, like automobiles, cell phones or luxury brands. To raise funds is essentially trying to invite donors to buy into who and what you are. Therefore, a solid brand and a relatable narrative are key.

Twenty years ago versus now – have you witnessed major changes in the profile of the local performing arts audience, e.g., average age, gender distribution, income and education level, etc.?

I don't have the exact social demographic stats, but from my casual observations, I would say that the performing arts audiences in Hong Kong are among the youngest and most culturally curious in the world. I went to a concert at the Edinburgh International Festival performed by the Philadelphia Orchestra conducted by the youngish Yannick Nézet Séquin in 2022. I looked around, and about 90% of the audience were grey-haired. A similar symphonic concert in Hong Kong by the two main orchestras would attract audiences 20 years younger on average. It's encouraging, but we need more of them to fill the halls.

What parts of your job as the Executive Director, Performing Arts Division, WKCD, do you find most rewarding? And which do you find most frustrating?

I am happiest when our audience leaves our shows or events touched and inspired by the experience. I am most frustrated when I can't find enough resources for the projects I believe in.

Why do we turn to art and music in times of crisis?

Nietzsche once said, "We have art in order not to die of the truth." Life can be difficult, and our world can be cruel and harsh. Whether it's an hour on Spotify listening to the sunny Mozart *Piano Concerto No. 21*, attending a live production of Shakespeare's *Much Ado About Nothing* or getting swept away by Keersmaeker's *Goldberg Variations*, you can find solace and inspiration. Sometimes, it's all it needs.

Are there any other interesting and inspiring stories regarding the WKCD that you wish to share with the readers?

The unique experience I have had so far working at WKCDA is the opportunity to help drive Lyric Theatre Complex's planning and construction, witnessing its development from a hole in the ground to the halfway point it's at now, and getting excited over its birth a few years from now. Visiting the building site in the middle of summer, wearing a hard hat and clunky safety boots is pretty challenging, but it is also a once-in-a-lifetime experience to be part of this cultural history that I wouldn't trade for anything else.

What would you like to be remembered for when you retire?

I hope that my work has touched someone's heart and made their life better.

Photo 1. Paul Tam.

Chapter 23

Scarlett Jie Chen, Former Head of Development for Performing Arts, West Kowloon Culture District

Introduction

A graduate of Master of Public Administration at Harvard University, Scarlett Chen served as the Head of Development, Performing Arts, West Kowloon Cultural District Authority (WKCDA) from 2019 to 2022. Before joining WKCDA, she served as the Chief Advisor for Harvard Wealth Strategy and Management (2016-19); Co-President at Harvard Kennedy School Arts and Culture Caucus (2018-19); Founder and Managing Partner at Jie Chen Music & Arts Academy (2017-19) and Founding Dean & Professor at the Department of Music, University of Shanghai for Science & Technology (2011-19). In the following interview, Scarlett discusses her leadership style as an arts administrator and how the performing arts performances at WKCDA complement the overall arts and cultural scene in Hong Kong. In addition to her many roles, Scarlett also maintains an active performing career.

What is your professional training and educational background? For example, what did you study at the university? Do you come from a family of performing artists, musicians, or creative people?

I often find self-introductions to be one of the great challenges in life. On the one hand, I would like to be as thoroughly detailed as possible so that no precious moments or important experiences are left out, but it is also important to me to paint as complete a picture of myself as possible for the readers. On the other hand, one runs a great risk of falling into the trap of becoming bored by sharing too much information.

Looking back on my life and career development so far, I realised that, in hindsight, some seemingly unrelated dots do indeed connect, making me into who I am today. Contrary to many people in the creative industry, I come from a family of highly educated and accomplished engineers, which explains why my musical education, taking piano lessons, was quite fortunate. I started playing the piano at age three and had no formal training in my early years. The piano felt like a very heavy piece of furniture to me, and my parents certainly hadn't overthought it until our neighbours recently acquired one. It then seemed to be quite an excellent addition to a well-rounded education. I started to win local music prizes, and people told my parents I might have some special 'talent.' Fast forward to winning the national audition for the Shanghai Conservatory and later on a full scholarship to the Curtis Institute of Music; amidst countless challenges and hardship along the way, I feel that ultimately it wasn't I who chose the path of learning the piano instead the piano chose me.

After earning your BA (Music), what motivated you to pursue an MA from the New School in 2009, an MBA from China Europe International Business School in 2016, and an MA (Public Administration) from Harvard University in 2019?

By the time I earned my BA in music, I already had an active performing career underway; this is mainly thanks to the many international prizes I had won. Frequent travelling required me to live in a metropolitan city with easy access to the airport. I had the opportunity to go to Yale in New Haven or Hannover in Germany, but ultimately chose New York for its convenience, its vibrancy, and richness of culture.

After studying in New York, I felt the need to attend business school; my career developed from performance to founding and managing the music department, as Dean, at the University of Shanghai Science and Technology (USST) over five years. This was a turning point in my career as, at that point, I had built up the department from zero to 1, and I realised that to scale it up, I needed more systematic and intensive training in management and finance.

One of the key experiences performing and touring the world provided me is that music does indeed communicate across languages, boundaries, races, and differences. I performed for the Indian Defense Secretary when the China-India border was under intense pressure. I have performed in small remote Spanish cities where none of the audience speaks English. I have also performed in poor rural areas for underprivileged communities where electricity was a luxury. These and other memorable experiences has led me to want to combine my skills and experiences with public services. The Harvard Kennedy School of Government is one of the most respectable names in this realm, and I truly enjoyed every moment.

What were the most valuable lessons and experiences earned at Harvard University?

I could spend pages on this topic as there are many unforgettable experiences. One of the most valuable lessons I learned is that instead of always focusing on finding the 'right' answers, we should ask ourselves if we are asking the 'right' question.

I attended the Kennedy School of Government, a public policy school at Harvard University. It is most well-known for its studies and research in public administration, politics, government, international affairs, and international development. It has also produced 17 heads of state, the most of any single graduate institution in the world. I was the first concert pianist ever admitted in the school's history, and I quickly realised that while they do have the best and brightest minds in almost all walks of life, awareness of the importance of arts and culture in today's social fabric, as well as the "what" and "how" modern government should play a role in this realm seemed to be overlooked. I then co-chaired the first Arts and Culture Caucus at Kennedy School, where together with a small team of like-minded schoolmates, we organised and hosted ARTS@HKS – a series of panel discussions exploring the role of arts and culture in the public sphere. Arts and culture, as well as THE ART OF LEADING – was a series of events including performances, interviews, and dialogues exploring the intersection and relevance of arts and policymaking in our society, the important role that various artistic mediums have played in propelling social movements and causes, and how we can collectively make things better.

Whilst at Harvard, I was given the opportunity to perform a recital at one of the most symbolic places on campus, the Memorial Church on Harvard Yard. Each year, the Memorial Church hosts the graduation ceremony. I gave the recital the title of "Dialogue without Words" in tribute to the vast diversity of inter-racial, inter-cultural, inter-religious, and inter-political student body. The power of this recital demonstrated to me how music is the language of the soul and how it transcends boundaries and differences. It brings people together into a judgement-free place and shares a moment without words. (One of the many beauties of art is that it's the one place where we give license to people to disagree. That's anomalous in our society today.)

Following on from "What motivated you to pursue an MA from the New School in 2009, and also an MBA from China Europe International Business School in 2016, and an MA (Public Administration) from Harvard University in 2019" – The next question is why did you not stay and further your career as a performing artist, instead of opting for a career in arts administration?

Steve Jobs famously said, "You can't connect the dots looking forward; you can only connect them looking backward. So, you have to trust that the dots will somehow connect in your future." I started performing and touring at age 15. By the time I finished my MBA and later MA from Harvard in 2019, I had already accrued about 20 years of a performing career, and I am grateful to say that I had what most people might call a "successful run" as a performing artist. Given the early start in my career, I had performed in almost all the top-tier venues around the world, including Carnegie Hall, Lincoln Center, Musée du Louvre, etc., with some of the best orchestras and conductors around the world. After a very intense 20 years of performing and touring, it came to a point where I started asking myself this question: with the longevity of life now expected and assisted by modern medicine, is it possible to devote the next 20 years of my life to something different? something that fascinates me in the same way performance has but is also beneficial to the world? In other words, I have a life philosophy that sees a lifetime in phases; I wanted to reinvent myself as I have so much curiosity in the world; I know piano will always remain in my blood, but it may take on a different part of my life and not be my primary focus.

"I have also performed in poor rural areas for underprivileged communities where electricity was a luxury" – what was the most valuable life lesson you learned from doing this?

Whilst the material world might differ from community to community, spiritual needs and emotional fabrics are more or less alike. We as human beings want to be understood, be heard, be empathised with, and be appreciated. Most importantly, we do not want to be alone; music offers exactly that companionship.

Could you describe your career path to becoming the Head of Development for the Department for Performing Arts, WKCD?

Before joining WKCD, I served as the Founding Dean & Professor at the Department of Music at the University of Shanghai for Science & Technology (2011-19), the first music department in a science and technology University at the time. In addition, I actively maintained my performing career and served on the juries for multiple competitions until I received the offer to study at Harvard Kennedy School as a Mason fellow.

Could you describe your experiences in this regard, and how much professional experiences contribute to your current work at the Department for Performing Arts, WKCD?

West Kowloon Culture District is one of the largest cultural projects ever built in human history. Spanning over 40 hectares of reclaimed land, we have art, education, public spaces, dining, and retail, with future commercial developments such as office buildings and hotels. Arts and culture are a vital part of any world-class city's economic and social fabric, and our vision is to not only be the main destination for Hong Kong, the GBA, and China, but a centre for the world.

When complete, it will provide about 23 hectares of public open space with two kilometres of the harbour-front promenade containing a host of arts and cultural facilities that will produce and host world-class exhibitions, performances, and arts and cultural events. It is rare to find such a rich combination of artistic possibilities, and I cannot wait to put into practice what I want to achieve; stay tuned!

Even though WKCD has been under construction for many years, it only started to open its doors in 2019 with the opening of our first venue, the Xiqu Centre. Therefore, in some respects, we are still growing like a big start-up. My previous experiences building up those two entities gave me the grit, entrepreneurial mindset, and perseverance to push through challenges.

As the Department for Performing Arts, WKCD, could you describe your typical day at work? Is there ever a typical day at work?

There's never a typical day. Sometimes we are in meetings all day communicating across departments both horizontally and vertically;

sometimes, we are out in the fields executing the work. But, to me, it doesn't matter what shape or form it comes in. Work is all about problem-solving.

As the Department for Performing Arts, WKCD, could you describe your main roles and areas of responsibility?

If I have to sum it up in one phrase, it would be to identify, mobilise and maximise all kinds of resources and possibilities to support and ensure the realisation, development, and sustainability of our artistic vision and mission.

As the Department for Performing Arts, WKCD, could you describe your management and leadership style? Would you describe yourself as a servant leader or a participative leader?

I don't micromanage and I don't dictate how things need to be done. I believe each individual should find their working styles, and hopefully, it will maximise their abilities. I like to inspire my team with a goal, empower them to make decisions, and encourage them to take up challenges.

What are the current difficulties and challenges in marketing faced by a majority of arts and cultural administrators in Hong Kong and other neighbouring regions?

I cannot speak for others, but for me, due to the disruption in the travel industry impacted by COVID-19, the influx of non-local audiences previously brought in by the vibrant tourism of this international hub city, as well as the rich resources of international artists have been put on hold. In other words, we are now marketing limited content to a limited audience market.

The COVID-19 crisis turned the world upside down. How have the Department for Performing Arts, WKCD, and you (as the Department Head) been coping with COVID-19?

Keep calm and carry on! I don't want to take up too much airtime and describe the millions of hurdles we had to jump over but let's just say that we are now used to having plans A, B, C, D, for any events that we put on. That being said, I trust we will come out of this stronger than ever.

Curtis Institute of Music versus Harvard University – what are the major differences in learning environments and students' learning attitudes and motivations between these two education institutions?

Before we start discussing what's different about them, let's look at what they share in common first. Both represent the top of their echelon, and acceptance is extremely competitive: Curtis had an acceptance rate of 3.9% in 2020, while Harvard was 5.2% that year. Needless to say, the students' learning attitudes and motivations are very similar, where insanely hard work and good ethics are valued, and everyone wants to make a difference in the world.

While both accept students from all over the world, the scale and scopes are quite different. Harvard University has 12 different degree-granting schools across 19 broad fields of study. While Curtis focuses on the classical music performance field, Harvard College admitted 2,037 new students in 2020, while Curtis only admitted 27 new students that same year. I am grateful to have studied in both institutions. I got perfectionist training from Curtis, while Harvard gave me a view of the world outside of the 88 keys on the piano.

The LCSD, Opera Hong Kong, and HK Arts Festival are already doing a great job in regularly bringing performing artists of international caliber into productions and performances. With the new establishment of the WKCD – how would it complement the existing LCSD, HK Arts Festival, and further enrich the Hong Kong arts and cultural scene as a whole?

That's a great question, and indeed, we are so grateful that HK already has such a rich array of presenting bodies. As you mentioned, they are doing a fantastic job in regularly bringing performing artists of international caliber. I think, as well as being a world-class presenter, we also see ourselves as an incubating platform for the next generation of possibilities in the realm of performing arts. We believe that young, emerging artists have the power to shape the future. Nothing is more rewarding than seeing today's young artistic talents become leading choreographers, composers, theatre directors, and superstars one day. At West Kowloon, we make their career trajectory our priority and focus.

Is the Development for Performing Arts Division, WKCD, also helping locate performing arts organisations (e.g., HK Ballet, HK Phil., and Opera HK) to find and build their new permanent homes at WKCD?

We already have long-term collaborative partnerships with these organisations. With the planning of the Lyric Theatre, which would be the next vehement venue under the Performing Arts unit scheduled to be complete by 2026, WKCD will no doubt become a place for everyone.

Photo 1. Scarlett Jie Chen (Former Head of Development for Performing Arts, West Kowloon Culture District).

Chapter 24

Ian Leung, Former Senior Programme Manager, Hong Kong Arts Centre

Introduction

Located in Wanchai, Hong Kong Island, the Hong Kong Arts Centre (HKAC) is a non-profit arts institution and art museum founded in 1977 with the mission to promote contemporary performing arts, visual arts, film and video arts, as well as to provide art education. The HKAC comprises presentation spaces and venues, including galleries, theatres, a cinema, classrooms, studios, restaurants, and offices.

Ian Leung is a quantity surveyor turned arts manager, currently serving as the Senior Programme Manager at the HKAC. Before joining the HKAC, he served as Programme Coordinator and Programme/Outreach Manager at the Hong Kong Arts Festival (HKAF) from 2008-2011. He is also the Founder and Executive Director of Thealosophers. Ian was also nominated for Best Director at the 2009 Hong Kong Drama Festival. In the following interview, Ian discusses the mission and philosophy behind the operations and programming of the HKAC. In addition, he also shares his view on the West Kowloon Cultural District project and its potential to create sustainable arts development in the City.

Could you introduce yourself, for example, your professional training and educational background? What did you study at the university? Do you come from a family of performing artists, musicians, or creative people?

My family can hardly be regarded as members of the artistic community. Like many families who migrated to Hong Kong since my grandparents' era, the mandate has always been to survive, strive and thrive. This has been passed down to me and is characterised as always seeking to gain recognition and approval.

So naturally, I chose a subject known to be secure in terms of career path - a professional career in Quantity Surveying. It was also during that period that I started to live a double life. In the day, I attended lectures and tutorials, and the rest of the time I devoted myself to the Drama Society at the Hong Kong Polytechnic University.

After working as a surveyor in Disneyland's private consultant and the Architectural Services Department, I realised I wanted to make better use of my time and decided to try merging my passion and training, so I ventured to Goldsmiths, University of London to pursue a MA in Arts Administration and Cultural Policy.

In 2019, you received the HKETO-NY Arts Activator Fellowship of Yale-China Association, and served as Research Fellow, Art/Architecture at Yale University. What were the most valuable lessons and experiences earned at Yale-China Association University?

All learning experiences are valuable, but I am still in awe of how many subjects students may opt-in to from their internal course selection system. They really spend time and effort making course selection easy. I could choose as many classes as I liked as long as I remained committed to the course output and managed my time well. As a result, one would often find students from other disciplines joining your class, which instilled faith in me that interdisciplinary practices are not only possible but also the way of the world.

During your time at Yale University, did you meet any notable alumni in person, or were you given any opportunities to learn and work alongside them?

Notable Yale alumni I have met include:
Joan Channick, School of Drama
Sheila Levrant De Bretteville, School of Art
Joel Sanders, School of Architecture

They have been instrumental in my learning journey. Joel even went so far as to offer an opportunity for the class students to opt in and work on my project - Via North Point, with two architects and one art student in his post-graduate class.

I also seized the opportunity to invite him to Hong Kong and join a roundtable and think tank with designers, art collectives, and advocacy groups from Taipei and Guangzhou. Together, they formed a solid foundation for the project I was about to embark on.

Could you provide a brief introduction to the Hong Kong Arts Centre (HKAC)? What are the mission, vision, and philosophy behind your Department's operations and management?

The Hong Kong Arts Centre (HKAC), in my view, is an independent creative hub for arts and culture in Hong Kong. It has always been the DNA of HKAC to push to new frontiers, enabling trail-blazing arts as well as supporting individual and small-medium size artists/groups to thrive. At the same time, it never ceases to expand its reach to the outside world, encouraging the permeation of both contemporary society and the Arts within the Centre. It is the destination-to-be for the arts of our times.

Under the Programme Department, I oversee Performing Arts, Public Art and Audience Development; three small but competent teams work not only in their subject areas but also in a task force to work on campaigns like the Cultural Masseur. Speaking of the philosophy behind driving my teams forward, I would say I celebrate their individuality and expertise from their unique areas of different forms of art. In the end, it is the spirit of interdisciplinary collaborations that makes our world turn. Progress can only be found in differences.

The HKAC operates without recurrent Government funding; the business model largely relies on the building rental income to support its own operation. In other words, all programmes we do, require additional funding support from other foundations, charities, corporations, or commissions from the Government. Hence, balancing funders' mission and vision with our own in serving the HK Art & Cultural scene always demands a delicate balance.

Could you describe your career path to becoming the Senior Programme Manager, HKAC?

When I graduated from Goldsmiths, the 2007 Global Financial Crisis meant that jobs were being cut everywhere, and it wasn't easy to find an internship. Luckily enough, I landed a job with the Hong Kong Arts Festival (HKAF) upon my return and have been with the Programme ever since.

During my tenure at the Festival, I worked as an executive producer for performing arts and progressed into programming for the HKAF's outreach and audience-building department. The journey has been intense and fascinating; I gained experiences from areas as diverse as an editor for scripts, subtitle, front of the house, off-site (non-conventional venue) technical coordinator, ticketing and merchandise. Also, as the touring manager when HKAF was tasked to bring two local commissions (百年回顧八和鳴 | 情話紫釵) to showcase HK's creative talents at the Shanghai World Expo 2012. From there, I moved on to oversee the HKAF PLUS and Young Friends Scheme with over 10,000 members, recruiting youngsters and organising activities to engage the youth during the Festival period.

By then, I saw what was lacking in my expertise, which was mainly the expertise of out and seeing things from different perspectives and weaving strategic alliances in the work I completed. That was when I recommended myself to Connie Lam, the Executive Director of HKAC then, and asked her if I could join the public art team. It was an area entirely different from my own field but offered the opportunity to develop partnerships with the outside world. Since I joined the public art team, I have been able to initiate, pitch, manage and produce a wide spectrum of public art projects covering collaboration with major transport corporations like the MTR and Airport Authority, commercial clients like Lanvin, Peninsula and Le Meridien Hotel, property developers like Hendersonland and Sino, funding bodies such as Lee Hysan Foundation, Urban Renewal Fund and the HK Jockey Club Charity Trust. The museum without walls project, Harbour Arts Sculpture Park 2018, prompted me to think if there is an alternative to a top-down model in the context of public art.

This gave rise to the recent project *Via North Point,* in which I adopted a hybrid model of both top-down and bottom-up to achieve a district-wide public art intervention campaign aiming at not only uplifting the urban landscape but also serving the community that addresses their concern. Until recently, my team and I have been happy to see some of the artworks still being celebrated by the communities from different districts. They are still serving the community's needs and interests.

In 2005, you graduated with a Bachelor of Science (Construction Economics & Management) from the Hong Kong Polytechnic University and also worked as a Quantity Surveyor Graduate on the construction of Hong Kong's Disneyland. Do you consider yourself a second-career arts administrator? What motivated you to leave your original career and pursue a career as an arts administrator instead?

My heart belongs in service to our society. I actively volunteered at the Leo Club in Repulse Bay for ten years. It taught me that doing something good doesn't require complicated planning; a simple act of goodwill can travel a long way. Nonetheless, how social services are being organised is very fragmented and KPI-driven. It lacks a value chain to connect the good that everybody else is doing. I see Art as the perfect medium to engage and thread through the social capital between the neighbourhood and the social services.

From 2011-2013, you served as the Outreach Manager at the Hong Kong Arts Festival (HKAF). In 2007, you co-founded Thealosophers (Theatre+philosophers) and were nominated Best Director in the 2009 Hong Kong Drama Festival. How do such professional experiences contribute to your current work as the Senior Programme Manager at HKAC?

I owe a lot to the theatre-making experience I gained from Thealosophers. I mostly worked as an actor and director, which gave me new perspectives on people and making decisions amidst a creative process. It aligns greatly with what I do now as a professional Arts Administrator. When my role shifts to a Producer, the edge it gives me is understanding the artist's conception before anything else is materialised. This enables me in a managerial framework to produce projects that can bring out the flavours of the artistry the artists have to offer and bring it under a budget and timeline which works for all parties.

You once said that philosophers aim to bring cross-disciplinary media together in interpreting the world we live in today. Could you elaborate more on that or perhaps give specific examples to illustrate your point?

One of the productions is titled *"Me. As a team."* We established the project would approach what constitutes the idea of "me." When we were in the rehearsal studio, we would pick up materials such as a news headline and distribute roles that we identified from the piece of information. These roles can be objects and do not have to be human beings. Afterwards, we will divide ourselves into groups and try to "speak" on behalf of the role; sometimes, the expression extends beyond words and can utilise a variety of mediums to communicate. Hence, we first identify the source from one media, in this case, a piece of newspaper headline. Then we formulate different mediums to try to communicate speculative content or what could have been missing in the original reporting. This was one of the typical days of rehearsal we worked on in our devising theatre process, and I owe the reference to Arianne Mnouchkine and Katie Mitchell.

As the Senior Programme Manager at HKAC, could you describe your typical day at work? Is there ever a typical day at work?

No day is the same, but there are some frameworks to guide what we do. First of all, I do not call meetings for progress updates. I trust my delegates, and they will all finish within a reasonable timeframe. If they encounter difficulties, they could come to me and share them. When that moment comes, besides coaching, I will also act as a facilitator to reallocate resources to ensure progress.

As the Senior Programme Manager at HKAC, could you describe your main roles and areas of responsibility?

I mainly oversee programme planning for the three disciplines under my care and always remind myself to look at them interchangeably or in an interdisciplinary manner. Once a programme idea is conceived, I will prepare internal pitching to my senior management, sometimes even further to outside funders.

In parallel, we will do budget scenarios about the same programme as we need to know what and how much risk we are taking, what is in our arsenal to combat issues and to measure between goodwill and value for money.

As the Senior Programme Manager at HKAC, could you describe your management and leadership style? Would you describe yourself as a servant leader or a participative leader?

My role is to be a good leader for the three teams that I manage. Being a leader does not mean being in the ultimate power position to give orders (though sometimes it does fall on you to make the final decision), but being an empathic listener and visionary. Never ceasing to prompt your teammates to look far and wide and consider the end game. I am still learning as we speak.

What are the latest trends in marketing and audience outreach/building amongst arts and cultural organisations worldwide? With the convenience of Internet connectivity and other mobile technologies, have you witnessed and experienced any major evolutions in marketing/outreach strategies in the context of arts and cultural management?

My first response would be to dismantle the categorical thinking of marketing/outreach; in terms of managerial or administrative reasons, it is understandable to be divided in such a way, but in terms of their direction and programming, they can no longer be divided because of the technological advancement we all experience today.

First, the ease of use of various creative content tools, which are web-based in existence in Web 2.0, allows both creators and consumers to find more ways to find their needs met in an on-demand mode, implying empowerment to consumer's choice even further and making it easier to find your own community regardless of how niche your community might be.

Second, Blockchain technology enables a decentralised ecology of content communities. This means ownership to the individual from every step of the way in the value chain until it reaches its user; the users act not only as consumers but circle back as active participators in influencing decisions or even joining as Decentralised Autonomous Organisation (D.A.O.) for a particular project.

Both of these informed us of a future where the community is more easily formed than ever, and the next-gen is no longer satisfied with spoon-feeding content from an institute or the top-down. In such an environment, my principle in navigating this landscape is to see marketing and outreach both under Audience Development, which is more human-centric and concerned more about the holistic development of your patrons, and see them beyond a mere consumer of cultural content.

What are the current difficulties and challenges in marketing faced by the majority of arts and cultural administrators in Hong Kong and other neighbouring regions?

Audience behavioural change, their expectation from the cultural experience, and the reasons why people are drawn to Arts are so different today. The pandemic accelerates this difference, where people are forced to stay home and find human connections and resilience.

This surfaces two core values to me as an arts administrator, namely:

a) the social dimension and the desire to relate to something larger than oneself have become a more dominant factor in the demand side of things.

b) technology literacy grows, revealing more talents across the globe, but at the same time, they are scattered; once a certain threshold is passed, an individual becomes known to others or him/herself, then like-minded creators and makers will gravitate towards one another and form community/collective. They operate on a project based on interest, further fragmenting the supply side.

What parts of your job as the Senior Programme Manager, HKAC do you find most rewarding? And which do you find most frustrating?

I want to say audiences applaud, but it comes second place to the smile and fulfilment when you and your team pull through just about any type or size of production where you also grow with the partners you choose to work with. It is always a collective learning experience. The most frustrating will always be the excruciating budget compared to the level and scale of things you set out to achieve. Nonetheless, that's where the muse comes from, and it always excites me.

COVID-19 has turned the world upside down. How have the HKAC and you (as the Senior Programme Manager) been coping with COVID-19?

I think what I experienced was largely shared by peers in the field; we went from programme->postpone to PlanB->cancel->PlanC and so on. Then it moved to programming for hybrid experiences; online was the standard with offline as a bonus, and now I am championing Concept Touring. What's worth traveling is the essence of an artistic project. I am striving for a certain artistic framework (i.e., like a recipe or formula) while allowing local/indigenous artists and communities to activate it. It is not only a way of answering to our own carbon footprint, but also a step beyond the conventional modes of consumer-performer ideology in "appreciating overseas artists" to conversing with visiting artists: body and mind, still non-verbal and transcending space and time.

In your opinion, what will be the impact of the West Kowloon Cultural District project in Hong Kong, and its potential in creating sustainable arts development in the City?

First, one must ask why the arts need sustainable development. To be more precise, if art is contented by itself with the art-goers and the market and all that, why bother? I am a believer in great nature, and it is in human nature that we want to keep everything "alive," so we can come back and visit whenever we please. Yet, sometimes beauty is at its most charming in the most ephemeral things or fleeing moments; the pursuit for the moment, the wait for the happening, is beautiful as well.

I think the West Kowloon Cultural District is in a challenging position to find this delicate balance with its institutional size. Perhaps a more holacratic mode of working where each complex is given room for arts administrators to work in a cross-team setting, forming task forces in a non-hierarchical manner on an individual level, creating safe room for errors and encouraging new ideas to spin and be tested. This orientation allows us to better cope with the VUCA environment more agilely and responsively. Without a doubt, we have the infrastructures gradually sinking in, now with some long-awaited centralised policy Bureaus backing behind it. It is in a pivotal position for the Hong Kong arts and cultural landscape to engage in exchange and dialogue with the world, not just importing excellence but also creating conditions for success and exporting our own cases.

Viewing your audiences beyond the status of visitors or the standard KPI of the number of visits could also be a good start. Trust in your artists and audiences, empower them and grow with them. Develop your audience through programming, marketing, and outreach all at once, with an ecological mindset instead of a linear one; beautiful things tend to happen in such conditions.

Any other interesting and inspiring stories regarding your work as the Senior Programme Manager, HKAC, that you wish to share with the readers?

I had my moment of doubt, so I applied for the Yale fellowship at the Yale-China Association, for which I am deeply grateful. The hanging question for me then was, "What makes Art art?" My underlying rationale in arriving at this question was: why it seems that no matter what I do or how much better I got at my job from experiences and learning, I still couldn't persuade my non-art friends to go to shows for reasons beyond our friendship and instead just to go for the sake of it?

With this question, I initiated the Tea House of Many Stories. As an Arts Activator (administrator stream) of the Yale Fellowship scheme, I was supposed to do an end-term presentation, but instead, I opted to run a series of one-to-one tea gatherings, totalling 74 people, and I presented my findings.

The Tea House is about curating a tea-tasting experience, where my guests will share whatever they feel like at the moment, and I would, based on what they share, pick 1 type of tea out of 5 to serve, and we drink together. Closer to the end, I would invite my guest to do a "task" together, and then I'd leave the room for the guest to enjoy a moment of solitude. Afterwards, I'd solicit their help to help me answer associated questions of "What makes Art art?" such as "What constitutes an artful experience?" "What we just experienced together, does it count as an art experience or just a simple social meeting of two strangers?"

The presentation was transformed into a lecture performance for a full audience at the Festival of Arts & Ideas, New Haven. What I am trying to land here is a reminder to ourselves that we do not have to hold tight to our definition of arts administrator/artist or programming/marketing or performance/exhibition or the arts equal to something to see/experience. In essence, I believe what makes Art art is that it contains an aesthetic experience (in other words, moments when you find beauty); you can absolutely trust yourself when you see something and instinctively say, "Awe, that's beautiful." And you can always trust that you can easily find these moments in everyday life if you choose to see them. In the Tea House, being an authentic me, having an honest exchange with another human being, is already an artful experience for all the guests I have served.

These 74 people and counting (I am still doing this in Hong Kong by the way) give me the strength to do what I am doing in the Arts Centre as a humble servant of the arts.

Photo 1. Ian Leung (Former Senior Programme Manager, Hong Kong Arts Centre).

Chapter 25

Anita Lam, Co-Founder & Curator, the Collective HK

Introduction

Founded in Hong Kong in 2013, The Collective HK is a cross-discipline design and technology studio specialising in creating digital and living art forms that range from installation to stage performance. Combining a variety of design disciplines, fine arts concepts and technology, the works of art created by The Collective HK are majorly interactive installations and immersive experiences. Anita Lam is the Co-Founder & Curator of The Collective HK. In the following interview, Anita Lam talks about the challenges faced in tackling the boundaries between art and technology and The Collective HK's unique approach to the human experience at the centre of technology.

Could we begin this interview by first introducing yourself and your affiliation with The Collective HK?

I am the current Creative Project Director and Curator in this studio (The Collective HK). As the Co-Founder, I established this studio with my business partner, Andy Stokes, currently serving as The Collective HK's Technical Director. The Collective HK is a for-profit organisation. However, we have recently created a non-profit technology platform, ALAN (Artists who Love Animals and Nature), to gather like-minded artists and creative technologists to create art pieces that would bring meaningful impacts on our society and positive change to our planet.

About my educational background, I majored in International Business Studies at the City University of Hong Kong (1994-97). Regarding my professional experiences, I spent many years working in the advertising and design industry. After earning my master's degree (majoring in Design Strategies) from the School of Design, Hong Kong Polytechnic University

(HK PolyU), I started this studio (The Collective HK) with my current business partner, Andy Stokes, in 2012.

How did you develop a keen interest in design in the first place?

I have always loved creating things that inspire and make people feel good. I have always preferred design over fine arts, because design involves more problem-solving elements, and I always like to find new ways to improve our ways of living. Living in terms of how we could change our planet for the better.

Regarding my professional training in Design, my friend (a product designer) recommended I pursue this master design in Design Strategies at the Hong Kong Polytechnic University (HK PolyU) -- it was truly a very inspiring programme. As soon as I completed this MA programme, I dedicated myself to the design industry.

What exactly are design strategies?

Design strategies refer to design thinking in our daily lives -- not just limited to art or design practices. Design thinking is more about developing the skills, techniques, and new concerts for problem-solving – which we could actually apply for tackling day-to-day challenges in innovative ways. Design strategies have opened the perspective that allowed me to push the boundaries and creativity, enabling me to apply different design concepts and skills to improve my business practices and daily life.

Could you provide an example to illustrate what design strategies are?

Design strategies involve applying design thinking and "play" into our everyday problem-solving practices. As we grow older, we develop some pre-set parameters and perceptions to guide our way to find solutions. Design thinking, however, deconstructs all pre-conditions, based on research and development, to guide us to find the solution. For example, I was at point A and believed point B was the best solution. In the past, I would focus on finding the path to reach B, to be "result-oriented." Design thinking, however, does not have any pre-set solutions. Through research and understanding the context, I discover where it leads me to be "process-oriented." I have learned that "plans are not made to follow; they are made to be changed."

I found one particularly inspiring activity during my study – "Spaghetti Tower Marshmallow Challenge." Each team has 18 mins to build the tallest free-standing structure possible out of 20 sticks of spaghetti, one yard of tape, and one yard of string that can support a marshmallow. Surprisingly, research shows that children achieved the best results among most humans, while most MBA students had rather disappointing performances. One argument is that children are not constrained by their experiences; they rather rely on trial and error, prototyping and free creative actions, while grown adults rely on discussion, assessment and results focused.

Can you provide a brief introduction to The Collective HK? Why did you choose the name The Collective HK for the organisation?

The Collective HK is a digital art creative agency/studio from Hong Kong. Our goal is to develop new art forms that bring people together, providing more engaging channels to convey messages more meaningfully. We chose the word "Collective" because business models or practices in the field of Design have undergone major changes over the years. We have recently witnessed a wide variety of new digital technologies and art forms continue to emerge in the market. Such a new landscape has undoubtedly revolutionised the relationships with digital technologies and art forms. With The Collective HK, we truly believe that by bringing professionals from diverse fields (e.g., arts practitioners and technology talents) to collaborate, new approaches could be achieved to bring new, inspiring and engaging experiences to the audiences.

In short, The Collective HK is a cross-discipline design & technology studio based in Hong Kong. We create digital and living art forms, ranging from installation to stage performance. Our works combine various disciplines, including interaction design, lighting, animation, programming and sculpture, with tools developed and customised specifically for each project. Our approach puts the human experience at the centre of technological development, with a strong visual impact and unique bespoke technologies created in-house.

When people talk about The Collective HK, what is the first image that comes to mind?

In Hong Kong, there aren't too many art- and technology-oriented design or creative studios to start with. So, what The Collective HK emphasises is not just combining all these elements (e.g., design, lighting, animation, programming and sculpture, etc.) together, but enhancing the inter-activeness between them is the key. There are other art and technology studios in Hong Kong. Some focus more on sound art, while others emphasise abstract installations or sculptures. Whereas with The Collective HK, since we first started as an animation studio (motion graphics design house), we tend to put a much stronger emphasis on the visual aspects and meaning of our artworks -- when it comes to the delivery of artistic experience for the audience with our art pieces. In other words, our ultimate goal is to bring more meaningful visual impacts and experiential experiences to the audience with our innovative art tech projects.

What are the missions, visions and philosophy behind The Collective HK?

Interactive installations with technology are so expensive to create -- because technological applications including R&D, software development, hardware acquisition, and maintenance all come with a high price tag. Based on the philosophy of "Art as a Platform, Technology as a Tool," The Collective HK wants to commit itself to creating interactive art installations that allow guests to stay longer in the exhibitions – thereby enabling them to truly feel the essence of the art pieces and to appreciate the thoughts of the artists. Hopefully, it would bring new insights and deeper meaning to the audience – in particular, to connect the millennials' interests and values, which technology is already part of our everyday lives.

Via The Collective HK's projects, we hope we can enhance the audience's awareness of the arts and encourage community involvement. In other words, we do not want our projects to be 'gimmicks,' 'eye candies,' i.e., carrying merely commercial values or no real purpose. In short, via The Collective HK using technology and new art-making approaches, we want our installations to carry the power to evoke an emotional response from the audience. I see art as a platform and technology as a tool. Technology consumes more energy and resources from our planet, and we don't believe in using technology as a gimmick or purely for photo opportunities. I should emphasise that our commissioned and art projects must carry meaning and purposes, and our ultimate goal is to drive social change.

We have been experimenting with different technologies to convey a message more effectively through interactive or immersive art, enhancing the audience's experience along the appreciation process. Meanwhile, The Collective HK is also developing augmented reality and machine learning. Due to the pandemic lockdown in the past two years, most physical installations have been postponed or cancelled. As a result, we spent our research on augmented reality for its high mobility without geographical boundaries.

Furthermore, since 2018 we have focused heavily on developing educational art pieces for non-commercial projects. We at The Collective HK believe that art should carry a message and that technology can enhance the experience, allowing more effective communication. In short, we aim to convey messages especially to the next generations, stimulating conversation and exploring possibilities.

As the Co-Founder, The Collective HK, can you describe your main roles and areas of responsibility?

I tell stories; I am a storyteller. Basically, when I come up with a new project, whether one installation or a collection of pieces, I need to develop a unique and interactive concept for telling the stories. I would then need to search for different potential artists who work together to create art pieces collaboratively and to tell these stories that would move or wow the audience.

Could you describe the staffing and organisational structure of The Collective HK?

The Collective HK's organisational structure is very flat. My partner Andy Stokes (Co-Founder) and I made up the whole organisation of The Collective HK. Meanwhile, designers and artists of a wide variety of creative backgrounds and expertise (e.g., animators, visual designers, programmers, etc.) work for The Collective HK freelance.

How would you describe your leadership style? Would you describe yourself as a participative or transformational leader?

I don't have specific terms or labels to describe my own leadership or management style. In terms of managing people, I also strongly emphasise 'fairness.' Because I understand the current young generation of the post-material era is increasingly focusing on building a fairer society, and the pursuit of social justice and equality are also central to their values and beliefs.

In terms of our organisational culture, under the umbrella of The Collective HK organisation, we put strong emphasis on co-workers having mutual respect for each other. We also emphasise work-life balance in our organisational culture. Because design and art-making are all about creativity, innovation, and change, designers, artists, and creative people need time and space to relax and refill their think tanks to rejuvenate their brain power.

In summary, under my management and leadership, The Collective HK aims to foster a casual, friendly, and collaborative working environment. However, when our colleagues are committed to a project, we expect ourselves to deliver not just 100%, but 110%. It is because when you aim high, you can be sure that 100% will be delivered in the end.

In what ways do you want The Collective HK to contribute to the overall design and creative industries in Hong Kong?

We never really thought about it that way. With The Collective HK, we really want to do something for the community. I adore some cities, like Copenhagen and Melbourne, where art is built for the community and people. Art is not about fame and trends; it is part of the culture and everyday life. Art is not only in museums, not only to display famous artists, not only for profits. Art is supported by the government, including local artists. As local artists, we hope to make a difference without following pre-set models and do something we believe in.

How do you want The Collective HK to develop in the next 5 to 10 years?

The pandemic taught me to live in the present and go with the flow. We had plans, but most were unsuccessful due to the social unrest and pandemic. I hope by the time readers read this interview, our Happy Zoo project will have been launched. That's our ultimate grand project to keep us going.

What would you like The Collective HK to be remembered for?

Along the way, we met good teammates, passionate artists, respectable corporate clients and sponsors. All these beautiful moments are built on kindness, mutual respect and trust. I hope people who worked with us on all these remarkable projects will remember the journey and the collective way in collaboration to achieve something great and fun together. And of course, the audience would see our values and thoughts in our artwork.

Photo 1. Anita Lam, Co-founder of The Collective and Wesley, the dog.

Photo 2. Break The Chain, augmented reality activated murals.

Photo 3. The Way We Dance, mixed reality dance performance.

Chapter 26

Louis Siu, Founder and Artistic Director, Toolbox Percussion

Introduction

Toolbox Percussion is considered a creative incubator, and was founded with the mission to make new music happen by commissioning, developing, collaborating, professional training, performing, recording and touring contemporary performances. Hong-Kong-born, Australian and US-educated percussionist Louis Siu is the Founder and Artistic Director of Toolbox Percussion. In the following interview, Louis Siu discusses the joys and challenges in reaching beyond the traditional classrooms and physical concert hall settings.

Could we begin this interview by first introducing yourself? For example, could you tell us about your professional training and educational background? Where did you study music? Do you come from a family of professional musicians or performing artists?

I started learning the piano when I was six years old. Percussion wasn't my first instrument. My first encounter with percussion instruments was in primary school in Hong Kong for a Chinese lion dance event. When I was in secondary school, my teacher asked us (students) if anyone could play the piano and read the music score – to accompany other string instruments -- so that the school could put an orchestra together. So, I volunteered to become the pianist for the school orchestra. When I was singing in the school choir, they asked me to play triangles and cymbals – I guess that was my very first experience with percussion music.

I later attended a boarding school in Australia. When I was at the Sydney Conservatorium of Music, I would attend their Saturday school, where I had the opportunity to join their ensembles, take music theory classes, and learn additional musical instruments. Then I started learning the marimba and recorder to perform in a chamber ensemble. I studied at the Sydney

Conservatorium of Music for about 3.5 years (2001-2003). After completing my high school education in Australia, I returned to Hong Kong to study at the Chinese University of Hong Kong, majoring in Music, and minoring in Accounting & Finance for one year.

One year later, I was transferred to the San Francisco Conservatory of Music to complete my bachelor's degree in Music, majoring in percussion performance. Soon upon finishing my bachelor's degree, I was offered a place to pursue my master's degree in Music at the Cleveland Institute of Music. Coincidentally, I received a call from the Hong Kong Philharmonic Orchestra (HK Phil), offering me a 12-week freelance position (when HK Phil was under the direction of Maestro Edo de Waart) to go on tour with the Orchestra, as well as doing some major recordings. So, I decided to return to Hong Kong to try out a career as a professional musician. In 2020, I received my master's degree at Central Saint Martins, majoring in Arts and Cultural Enterprise. I am also building a partnership with the Chinese Culture Center of San Francisco and the Asian Art Museum, which I have spent many years cultivating.

My orchestral presence as a professional percussionist includes my former engagement as the principal percussionist of the Macao Orchestra. I was also an ExxonMobil New Vision Artist at the 40th Hong Kong Arts Festival, and a Teaching Artist at the San Francisco Symphony. I am currently working as an art-time instructor at the Music Department of the Chinese University of Hong Kong (CUHK).

Could you describe the audition process for the percussion position for the HK Phil and the Macao Orchestra (MO)?

HK Phil does not hold auditions for freelance orchestra positions regularly. But for that particular year (during Edo de Waart's era), every single orchestra player had to go through the re-audition process. Regarding the audition for the freelance percussion position (I was still a freshman at the San Francisco Conservatory of Music), the HK Phil would give you a list of excerpts that they would want you to play – you then apply – and they would then give you a timeslot for your audition. Then I had to fly back from San Francisco to Hong Kong (at my own cost) to audition for the HK Phil. Regarding the audition list, the HK Phil asked for many accessories, including many tambourine and triangle excerpts. However, Maestro de Waart did not listen to my whole audition, and the HK Phil percussionists listened to the rest.

In 2010, the MO offered me a full-time position as a percussionist (full-time for 3 years as principal percussionist and another 2 years as guest principal), as the local Macao Government funds MO. The cultural scene in Macao is different from that of Hong Kong. Macao has a cultural bureau and a strong heritage conservation policy, which all give positive vibes to the boutique cultural landscape. Although the population in Macao is very small, there is only one symphony orchestra (i.e., MO); hence, there is room for me to propose programme to the management, such as the interesting collaboration at Mandarin House (鄭家大屋) in the theme of Le French May Festival. Eventually, I worked for MO for three years as a full-time orchestra member, and then I stayed with MO for two more years, exclusively performing for concerts conducted by Maestro Lü Jia and education series.

Could you describe your experience in performing in Wagner's Ring Cycle with the Hong Kong Philharmonic Orchestra (HK Phil)?

It was an interesting and challenging experience, especially with eight percussionists playing anvil backstage!

Do you mean that, as a percussionist, there is freedom for individual self-expression when you are playing in an orchestra?

When I was working as an orchestra member, I considered myself mostly a technician because when playing in an orchestra, I often didn't get to choose the kinds of sound I wanted to produce. When we are playing the Beethoven or Liszt piano concertos, there are only very small orchestral parts that you (as a percussionist) get to play the triangle. Certain conductors would always say, for example, that your triangles are out of tune! Or the sound you are producing is either too high or too low!

Some conductors (maybe he was trained in the traditional German school earlier) might always be looking for this shallow metallic brass sound in the percussion section. Interestingly, there was this one incident when we were performing the Liszt Piano Concerto – the conductor heard me producing these light, tiny shimmering sounds with the triangles -- he got furious – because he was obviously looking for a much deeper sound with a lot more weight and bell-like sound.

The funny thing is that as a percussionist, sometimes it is about how you "look" rather than the actual sound that you are producing – for example, sometimes you just have to make large gestures -- to give the conductor the impression that you are playing very loudly with a lot of power, instead of actually playing really loud. In addition, it also has a lot to do with the acoustics of the concert halls, and how well and far the sound could travel inside, particularly concert halls, instead of having us orchestra players playing very loud all the time. These sum up why I see my work as an orchestra player as a technician rather than an artist. On the other hand, when I do my own projects, I have the total freedom to create any kind of sound, such as musical messages that I want to communicate to the audience, in addition to the freedom I have to express my own artistic ideas. Furthermore, I would also have total freedom to explore different percussion repertoires.

What motivated you to found Toolbox Percussion? In addition, could you provide a brief introduction to Toolbox Percussion?

I decided to found Toolbox Percussion as I realised that I could not further my career as a musician by performing percussion music only, except by venturing into collaborations with other musicians or artists of different art forms (including dancers, designers, visual artists, etc.), aiming to create a more holistic and impactful experience for the audience. Our collaborative projects include holding site-specific performances at art galleries in Hong Kong. The installation included video and John Cage's "Radio Music," a piece composed for radio frequencies. Post-show, the public can write and send postcards to share what they heard, saw and, above all, felt.

I am the producer, artistic director, grant applicant, and more for the performances and collaborative projects launched by Toolbox Percussion. In short, Toolbox Percussion is constantly thinking of how to develop beyond the traditional concert hall venues. For details, please refer to "Transforming Everyday Objects into Music."

Toolbox Percussion was founded in 2012 with the mission to function as a platform for artistic experimentation, collaboration, and performance. Commissioning and touring work play an important part in our creative strategy, and Toolbox Percussion has been invited to perform in Gwangju, San Francisco, and Shanghai. Furthermore, Toolbox Percussion hosts an annual innovation lab, the Toolbox International Creative Academy, and leads outreach programmes for children and students. I am proud to say that Toolbox Percussion has been driving percussive arts programming in Hong Kong since 2012, and has curated diverse innovative music projects. In 2021, Toolbox Percussion served as a Leisure and Cultural Services Department (LCSD) Community Cultural Ambassador and, for Jockey Club New Arts Power, is curating family workshops that are based on the idea from John Luther Adams' Inuksuit, a nature-inspired piece performed by multiple percussion players dispersed among a natural site, creating a truly magical soundscape.

Furthermore, Toolbox Percussion is considered a creative incubator, and our mission is to make new music happen by commissioning, developing, collaborating, professional training, performing, recording and touring contemporary performances, etc.

Toolbox Percussion is "not just a percussion group." Instead, we see ourselves as a platform for new artistic creation and collaboration in forms designed to meet audiences where they are – our events and concert programmes are often carried outside the regular auditorium or concert hall. In the last decade, we have proven successful in creating cutting-edge and innovative programmes that challenged local artists, enhanced cultural exchange by collaborating with world-class musicians and developed a series of outreach and professional educational activities. In short, Toolbox Percussion operates with a strong belief in cultivating local young talents, and we are committed to empowering audiences of different age groups to discover the versatility of daily soundscapes by relating its work closely to the actuality of today's Hong Kong. It is our mission to encourage people to learn about creativity and how to listen.

The music scene in Hong Kong has been dominated by Western classical music, particularly in terms of our education system (both elementary and secondary schools). Hence, our goal is to reach beyond the traditional classroom and concert hall settings. I strongly believe that audiences in Hong Kong have a big appetite for programmes that would engage and invite reflection and explore different new art forms. Hence, I am optimistic that our work and innovative presentation style could reach an ever-expanding audience as well as create opportunities for other artists.

As the Founder and Artistic Director of Toolbox Percussion of the Toolbox production, what are your main roles and areas of responsibility?

My main role as the Artistic Director is to design artistic programmes for Toolbox Percussion for the upcoming year and identify various funding opportunities for supporting our artistic programmes. (Toolbox Percussion is a three-year grantee of the Hong Kong Arts Development Council.

Touring and performance tours play are very important for showcasing our new commissions. Hence, as the Artistic Director, I have to do a lot of PR and external liaison, i.e., to identify noteworthy collaborators and other people who are interested in what we are doing – to help us put performance tours together. During the 2018-19 season, Toolbox Percussion travelled to Asia Culture Center in Gwangju, South Korea, and made our North American debut at the San Francisco International Arts Festival. Invited by the Chinese Culture Center of San Francisco, Toolbox Percussion also curated a sound-based exhibition titled A Double Listen to showcase its works. The exhibition was reprised at H Queen's in Hong Kong in 2021 in collaboration with different cross-media artists. In terms of artistic programming for our future seasons, we are currently focusing on showcasing Hong Kong music by local musicians, composers, and artists from Hong Kong.

Supported by the Arts Capacity Development Funding Scheme, Toolbox Percussion launched its annual festival, Toolbox International Creative Academy (TICA), in collaboration with mainland and overseas universities in 2019. The academy aims to provide professional apprenticeship opportunities through specifically focused areas of study and learning occasions with industry professionals.

In terms of experimentation and commission of new works, Toolbox Percussion has been collaborating with leading figures on exploring the frontiers of music, sound, and performance. These include the Japanese-American sound artist and composer Ken Ueno, who is Toolbox Percussion's Creative Director-in-Residence and holds the Jerry and Evelyn Hemmings Chambers Distinguished Professor in Music at the University of California, Berkeley. Likewise, Hong Kong native Samson Young, whose sound performances and installations have been commissioned by Art Basel and shown at museums and festivals around the world, has contributed compositions and serves on the company's Board of Directors.

What parts of the job as the Founder and Artistic Director of Toolbox Percussion do you find most rewarding, and which do you find frustrating?

The work at Toolbox is always about collaboration; being able to co-curate with other partners and artists is the most rewarding part of the work. However, with the contemporary music scene in Hong Kong still at an early stage, it would be challenging for the audience development process.

In what ways do you want Toolbox Percussion to develop in the next three to five years?

I hope the collective could be more independent and able to have more guest artistic partners for various projects and encourage our own artists to lead more projects for arts education and local development.

What would you like to be remembered for when you retire?

I don't need to be remembered. Rather, I hope all artists and collaborators can remember their good times with the art group.

Photo 1. Performing Steve Reich's Music for Pieces of Wood.

Photo 2. Snapshots of Steve Reich's Nagoya Marimba.

Photo 3. Steve Reich's Clapping Music with Multi-media Projection.

Photo 4. Louis Siu Performing John Cage's Radio Music.

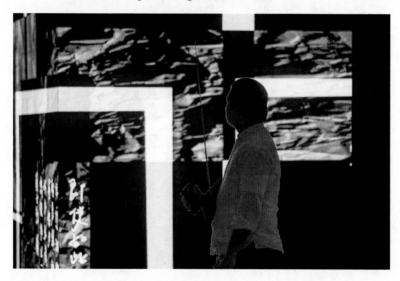

Photo 5. Experimenting performance with Multi-media and Digital Art.

Photo 6. Performance of "Toolbox Manoeuvre." Percussive Theatre of Jockey Club New Arts Power 2021.

Photo 7. Louis Siu, Executive Artistic Director of Toolbox Percussion.

Photo 8. Little Toolbox Percussion at Tai Po Arts Centre.

Photo 9. First Collaboration with Third Coast Percussion (USA) at HKUST in 2020.

Photo 10. Participant of Little Toolbox Percussion with Brian Chan (Teaching Artist of Toolbox Percussion).

Photo 11. Performance of Toolbox Voyage, LCSD Community Cultural Ambassador Scheme.

Chapter 27

Chi-Yung Wong, Installation Artist & Artist-Curator

Introduction

Born and educated in Hong Kong and Europe, Chi-yung Wong is a cross-disciplinary artist and artist-curator whose work encompasses experiential installations, light installations, creative education, and cultural exchange between the arts and sciences. As an artist-curator, Chi-yung produces his own projects and curates projects for other artists and institutions, presenting a range of interdisciplinary collaborations, including installations, research, publication, workshops, and seminars. These programmes provide opportunities for exchange between artists, scientists, technologists, researchers, journalists, and students. Chi-yung has hosted master classes and workshops on art and mental health awareness, interdisciplinary collaboration, and creative education. In 2020, Chi-yung Wong was selected as an Arts Fellow by Yale University due to his dedication to the field of arts and mental health.

His recent collaborators include the Theatre of Liège in Belgium, the West Kowloon Cultural Authority, the Hong Kong Arts Centre, the Zurich University of the Arts, ETH Zurich (Swiss Federal Institute of Technology in Zurich), the Artists-in-Labs Programme (Zurich), and the Hong Kong Academy for Performing Arts, Hong Kong Design Institute, Hong Kong University of Science and Technology, The Education University of Hong Kong (EduHK), Leisure and Cultural Services Department Hong Kong, and many other institutions.

In the following interview, Chi-yung discusses the sources of inspiration for his installation designs, as well as the importance of interdisciplinary collaboration between scientists, artists, and institutions of different cultural backgrounds.

Can we begin this interview by first introducing yourself, your professional training, and your educational background? What did you study at the university? Do you come from a family of artists, art historians, museum curators, or creative people?

I am Chi-yung Wong, a cross-disciplinary artist and curator whose work encompasses experiential installations, light installations, creative education, and cultural exchange between the arts and sciences. My educational background includes; a bachelor of fine arts in Theatre Lighting Design from The Hong Kong Academy for Performing Arts (HKAPA), where I graduated with a first-class honour, training in French language and civilisation at La Sorbonne Université in Paris, a Visual Arts Degree from Paris VIII, Université Saint-Denis, it was supported by the Alexandre Yersin Scholarship from the French Consulate in Hong Kong and recently, a Master of Arts in Transdisciplinary Studies in The Arts from Zurich University of The Arts. I was also the first Asian student to attend The Theatre Academy of Finland, where I took part in an exchange programme. These diverse experiences from studying in different cultures gave me a strong foundation in performing and visual art.

I do not come from a family of artists or creative professionals. However, I have always had a passion for the arts and have had many creative friends. At age 16, I joined an experimental art group. This group included creative photographers, performers, illustrators, graphic designers and musicians and was influential to me. These collaborations have helped inspire and support my creative pursuits, and I have learned much from these people. Many of them are important figures in various organisations now.

At what stage did you decide to pursue a career as an artist specialising in installation, such as lighting installations?

When I was 16, I became financially independent as my family kicked me out. I decided to become an artist and study art, and I was hanging out with much older people, aged 20 - 30. This influence led to me deciding what I would like to do. I wanted to do installations using lights as the subject became very interesting. In the 1990s, you couldn't study lights in university. My installation work is like sculpture or painting but using lights and video. I developed a mixture of interest in theatre and installation, so I hired a small office and went to the theatre to study theatre lighting.

Could you tell me what inspired you to create your first art installation light?

The art of light has been a constant source of inspiration for me since my introduction to it as a member of the experimental art group. Through interactions with other artists and designers, I explored various mediums and techniques, and the magic of lighting particularly struck me. In one of our performances at a small theatre, I saw first-hand how light can transform a space and bring our imagination and feelings to life in an instant. This experience solidified my appreciation for the art of light and its ability to engage the viewer uniquely and powerfully.

Inspired by this experience, I decided to pursue formal education in theatre lighting design. I was drawn to the idea of using light to create immersive and dynamic experiences for audiences, and was eager to learn more about the technical aspects of lighting design. Through my studies, I gained a deep understanding of the different applications of light in performances and spatial designs. The study helped me to master the use of colour and intensity, and the importance of creating a cohesive lighting design that supports the overall concept of a production.

As I continue to explore lighting as a medium in my art, I am constantly amazed by its versatility and power. Light has a profound influence on our lives, both physically and emotionally. From a biological perspective, light is necessary for producing vitamin D and regulating our sleep-wake cycles. It also plays a crucial role in our ability to see and perceive the world around us. On an emotional level, light has the power to affect our mood and behaviour. Bright, natural light has been shown to improve productivity, reduce stress, and improve overall well-being. In contrast, a lack of light can lead to sadness and lethargy.

In the world of art, light is often used as a medium to create immersive and dynamic experiences. Whether it be through the use of traditional light sources or cutting-edge technology, the possibilities for creating art with light are endless. From performances and installations to photography and film, light can transform a space and engage the viewer uniquely and powerfully. Overall, light is an integral part of our lives and can influence us in many ways. Whether through its impact on our physical and emotional well-being or through its use as a medium for creating art, learning about or coming across the art of light is very useful as it helps us understand how we experience the world around us.

In your experience with lighting installations, what are some examples of major evolutions in materials and technologies that have occurred over the past 20 years compared to the present day?

Lighting installations have come a long way over the past two decades, thanks to the development of new materials and technologies. These advances have opened up new possibilities for artists and designers, allowing them to create more dynamic, interactive, and immersive experiences for viewers. One of the most significant evolutions in lighting technology over the past 20 years has been the widespread adoption of LED (light emitting diode) lighting. LED lights are energy efficient, have a long lifespan, and can be used to create a wide range of colours and effects. They are also easily programmable and controllable using computer software, making them a popular choice for lighting installations.

Another major development in lighting installations has been incorporating interactive technologies such as sensors and touchscreens. These technologies allow the artist to create dynamic and immersive experiences that respond to the viewer's actions or movements. For example, an installation might use sensors to detect the presence of a viewer and change the lighting or sound in response. Projection mapping, which involves projecting video or other visual content onto irregular surfaces, has also become more accessible in recent years. This technology has been used to create impressive and large-scale lighting installations, such as projections on buildings or sculptures.

The development of wireless and battery-powered lighting technologies has also made creating installations in remote or off-grid locations easier. This has opened up new possibilities for creating temporary or site-specific installations not dependent on a power source. Finally, the emergence of augmented and virtual reality technologies has also impacted lighting installations. These technologies can be used to create immersive and interactive experiences that combine the physical and digital worlds.

How do you see the future of light art and light technology?

In addition to its use in the arts, lighting technology has also had a significant impact in the fields of science and medicine and continues to play a crucial role in various research and treatment applications. One example of the use of lighting technology in medicine is light therapy or phototherapy. This type of treatment uses specific wavelengths of light to help heal or alleviate various medical conditions, including skin conditions like eczema and acne, as well as mood disorders like seasonal affective disorder (SAD). Lighting technology is also used in scientific research to study the effects of light on various organisms and processes. For example, scientists may use specialised lighting systems to study the growth and development of plants, or to investigate the impacts of light on human health and behaviour.

The future looks promising for the role of lighting art and lighting technology in changing the world. Recently, during my artist-in-residency in Switzerland working with neuroscientists, I proposed an idea for how a light artist and scientist could collaborate to use light art as a tool to help reduce stress in the field of medicine or therapy.

In my proposed art-science collaboration, the lighting artist and scientist could work together to design an installation that incorporates stress-reducing wavelengths of light, that is designed to be viewed in a therapeutic setting such as a hospital or wellness centre. The installation would allow the viewer to focus on their biofeedback training with the experience of the intensity and colour of the light. The goal is to help viewers practise mindfulness and awareness between their feelings and physiology. The light artist and scientist could also incorporate other elements into the installation, such as sound or scent, to create a fully immersive and relaxing experience.

I'm curious: how has your experience working as a lighting consultant for commercial brands like Louis Vuitton and Chanel influenced your artistic career or journey?

As an artist, I am constantly seeking ways to push the boundaries of what is possible in my artistic exploration. I am always curious to know what will happen if I try a different role in a different culture and system, which is why I have travelled, studied, and worked between Europe and Hong Kong. I am simply interested in finding ways to connect the world and connect people. When I was offered the position in the retail world as a light consultant for Chanel and Louis Vuitton, I was curious about how my craft would develop within this context. This experience greatly enhanced my skills in artistic leadership and management, and I have had the privilege of meeting many remarkable professional people from various industries.

From a pragmatic standpoint, working in the commercial field has allowed me to work on projects with varied timelines, budgets and missions, which has honed my skills as a professional and taught me how to manage my time and resources effectively. It has also allowed me to apply my skills to different projects and explore diverse roles, which has helped me to reflect on why we collaborate and how to form successful collaborations.

After working in the commercial field, I joined an interior design firm specialising in hospitality design and was appointed lighting design director. I then moved on from working on a project to creating my own projects. This is why you may have seen me presenting multiple art installations, seminars on art and mental health, exchange programmes with scientists, and educational programmes on cross-disciplinary practice. It has allowed me to learn from a different perspective and reshape my understanding of my artistic journey. The experience has been incredibly inspiring to me, and has helped me see the value of collaboration and teamwork on a global scale.

Could you tell us about your experiences working with neuroscientists and psychiatrists in Zurich as part of the artists-in-labs programme?

Collaborating with scientists and scholars in these programmes allowed me to see first-hand how art and science can intersect and how they can be used to complement and enhance each other. During my residency, I worked with scientists from the Translational Neuroimaging Units at ETH University. At the start of our collaboration, we faced the challenge of our differences in artistic and scientific methods. However, I approached this challenge by asking questions that might interest the scientists, such as how art could be a resource for stress reduction and what the essential factors are for a successful arts-sciences collaboration.

Could you tell us more about how you plan and work with scientists?

Over 6 months, I have developed a model for our exchange, focusing on four major activities as the pillars to support our collaboration.

The first pillar was weekly workshops, where we exchanged our professional practices. The second pillar was collaborating on prototypes. We picked a scientific prototype and brainstormed creative possibilities for it, and also picked an art installation I was working on and invited the scientists to brainstorm on its potential as a scientific tool.

The third pillar was visiting and interviewing other scientific experts to understand how they work and collaborate in an interdisciplinary environment and how they research topics such as stress and mindfulness. These experts included neurologists, neuroscientists, computational psychologists, engineers, neuroimaging experts, mathematicians, and physicists.

The fourth pillar was participating as a control subject in the scientists' experiments, which allowed me to understand their research methods and the technology used.

We are also curious to know the result and impact on your artistic practice.

As a result of this experience, I have created a series of art programmes to continue this exploration and facilitate exchange between the artistic and scientific communities. These programmes include my recent experiential installation series, Solis Occasus, To See A World in a Grain of Sand, and To See A World in a Grain of Sand (mobile app version), Heaven in a Wild Flower, and Auguries of Innocence, as well as talks and workshop series on mindfulness and creativity, combining artistic and scientific approaches to stress reduction, exploring the topics with artists, scientists and students, how we come up an innovative approach to using art as a tool for non-pharmaceutical intervention in the future. These experiences have had a lasting impact on my artistic journey and continue to inspire me in my work.

Could you share your experience as an artist fellow at Yale in 2020? How did this fellowship impact your artistic practice and development?

As the Art-Activator, I facilitated cultural and knowledge exchange through various projects and activities. One of the highlights of my fellowship was collaborating with scientists and bringing my experience from working with the Translational Neuroimaging Units at ETH University to Yale. This enabled me to continue discussing and learning about the latest research methods and technologies in neuroscience, and even led to my introduction to biofeedback training, which significantly influenced my series of experiential installations. Over six months, I could design my fellowship according to my goals and interests. I adopted a "cook-and-see" approach, creating a list of exchange opportunities with different groups at Yale. I could start conversations and explore collaborations with Yale's scientists, faculty mentors, experts, cultural partners, and students by targeting specific groups. By the end of my residency, I had achieved my four main objectives: sharing, learning, exchanging, and exploring. I reached a total of 990 experts, professors, and students from the Yale New Haven and Hong Kong international communities. I finished the residency by presenting an online forum to discuss the future of art-sciences collaboration and education. I had the chance to meet the research department behind the Yale Art Gallery, programme directors and professionals to learn about the design of art, science, and technology teaching programmes, and so much more.

How did you become interested in contemplation and experiential installation? How did these bring you to research mindfulness and lead you to work with scientists?

My artistic interest is to combine scenography and immersive experience in my installations, aiming to create a contemplative space. With these things in mind, I began to question how theatre or installation arts could improve mental health, and whether artists and scientists could orbit around mental health and create collaborative research. These questions led me to begin a journey to explore mindfulness with scientists. Initially, the concept was to develop an art and science exchange that allowed scientists and artists to discuss and explore how to enhance mindfulness practice with experiential installation. In our collaboration, we hypothesised that an experiential installation would enhance mindfulness practice, so we started by sharing our research and views related to mindfulness.

Can you share how your research lead you to create for your series of works that relates to experiential installation and mindfulness, such as the online programme "Exploring Arts and the Mind," and the online digital artwork "Auguries of Innocence," and your recent large scale experiential installation "Solis Occacus"?

This journey of collaboration and exploration ultimately led me to the positions for my recent projects, such as "Exploring Arts and the Mind," "Auguries of Innocence" and "Solis Occacus," which have occurred through innovation and experimentation with new ideas and approaches. Through listening to and exchanging feedback with experts from different disciplines, I can better understand the challenges and potential of using artistic creation to enhance mindfulness practice and reduce stress.

One approach I often use in my artistic practice is the cook-and-see approach, a method of experimentation and exploration in which an idea or concept is developed and then tested or implemented to see how it works in practice. It involves a series of trial-and-error, where the experiment results are observed and used to inform further development or improvement. This approach allows me to open up, test, and refine ideas flexibly and iteratively.

It can also be a useful method for understanding the potential applications and limitations of a concept, and for identifying areas for further research and exploration.

Can you share more about your "Heaven in a Wild Flower" installation project and how you integrated it with educational workshops at the Dance School of the Hong Kong Academy for Performing Arts?

"Heaven in a Wild Flower" was a truly memorable and enriching experience for me as an artist. The installation was a contemplative space where visitors could immerse themselves in a sensory experience with light, music, and touch. As part of the project, I collaborated with the Hong Kong Academy for Performing Arts to host educational workshops and developed a dance performance with students and their teaching artists. This workshop, "Concept on the Move – Exploring Our Artistic Practice with Mindfulness," allowed the students to explore the relationship between movement, observation and introspection, and to translate that exploration into dance creations that interacted with the installation. The installation became their stage, and it was a wonderful opportunity for the students to review and explore the possibilities and interactions between performing arts and installation arts.

Through our insensitive activities, spending three weeks together, the students learnt about my artistic research on contemplation, mindfulness and experiential installation. We give them learning and creative opponents to explore how to reflect and understand our own physiology, introspection, movements, and emotions. It was an excellent opportunity for them to learn about cross-disciplinary artistic research and explore alternative ways of creating dance with an experiential installation and mindfulness. I believe that these workshops helped the students develop a deeper understanding of their own creative roles and practices and explore new areas of growth as artists.

Collaborating with the dance school allowed me to introduce a new perspective and approach to the student's education. By incorporating mindfulness and experiential installation elements into their dance practice, the students could explore and experiment with new ways of creating and performing. This interdisciplinary collaboration helped broaden their understanding of the arts and opened up new possibilities for their creative expression. Moving forward, I see education and interdisciplinary collaboration playing a crucial role in my artistic practice.

How has the COVID-19 pandemic affected your artistic practice and projects, and what creative solutions have you come up with to navigate these challenges?

The COVID-19 pandemic has certainly had a significant impact on my artistic practice and projects. At the beginning of the lockdown, I found myself with a lot of extra time on my hands, and I spent a lot of that time reflecting on my own personal experiences with grief and contemplation. I realised that these were themes that many people around the world were also experiencing due to the pandemic and the loss of loved ones, jobs, and normalcy.

However, it has also presented new opportunities and challenges that have inspired me to be creative and adaptable. One of my recent projects, for example, focused on contemplation and grief, and was inspired by the isolation and reflection that the pandemic brought about. In order to create this project, I took time to meditate and practice mindfulness in my own life. I produced an experiential installation called "Solis Occacus," which translates to "sunset" in Latin. The installation was designed to be a space where visitors could reflect on their experiences with grief and loss in a peaceful and contemplative setting. To bring my vision to life, I worked closely with a team of artists, scientists, and researchers to create a multi-sensory experience incorporating sound, light, and scent elements. We also designed a series of educational workshops in conjunction with the installation, allowing visitors to learn more about the science of grief and how to cope with loss healthily. Overall, the COVID-19 pandemic has been challenging for all of us, but it has also inspired me to create some of my most meaningful and impactful projects to date.

Before we finish, is there anything you want to share with us?

I think exploring the intersection of art, science, technology, and mental health is an intriguing aspect of contemporary artistic practice, and there are many uncharted territories between art, mental health and education paradigms. By researching and collaborating with individuals and organisations from different disciplines, artists can bring new ideas and approaches to their work and continue learning and growing as artists. Such interdisciplinary collaboration is also important for fostering meaningful exchange and understanding between different cultures and artistic communities.

Photo 1. Chi-yung Wong.

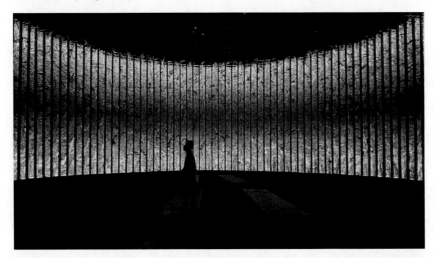

Photo 2. Solis Occasus (Photo credit: Yvonne Chan).

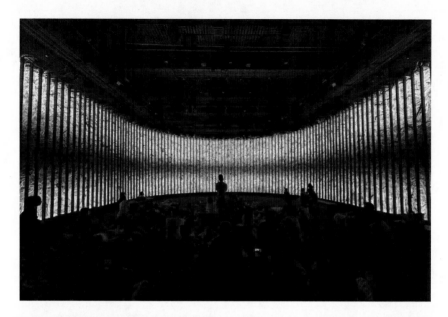

Photo 3. Solis Occasus (Photo credit: Eric Hong).

Photo 4. Online Forum – In-Between Two Realms.

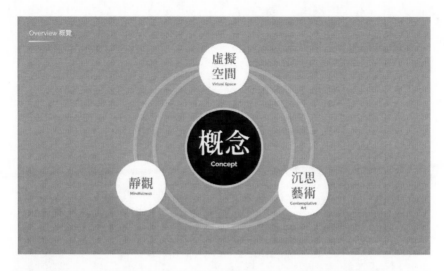

Photo 5. Concept: (Virtual Space) + (Mindfulness) + (Contemplative Art).

Photo 6. Exchange Brought New Inspirations.

Chapter 28

Andrew Strachan, General Manager Asia, Member of the Executive Committee, Art Basel

Introduction

Established in 1970 by Basel gallerists Ernst Beyeler, Trudl Bruckner and Balz Hilt, Art Basel is a for-profit, privately owned and managed international art fair staged annually in Basel, Miami Beach, Hong Kong, and Paris. While Art Basel functions as a business platform for galleries to showcase and sell their work to buyers, it has also gained a large international audience of art spectators and students by working with each host city's local institutions to grow and develop a variety of visual-arts-related programmes.

Established in 2013, Art Basel Hong Kong features premier galleries from across Asia and beyond, providing an in-depth overview of the Asia-Pacific's astonishing diversity, as well as global artistic perspectives, through modern and contemporary works of art. Over the years, Art Basel's Hong Kong fair has affirmed the city's position as one of the busiest cultural tourist destinations in the region.

From 2011 to 2022, Andrew Strachan served as General Manager (Asia) of Art Basel, based in Hong Kong. Before joining Art Basel, Strachan spent years working in international event management in Asia and Europe. In the following interview, Strachan discusses the thinking and operations behind Art Basel Hong Kong, as well as its contributions to the cultural economy and cultural tourism in Hong Kong.

Could you describe your career path to becoming General Manager Asia of Art Basel?

I studied International Business at the University of the West of England in the UK. I went on to work at the International Festival of Extreme Sports (FISE) in France, the largest extreme sports festival in Europe, where I began my event management career before moving to London, where I grew to the position of Group Show Director for Brand Events, a major consumer events company, between 2000 and 2005. From there, I moved into sports marketing in my role as Event Director at Quintus Asia Pacific in Singapore and Hong Kong from 2006 to 2009, and subsequently led a ground-breaking 10,000km endurance running expedition along the Silk Road before I was appointed to the position of the General Manager Asia of Art Basel in 2011.

My family is not from an arts background, and I didn't receive any formal training in the art world. I essentially learned by doing and listening carefully to various experts in the arts, while bringing my international business experience specialising in event management to Art Basel. Because of the international companies I worked for, I have worked around the world, from Asia to Europe and America, and I've been incredibly fortunate to work across a wide range of events, from consumer exhibitions and festivals to touring theatre shows and extreme expeditions!

Could you describe the missions and visions of (1) Art Basel in Basel and (2) Art Basel in Hong Kong, and the philosophies behind their operations and exhibitions?

Art Basel is a for-profit international art fair started by Basel gallerists Ernst Beyeler, Trudl Bruckner and Balz Hilt in 1970. Art Basel Miami Beach was first introduced in 2002, and Art Basel Hong Kong was launched in 2013. Today, Art Basel is staged annually in four different cities: Basel, Miami Beach, Hong Kong, and Paris, where we launched Paris+ par Art Basel in 2022. Working in collaboration with local institutions in each respective host city, Art Basel functions as an international platform for leading galleries around the world to show the best of modern and contemporary art.

The themes and uniqueness of the exhibitions of Art Basel in Basel, Miami Beach, Hong Kong, and Paris are reflected in the following aspects: (1) participating galleries; (2) artworks presented; and (3) concepts of the parallel programming that each of the shows produces in collaboration with local and regional institutions. All these aspects are meant to create unique artistic and cultural experiences for both visitors and potential art buyers.

Each Art Basel fair reflects the energetic spirit and personality of its host city. In the case of Art Basel Hong Kong, we have aimed to feature leading galleries from Asia and around the world since we began in 2013 to present an in-depth overview of the Asia-Pacific's astonishing artistic diversity through modern and contemporary artworks by established and emerging artists. From the beginning, our Hong Kong show's core mission has been to become Asia's premier international art fair featuring the best of Asia's galleries alongside leading galleries worldwide. With a balance of approximately 50% of galleries operating spaces in Asia and 50% with spaces in the rest of the world, the aim is to act as a bridge to foster closer relationships between art scenes across Asia and bring East and West together under the same roof.

It is worth noting that Art Basel Hong Kong is widely considered the most globally representative art fair for galleries and artists, and I want to highlight the thirst for knowledge that is particularly evident in our Art Basel Hong Kong shows. That thirst for knowledge refers to research conducted at the fair by arts professionals, from curators to art critics, to buying patterns, with collectors doing significant amounts of research to gain an in-depth understanding of the artworks they are collecting. We see many young collectors launching their collections through the fair and young arts professionals developing their careers based on the momentum the fair creates across Hong Kong's arts ecosystem and beyond.

Can you describe the staffing structure of Art Basel Hong Kong?

We operate with a team of around 20 people based in Hong Kong covering the following: (1) Operations, (2) Gallery Relations, (3) VIP Relations, (4) Marketing, Content & Communications, (5) Partnership, (6) Digital. Our organisational structure at Art Basel Hong Kong is rather flat compared to a top-down command and control structure. We don't have any hierarchical structure, and our team of 20 staff becomes a team of about 30 in the month before the show. We also have staff teams servicing our global shows based in Basel, Paris, and New York. In addition, Art Basel has a network of VIP representatives operating in 26 key art markets worldwide. In Asia, we work closely with our representatives stationed in Mainland China, Japan, Taiwan, Southeast Asia, India, Australia, and Korea, all working across our four international fairs.

Who are Art Basel Hong Kong's major partners? What are the advantages of such partnerships and collaborations?

Art Basel Hong Kong's major partners include UBS, Audemars Piguet, BMW, Hong Kong Tourism Board, La Prairie (Switzerland), Ruinart, Sanlorenzo, and Swire Properties.

In multi-year agreements, we work in partnership with select commercial brands across our four shows and view these relationships as going beyond traditional sponsorship arrangements. We tend to work with partners committed to the arts in long-term strategic ways – we do not simply put their logos on our Art Basel posters! For example, Art Basel and BMW launched the BMW Art Journey together in 2015. The prize has enabled every winning artist to go on their own journey of creative discovery almost anywhere in the world, so they can develop new ideas, discover new themes, and envision new creative projects.

Our Lead Partner, UBS, has a long history of supporting contemporary art and artists. As well as having one of the world's most important corporate art collections, UBS demonstrates its commitment to the industry and its partnership with Art Basel in many ways. One example is the co-published *Art Basel and UBS Global Art Market Report,* which is written by the leading cultural economist, Dr. Clare McAndrew.

In addition to our commercial partnerships, we also work closely with local educational institutions, collaborating on educational, outreach, or visitor engagement programmes regularly and continuously. Every year, Art Basel Hong Kong gives between 5 and 10% of the tickets to schools and universities so that art students can attend the annual show for free, helping build engagement and hopefully inspiring the next generation of artists and arts professionals in the city.

We value our public role at Art Basel Hong Kong, since we allow the public to see an incredible swathe of art from across the world, giving insight into different art histories while showcasing new developments in contemporary art. Beyond staging a fair at the world-class Hong Kong Convention and Exhibition Centre, we have initiated and supported a number of public projects through the years. For example, the Artist Tram Project in 2022 was commissioned by Art Basel and co-presented by the Hong Kong Tourism Board, with Hong Kong artists Cherie Cheuk, Stephen Wong and Shum Kwan-yi presenting their art on the exteriors of Hong Kong's iconic trams.

What are the roles and responsibilities of VIP Relations of Art Basel Hong Kong? Who are the current and regular VIPs of Art Basel Hong Kong?

AS: Between 2020 and 2023, the visitors of Art Basel Hong Kong were predominantly made up of Hong Kong residents because of COVID-19 travel restrictions. However, before that, regular VIPs would be made up of major institutional buyers, private collectors, and government officials from around the world – a composition that will resume from March 2023, when we stage our first fair since the lifting of most COVID-19 travel restrictions to the city. The fair also welcomes representatives from local arts councils in Hong Kong and other parts of the world.

One of the main roles of our VIP Relations Team is to connect major buyers with the galleries being presented at Art Basel Hong Kong – with the hope of facilitating conversations between both parties. Meanwhile, our global team is responsible for bringing thousands of VIP collectors, curators, influential critics, and journalists to our Art Basel fairs in Hong Kong. In a normal year, we would expect several thousand VIPs outside Hong Kong to attend our Art Basel show. For example, a US-based VIP Relations manager might bring six or seven museum groups from the United States to Hong Kong. The local VIP Relations manager would connect those VIP buyers from the museums with the galleries. In terms of facilitating this conversation, the VIP Relations manager needs to establish an ongoing dialogue between the buyers (for example, the art museum and the galleries) providing the artwork. But these connections go beyond sales. Through their ability to network with the Art Basel community, our VIP representatives facilitate a meeting of minds, which is integral to the function of Art Basel Hong Kong and every other Art Basel show. They help connect museum groups to local and visiting institutions, as well as like-minded museum groups who share a common interest and are present in Hong Kong during the week.

Beyond their presence at each of our fairs, Art Basel's VIP representatives also function as our eyes and ears on the ground wherever they are, helping us keep a finger on the pulse in their respective art scenes and territories, and sharing news and updates on developments. True to their title, they function as representatives or ambassadors for Art Basel year-round.

As General Manager Asia, Art Basel, could you describe your typical day at work? Is there ever a typical day at work?

As General Manager Asia, Art Basel, there was rarely a typical day at work! With a 12-month planning cycle, there are different focuses throughout the year at different times. For example, immediately after the show finishes, we begin to debrief and start planning the following year's show, including show architecture and design, content strategy, opening applications for galleries, ticketing planning, financial and resource planning, citywide programming, and so on. A typical day could be as varied as developing innovative ideas, such as introducing holograms in the show, which we pioneered in 2021, or working with our legal team on agreement structures.

In recent years I have also been working with Art Basel's partners across Asia to plan or support events such as Art Week Tokyo and SEA Focus in Singapore.

Could you describe your main roles and areas of responsibility?

The General Manager is responsible for managing the team that delivers the shows. That involves operational excellence, commercial performance, team leadership, and strategic planning, among other areas.

How would you describe your managerial and leadership style?

AS: I like to see myself as an entrepreneurial facilitator, leading energetically and ambitiously – and ideally maintaining a strong positive team spirit, even under pressure!

When people talk about Art Basel Hong Kong, what is the first image that comes to your mind?

They see an art show and parallel cultural programming full of energy and vibrancy in an incredibly dynamic, fast-paced, and fascinating city. Hong Kong's art scene is unlike any other in the world. Then there's the food!

How about Art Basel's Conversations programme? How do such conversation programmes contribute to the overall operations, marketing, and branding of Art Basel, as well as art education, art promotions, and art participation as a whole?

Art Basel's Conversations series, whether online or with a live audience, covers all topics concerning the global contemporary arts scene, with panel discussions promoting dynamic dialogues and exchanges between prominent members of the international art world. Art Basel Conversations aims to provide unique perspectives on a broad range of topics concerning art, from collecting, making, and exhibiting art to how art histories are made. In short, across all four Art Basel fairs, Conversations is a valuable platform for connecting people to the entire world of visual arts, regardless of background and interest. In Hong Kong, all talks are presented with simultaneous translation into English, Mandarin and Cantonese, and are filmed and archived online as an openly accessible resource.

Could you explain why and how Hong Kong has recently become Asia's cultural and commercial arts hub, particularly in the art trade and cultural exchanges? Furthermore, what are the practical reasons for Art Basel to set up its Asian regional base in Hong Kong?

Hong Kong is a friendly, sales-tax-free city where English is widely spoken. Hong Kong also has a great selection of hotels, combined with a huge number of galleries. Major auction houses like Sotheby's, the biggest auction house for contemporary art in Hong Kong since 2013, alongside Christie's, Phillips and Bonhams, have set up their bases in Hong Kong and continued to invest in contemporary art. It is a combination of all these practical reasons that makes Hong Kong the ideal place for Art Basel to operate in Asia currently.

How do you think the introduction of Hong Kong's national security law will affect Hong Kong's cultural tourism industry, as well as the city's position as one of the world's top art markets in the long run?

We at Art Basel have not been asked to do anything differently or adapt our operations since the introduction of the national security law in Hong Kong, and we hope that remains the case.

What parts of your job as General Manager Asia, Art Basel do you find most rewarding? And which do you find most frustrating?

I find watching the first viewing – the unveiling – of our fairs and launching new partnerships and projects in Hong Kong and around the region incredibly rewarding. Equally rewarding is watching Hong Kong artists succeed on an international stage, and for our colleagues working with Art Basel to develop professionally in their careers. The COVID-19 years were clearly the most unimaginably frustrating experience!

In what ways do you want Art Basel Hong Kong to contribute to the cultural economy of Hong Kong and cultural tourism to the city?

Since the introduction of Art HK and subsequently Art Basel to Hong Kong, the city's arts and cultural scene has never been the same. The momentum driven by Art Basel has unquestionably added more layers to Hong Kong's fast-moving and evolving cultural landscape. For example, in addition to creating positive impacts – like bringing in more business – for local galleries and artists, the fair has also led people to recognise Hong Kong's new positioning in the global art market and art and cultural sector. During its first year in 2013, Art Basel Hong Kong attracted over 60,000 visitors for five days. The 2018 edition of our Hong Kong show attracted an attendance of 80,000, with the 2019 edition drawing an attendance of 88,000. The fact that around 50% of the total attendance comes from outside Hong Kong simply speaks for itself, and probably makes the Art Basel show the most important tourism event in Hong Kong.

In what direction do you want Art Basel Hong Kong to develop in the next three to five years?

I would like to see the influence of Art Basel Hong Kong radiate into other key markets around the region, thereby supporting the long-term and ongoing developments of art scenes throughout Asia. Via Art Basel, I also want Hong Kong's arts and cultural institutions to gain appropriate recognition worldwide. Based on our digital offerings, Art Basel Hong Kong has witnessed significant acquisition growth from collectors and institutions from overseas in the last few years. I sincerely hope we will continue growing and developing in this direction.

COVID-19 has turned the world upside down. How has Art Basel in Hong Kong and your clients been coping with COVID-19?

Going back to the beginning of the pandemic crisis, we were the first international event in the world to cancel our physical exhibition. In March 2020, we immediately launched online viewing rooms for galleries to connect with collectors virtually.

Because many people could not travel due to COVID-19 travel restrictions, we decided to launch the Hong Kong Spotlight by Art Basel in 2020 to showcase local Hong Kong galleries. Hong Kong Spotlight was organised in collaboration with Fine Art Asia as a united response to support the city's arts community during the COVID-19 crisis and connect local buyers with Hong Kong's leading galleries. Hong Kong Spotlight's presentation comprised precisely curated projects, ranging from thematic solo and group exhibitions to art-historical showcases and film screenings.

In 2021, even under COVID-19 constraints, Art Basel Hong Kong became the first truly hybrid event, with an international physical show and significant digital amplification that featured 104 galleries altogether. In a pioneering move, we employed and trained a team of local staff in Hong Kong to set up and attend satellite booths for 55 overseas galleries, which enabled overseas galleries to ship their works to Hong Kong and present them at Art Basel Hong Kong, even when their representatives could not be physically present at the fair. In 2022 we were forced to repeat that initiative due to ongoing pandemic constraints, with 130 participating galleries. Strong sales were reported, driven by a passionate and loyal collector base in the city, and a strong show of support from international collectors who engaged with Art Basel Hong Kong digitally.

Would you like to say something inspiring to our readers to conclude this interview?

Art Basel is committed to supporting Hong Kong to become the true international hub of the Global Art World.

Photo 1. Andrew Strachan.

Photo 2. Art Basel Hong Kong 2022.

Photo 3. Art Basel Hong Kong 2022.

Photo 4. Art Basel Hong Kong 2022.

Photo 5. Art Basel Hong Kong 2022.

Conclusion

This conclusion provides insights based on conversations with Hong Kong's leading arts and cultural administrators, educators, producers, and presenters who are major players in Hong Kong's Arts and Cultural Scene. The Introduction discussed statements made by Poposki and Leung (2022) that "in Hong Kong's art ecology, the dominance of the top end of the art market has created opportunities as well as problems that have led to many challenges in terms of the role of art institutions in Hong Kong. This situation could potentially have a significant impact on the development of art institutions and fine arts practices in Hong Kong, including on the quality of the local art scene in Hong Kong and on supporting and nurturing the development of the arts in Hong Kong." With that said one of the hopes of this publication is that it will bring additional light voices and provide new recognition to those working in the arts profession in Hong Kong. The interviews featured in this volume demonstrate some clear strategic successes, whilst presenting some challenges facing the scene. Addressing the 'elephant in the room,' that being the question, "Is Hong Kong a cultural desert?" each interviewee led to a defiant stand across all organisations to say, "No, Hong Kong is not a cultural desert!" The scope of this book was not to collect quantitative data to justify but rather to provide qualitative evidence from those directly involved across the sector to show evidence that the City's cultural scene is rich, thriving, and evolving.

Three commonalities from the interviewees' statements are summarised as follows:

- The first commonality indicates that the interviewees' professional training and development rely heavily on business or science and technology rather than the arts.
- The second unifying element consists of the fact that almost all interviewees have had some training in Europe.

- The third common place is represented by the level of academic achievement amongst the staff, which is level 7+, with all interviewees having some sort of postgraduate qualifications.

In 2016, Forbes produced a short-form reader contribution blog article titled "Why Art and Science Are More Closely Related Than You Think" (2016) that made the readership conclude with the equation: "Art = Science and Science + Art." In the UK, a vast cultural heritage is available, including arts and sciences. However, in recent times, since the Global Financial Crisis of 2008, the UK has seen significant cuts to arts funding with increased science funding. This is one of the stark comparisons between Hong Kong's cultural scene and the UK's. Where the UK has significantly reduced funding for the arts sector, Hong Kong has significantly increased its investment to become a world-leading location for arts and cultural innovation in the 21st century. The role of art and culture in Hong Kong has taken on increasing prominence in the City's search for an identity since China resumed sovereignty over the territory in 1997. Previously under the auspices of the two Municipal Councils, cultural matters now fall mainly under the purview of the Leisure and Cultural Services Department (LCSD) and the Hong Kong Arts Development Council (ADC). The government's formal cultural policy statement and funding amounts are available on the website of the Culture, Sports and Tourism Bureau.[1]

The second notable commonality among the interviewees is their connections to Europe, particularly studying in the UK and Germany. One has to praise the foresight of the administration of Hong Kong in selecting their departmental staff to include such experiences. By all interviewees' accounts, this preparation has influenced the culture they try to foster in their audience engagement, concert programming, key performance indicators, and leadership styles.

The potential issue with the commonality of staff academic achievement being reported so high is the approach to engagement, events, programming, and accessibility that may unintentionally lead to discrimination. There is arguably an imbalance in the upper administration, which would benefit the scene if addressed. The imbalance manifests itself as 'the soloist' striving for excellence. A culture of excellence may struggle to shake hands with a culture

---

[1] Culture, Sports and Tourism Bureau (n.d.). *Culture and the arts.* Retrieved from: https://www.cstb.gov.hk/en/policies/culture/culture-and-the-arts.html.

of true innovation. Innovation requires pioneering projects, which may not result in immediate excellence.

There is a determined willingness for innovation. However, perhaps the 'cork is a little stuck' due to their not exhibiting:

- a curation of the strong culture of amateur arts and culture amongst the general public?
- a lack of opportunity for alternative cultural or demographic-based diversity in communities and groups as one commonly finds in Western counterpart environments?
- a new area of development in the field of traditional music from Hong Kong. There are only 8 staff members specialising in this field: Chinese painting, calligraphy, art and culture, and history. Musically, there seems to be a large international success with the Hong Kong Chinese Orchestra, and these types of activities should receive significant investment to support research and future innovation projects as this will give depth to the scene while engaging the entire community of Hong Kong.

In 2022, the distribution of the global market industry in art and culture saw China ranking at 17% of the market, third to the USA at 45% and the UK at 18% in terms of global art market value. The collection of interviews included in this volume leaves a significant lasting impression. As we step into a post-COVID future, Hong Kong will be considered the world's leading innovation capital of arts and culture on a scale never before attempted. The primary example is the West Kowloon Cultural District Arts and Culture Complex. A purpose-built arts and culture district due for completion in 2026. The overarching goal of the complex is to develop attending art performances as a habit that integrates into daily life. The focus of all the organisations featured in this collection of interviews is to engage not only new audiences but also existing audiences. The approach does appear to be top-heavy rather than utilising grassroots arts and culture movements. Grassroot projects on a local scale where the aim is innovation and community rather than competition would lead to a more competitive environment in the future.

The Hong Kong arts and culture scene benefits from significant government funding underpinning all the major arts organisations, artists, and orchestra ensembles. In some ways, this approach means that maintaining standards and quantities of players will remain consistent. However, it can cause a level of complacency, some of what these interviews indicate. There are many government-funded arts administration roles, meaning that diversity and local-level community arts engagement remain at arm's length. The quality of the acoustic, studio and exhibition spaces is world-class quality; what is excellent is the scene that is providing permanent homes for its arts organisations, enabling community engagement and outreach to take place on a wide spreading level.

Benedikt Fohr, former Chief Executive of the Hong Kong Philharmonic Orchestra, commented that he was shocked by the homogeneous nature of the sound quality of the Hong Kong Philharmonic Orchestra Brass department. This shock was both exciting but pointed to potential concerns: is the repertoire being performed in the Hong Kong cultural scene diverse enough to entice listeners to attend concerts? Perhaps go back to the drawing board and ask: Why should attendees come to listen to or view arts in Hong Kong? What are the orchestras and art galleries in Hong Kong offering that is different from New York, London, or Paris? Should it be different? Is the appeal primarily for tourism or is it to have a busy local culture? What are the proposed mechanisms underlying the cultural influence in the scene or cultural perception and value in 2022? Has the balance between culture, heritage, and community been weighted in the most appropriate fashion in a post-COVID economy?

There is a vast array of festivals in the Hong Kong arts scene, from chamber music to drama, film, dance, traditional music, and more. One of the simplest but perhaps effective models being put into practice with students is the normalisation of engaging with one arts event every month. What would impact the arts scene if this became a national initiative, for example? From month 1 to month 12, an assessment of culture could then see the impact, particularly on mental health, well-being, productivity, and job satisfaction in the wider workforce. The scene is creating a labyrinth for audiences through new buildings, music, and art commissions. How will this journey connect with spiritual values on a national level?

There is a noticeable difference in the offer of creative arts as a commonplace subject at the university level in both undergraduate and postgraduate training. It is little to almost non-existent. Fostering creative practice feeds into innovation and building a scene in the long term. Presently there is excellent infrastructure. However, the cross organisation and interdisciplinary culture are new concepts. There is a trend amongst the organisations and artists mentioned to engage in mentorship programmes instead of outreach programmes. Again, this focus is on results rather than supporting the process. There is a vast difference between an orchestra mentoring a promising young musician and working weekly in outreach programmes across the city with children and young persons without access to high-level arts and culture. This would be an obvious next step for the scene.

Michael Kaethler's article in the *Journal of Organisation Design* took the concept of curating creative communities of practice: the role of ambiguity (2019). "Communities of Practice (CoPs), it is argued, are loci for creativity, innovation and problem-solving. Instigating a CoP and harnessing this creative energy from an external position (be it institutional or individual) is, however, problematic. The literature surrounding CoPs emphasises the delicate manner in which they are formed and sustained. Those instigating these communities from an external position, such as curators, managers, or educators, do so at the risk of undermining some of CoPs' fundamental qualities. Namely: the fluid social relations, the level of informality and the processes of self-selection and moderation that characterise CoPs, asking 'how, if possible, can one instigate creatively-oriented CoPs?"

The loyalty issue is a major consideration for the arts and cultural scene of Hong Kong as the development of loyalties to a shared problem or goal orients actions and attitudes and provides what Lindkvist (2005) describes as a relevance structure based on self-organised discovery. Problem orientation provides a platform for a shared identity and, in some cases, can lay the foundation for deepening social ties while still allowing for a high turnover of participants. Wenger (1999) argues that participating in common problems forges strong social bonds. Brown and Duguid's (1991) research provides an account where problem-solving through situated approaches and reformulating canonical methods is the pinnacle of creative collaboration.

As far as peer recognition and trust are concerned, a community is formed not only by mutual recognition of those on the 'inside' of a community (Wenger 1999) "but also through a recognition of the qualities that those individuals possess as being of value to the community," supported by Slack space. "Slack space is unsanctioned space, which, as Thompson (2005) states, allows a group to 'consciously cultivate informality.' Amin and Roberts (2008) note that 'informality, iterative purposefulness, and productive idleness' are commonly found in groups, from scientists to artists. This involves elements of freethinking, imaginative play, 'serendipity,' and so forth.

The interview about the Academy of Visual Arts discusses students in Hong Kong focusing their art on telling 'personal stories' rather than collective or political stories. Critical engagement with this as a cultural tool for innovation could lead to some high-impact results on the education system, opportunities, and excellence in delivery. There is a strong link across all the organisations between science and the arts scene, this link is not as strong in other world-leading countries. Continuing the development of technology, instruments, and infrastructure will ensure that artistic expressions of culture may be captured for future generations. The primary consideration, then, is the cost in real terms to the citizens of Hong Kong, is the arts and cultural scene affordable to those on a minimum/low salary?

Thematic approaches across outreach and organisations would be an innovative way to approach interdisciplinary collaboration and creative practice between organisations in a non-threatening way; for example, the theme for a spring/summer arts season could be the topic of "Oceans or Coral." All arts organisations across the city could engage with the theme in their disciplines, this would give the local community opportunity to 'follow' the theme around Hong Kong, by taking a theme that is common to humanity it can break down barriers that high-level arts cultures can create.

There is a tremendous amount to gain from reading this book, particularly a sense of the scale of innovation and investment taking place in the Hong Kong arts and culture scene. The notion of 'scene' is an interesting point to consider for readers as it is a snapshot of a cultural space that, in this case, is open and willing to foster dialogue about the future and sustainability of art and its future role in the culture of the country.

For those who are in Hong Kong and plan to enter the business of Arts Management, this book is a must-read; it maps the locations, cultural venues, and spaces available. There is huge potential and opportunity for new businesses and artists in Hong Kong. Recognising the potential impact and importance of public art and finding new ways to engage each various strata of the local community would be an interesting place to start developing your business model. For those not based in Hong Kong and looking into this scene, we can gain a new perspective on what innovation looks like. The use of space and investment in the arts at all levels of society should be impactful in our future planning. This book provides some staggeringly positive examples of the holistic use of resources and the importance of art for promoting public health, the wider workforce, and well-being. This book would be an asset to any cross-subject course that includes a module on professional or creative practice. Arts, Sciences, and Humanities would all take lessons away from this text.

References

Amin, A. & Roberts, J. (2008). Knowing in action: beyond communities of practice. *Research Policy*, 37(2): 353-369. https://doi.org/10.1016/j.respol.2007.11.003.

Brown, J. S., & Duguid, P. (1991). Organizational learning and communities-of-practice: toward a unified view of working, learning, and innovation. *Organization Science*, 2(1): 40–57. https://doi.org/10.1287/orsc.2.1.40.

Culture, Sports and Tourism Bureau (n.d.). *Culture and the arts*. Retrieved from: https://www.cstb.gov.hk/en/policies/culture/culture-and-the-arts.html.

Kaethler, M. (2019). Curating creative communities of practice: the role of ambiguity. *Journal of Organization Design*, 8(10). Retrieved from: https://link.springer.com/article/10.1186/s41469-019-0051-z.

Mørk, B. E., Aanestad, M., Hanseth, O., & Grisot, M. (2008). Conflicting epistemic cultures and obstacles for learning across communities of practice. *Knowledge & Process Management*, 15(1): 12-23. https://doi.org/10.1002/kpm.295.

Statista Research Department. (2023). *Distribution of the global art market value in 2022, by country*. Retrieved from: https://www.statista.com/statistics/885531/global-art-market-share-by-country/.

Thompson, M. (2005). Structural and epistemic parameters in communities of practice. *Organization Science*, 16(2): 151-164. https://doi.org/10.1287/orsc.1050.0120.

Wenger, E. (1999). *Communities of Practice: Learning, Meaning, and Identity*. Cambridge: Cambridge University Press.

Why Art And Science Are More Closely Related Than You Think. Forbes, 16 March 2016. Retrieved from: https://www.forbes.com/sites/quora/2016/03/16/why-art-and-science-are-more-closely-related-than-you-think/?sh=6e33e98569f1.

Index